2006

AMERICAN HISTORY AND
CONTEMPORARY HOLLYWOOD FILM

AMERICAN HISTORY AND CONTEMPORARY HOLLYWOOD FILM

Trevor B. McCrisken and Andrew Pepper

RUTGERS UNIVERSITY PRESS

New Brunswick, New Jersey

For my parents, Alison and David Pepper

– A. P.

For my parents, Jenny and Ray McCrisken

– T. M.

First published in the United States 2005
by Rutgers University Press, New Brunswick, New Jersey

First published in Great Britain 2005
by Edinburgh University Press Ltd
22 George Square, Edinburgh

Library of Congress Cataloging-in-Publication data

McCrisken, Trevor B., 1968–
    American history and contemporary Hollywood film / Trevor B.
    McCrisken and Andrew Pepper.
        p. cm.
    Includes bibliographical references and index.
    ISBN 0-8135-3620-0 (cloth : alk. paper) – ISBN 0-8135-3621-9 (pbk. : alk
    paper)
        1 Historical films–United States–History and criticism. 2. Motion
        pictures and history.
    I. Pepper, Andrew. II. Title.

PN1995.9.H5M43 2005
791.43'658–dc22   2004051365

Printed in Great Britain

CONTENTS

ACKNOWLEDGEMENTS

I would like to give a massive note of thanks to my co-author Andrew Pepper and our editor at Edinburgh University Press, Nicola Carr, for their support, understanding and patience during what has been an often difficult and challenging period for both personal and professional reasons – it wasn't always easy but we got there in the end! I owe a huge debt of gratitude to Lois Vietri at the University of Maryland, with whom I first explored in depth the relationship between film, history and politics, and whose friendship and support I continue to cherish. I am grateful to the students I have taught over the years, especially those in my 'America in the Modern World' seminars at Sussex, who have also contributed much to my understanding of film and history. I would like to thank my colleagues and friends at the University of Sussex, Lancaster University, the University of Oxford, UWE Bristol and the University of Warwick. Andrea Beighton and Gillian Fullilove, in particular, gave me invaluable support during my time as a Visiting Fellow at the Rothermere American Institute at Oxford. At Warwick, I would like to give special thanks to David Baker for keeping the banter going across the corridor and for reading and making helpful comments on draft chapters, and to Lorraine Elliot and Ben Clift for their support and advice on some of the ideas contained here. Many thanks to Clive Webb, David Ryan, Alan Ware, Michael Dunne and Steve Burman, who have all provided essential support and encouragement during the writing of this book. I am especially grateful to Rob McMahon and Claire Castling, who continue to be great friends and helped make my time at Oxford so enjoyable.

My greatest debt of gratitude goes to my family and friends, both near and far, who provide an unlimited amount of love and support – and have also spent a good deal of time watching movies with me! My grandmother, Kathleen Hind, was always a source of great inspiration for me and is now dearly missed. My wife, Sarah Brammeier

McCrisken, will never cease to amaze me with her depths of love, patience and understanding – I cannot thank her enough for all that she does. Our beautiful daughter Kate has opened up all manner of new perspectives on the world and is a source of daily surprises! My parents, Jenny and Ray McCrisken, have supported and loved me unconditionally and I can never thank them enough. They are going through the most difficult of times as I write this. They are remarkable people and will always be with me. I have dedicated this book to them.

Trevor McCrisken

I want to underscore the debt that we owe our editor, Nicola Carr, for not giving up on the book even as we missed our umpteenth deadline. I'm sure that we wore her patience fairly thin but the very fact of the book's existence is a testimony to the fact that it never actually snapped. I would also like to acknowledge the support and friendship of colleagues at Middlesex University, London Metropolitan University and latterly and most importantly Queen's University Belfast. Thanks, in particular, to those in the School of English at Queen's, who have sat through dull seminar papers drawn from sections of this book and offered constructive and insightful feedback and those who have listened with patience and understanding as I've tried to articulate my own difficulties and anxieties related to the task of writing this book. Given that I have presented parts of this book at various conferences in the UK and Europe over the past few years, I would also like to acknowledge the advice and criticism I've received from American Studies colleagues, even where excessive alcohol means that I haven't been able to recall everything that was said to me the following day. This book is dedicated to my parents, who continue to give me their unconditional support and love, even if the content of what I write about remains something of a mystery. Above all, though, this is for Debbie Lisle, whose razor-sharp insights and selfless assistance throughout the time of writing the book have been as invaluable as they have been constant and unstinting. Her amazing warmth, generosity and love are daily reminders that there are more important things in life than the business of intellectual criticism.

Andrew Pepper

PREFACE

In the early stages of planning for this book, we were struck by a number of related circumstances. First, working as we both did then in American Studies departments in the United Kingdom, we had noticed a growing preference for using films to 'teach' American history and were both excited and concerned by such a development. From our own experiences, we knew that films which featured episodes and events from American history engaged the interest of students and potentially raised some intriguing questions about historical truth, realism, genre, Hollywood and ideology. The assumption that Hollywood films constituted unambiguous and unproblematic historical texts, however, needed to be well and truly resisted. About the same time, we started to notice the sheer number of contemporary Hollywood films being made that focused on American history as their subject. Indeed, a steady flow of new releases throughout the late 1980s and 1990s suggested a growing interest both on the part of filmmakers and audiences in questions of public history, nation and national identity. *Glory*, *Born on the Fourth of July*, *Heaven and Earth*, *Malcolm X* and *JFK* were followed in quick succession by *Saving Private Ryan*, *Nixon*, *The Thin Red Line*, *Three Kings*, *Amistad*, *Ride with the Devil*, *U-571*, *The Patriot*, *Pearl Harbor* and *Black Hawk Down*. The initial impetus for this book, therefore, came from a desire to explore Hollywood's renewed interest in American history and analyse these films in pedagogical terms. In this task, we were keen to 'rescue' these films from both their celebrants and detractors: those who would either use Hollywood films to exemplify and explain particular historical moments and those who dismiss them as inaccurate 'entertainments' without any value as historical texts.

There is no shortage of critical studies examining the relationship between film and history in general and of Hollywood's role as American historian in particular. Of these, we were especially interested in Peter Rollins' *Hollywood as Historian: American Film in a*

Cultural Context (1983), George Custen's *Bio/Pics: How Hollywood Constructed Public History* (1992), Robert Burgoyne's *Film Nation: Hollywood Looks at US History* (1997), Robert Brent Toplin's *Hollywood as Mirror: Changing Views of 'Outsiders' and 'Enemies' in American Movies* (1993) and, best of all, Robert Rosenstone's *Vision of the Past: The Challenge of Film to Our Idea of History* (1995) and *Revisioning History: Film and the Construction of a New Past* (1995). We were not convinced, however, that any of these books had wholly addressed the subjects and concerns that interested us. Rollins' study focused on historical films made throughout the twentieth century; Custen's addressed only historical biopics; Toplin's study considered the representation of broader historical themes in American films (for example, slavery, immigration, the Cold War) but focused largely on films made between the 1930s and 1960s; and Rosenstone's critical preoccupations often took him beyond the geographical and cultural limits of America and Hollywood. Perhaps only Burgoyne's *Film Nation* significantly overlapped with our own plans for this book, given its twin focus on contemporary Hollywood films and their attempts to reconfigure what Burgoyne calls the 'official' or 'master' narrative of the United States. We were not entirely convinced, however, by his quite optimistic assertions about the ability of Hollywood films to contest and disrupt this 'official' or 'master' narrative, nor did we think that the range of films that he addressed was sufficiently broad. We certainly owe a critical debt to others in the field, Rosenstone in particular, whose criteria for judging the worth of historical films we have found especially useful. We remained convinced, however, that there was room in the field for a wide-ranging analysis of the relationship between American history and contemporary Hollywood films.

Of course, it is not easy to define what the term 'contemporary Hollywood films' means, or indeed to determine what constitutes an appropriate engagement with American history. As such, we were led by a number of guiding principles. First, we decided to confine our interest to films made after the fall of the Berlin Wall in 1989, an event that signalled the ending of the Cold War. In certain instances we allow ourselves to consider films made prior to this moment (for example, *Revolution*, *Platoon*) but only where they exemplify particular trends that relate to more recent films or act as effective points of comparison with such films. We decided that the end of the Cold War was a significant moment because it marked the beginning of a period of critical reassessment and reflection that seemed to centrally preoccupy many Hollywood filmmakers, as well as much of the academic community. During this period, the already contested terrain of nation and national identity underwent intense scrutiny and revision, as did the question of what 'America' constituted domestically and internationally following the demise of its only rival superpower. Such inquiries became an implicit jumping-off point for films made after the end of the Cold War as diverse as *Saving Private Ryan* and *The Patriot*.

If the Cold War is one of the bookends for our study, then 11 September 2001 is the other. We planned and started to write our book before the attacks on the World Trade Center and the Pentagon and the fraught aftermath: the outpouring of patriotism within the United States, the establishment of the Department of Homeland Security, the wars in Afghanistan and Iraq, and US-led clampdowns elsewhere in the world. Though we address the possible impact of the events of 11 September 2001 on the representation of American history by Hollywood filmmakers in our concluding chapter, we feel that it is still too soon to assess with any certainty what this impact might be. As such, it has not been our intention, except where September 11th has explicitly affected either the production or reception of particular films (for example, *Black Hawk Down*), to reread films made before 11 September 2001 through a post-September 11th critical lens. Nor are we prepared to accept that the events of September 11th and their aftermath invalidate the basic tenets of our argument. Certainly September 11th has significantly affected Americans' perception of their nation both domestically and internationally. The events of that day and their aftermath have necessarily provoked much debate inside and outside the United States about what concepts such as nationality, sovereignty, security and global politics now mean. Still, whether September 11th has ushered in an entirely transformed social, political, cultural and economic landscape or whether it merely exacerbated tensions and fault-lines already present in the post-Cold War United States and the world remains to be seen.

Though we have been aware, from the start of this project, of the problems associated with recovering an objective, neutral, disinterested history, we quickly decided that we would focus only on those films that engaged predominantly with episodes and events of particular national significance, even if their treatment of these events was entirely or largely fictionalised. In addition, we decided to allow for a quite loose definition of what constitutes a 'Hollywood' as opposed to a 'non-Hollywood' film. In part this was to acknowledge the often problematic distinction between Hollywood and independent filmmaking. In other ways, it was to draw attention to the global nature of film financing, production and distribution. The assimilation of previously autonomous film studios like Columbia and Paramount into giant multinational conglomerates has further embedded Hollywood in newly emerging systems or networks of global politics and economics. While this may not necessarily have an explicit impact on what gets made and how it gets made, it would be foolish to claim that such changes have had no impact whatsoever. In this respect, we prefer 'Hollywood' to 'American' filmmaking simply because the financing, production and distribution of most, if not all, feature films made by one of the major studios (Columbia, Fox, Paramount, DreamWorks, Universal, and the like) is no longer entirely confined to the geographical boundaries of the United States.

Having established a set of criteria that would determine the films that we would focus upon, our final task was to agree on a structure for the book – that is, how we would both organise the material and then divide up the work. This was both the easiest and hardest task that we faced. It was the easiest task because the categories or rather chapter headings practically chose themselves. Due to the sheer quantity of films being made about particular subjects or events, we quickly decided that there would have to be chapters on World War II, the Civil War, Civil Rights and Black Nationalism. We decided that the American Revolution and slavery would make interesting chapters, even if the field of available films to examine was less rich. We also decided that because the most significant Vietnam films had been made prior to our starting point (that is, 1989) we would roll our analysis of Oliver Stone's Vietnam trilogy into a single chapter which also considered *JFK* and *Nixon*. Finally, we decided that we would conclude with a chapter that considered Hollywood's first forays into the history of the post-Cold War era itself by looking at films about US military interventions during the period. In making these choices we obviously could not assess every historical film made by Hollywood. There are certainly some gaps in our coverage. There are no chapters, for instance, on labour history or women's history, but this is largely because mainstream Hollywood filmmakers have themselves tended to overlook such subjects. Perhaps more controversially, we have also not included a chapter dedicated to the western. This was both a reflection of a perceived waning of interest in the genre on the part of filmmakers and audiences in the post-Cold War period and an admission that we could add little to the vast body of criticism already published on the western. Still, the western is less an absence than an absent presence in our book because we do argue that the genre has, for much of the twentieth century, set the terms and the limits for Hollywood's engagement with American history. It is practically impossible, for example, to conceive of Mel Gibson's struggle against the forces of the British Crown in *The Patriot* or *Ride with the Devil*'s re-staging of the Civil War without first paying attention to their self-conscious assimilation of the multiple codes and conventions of the western.

Finally, it is perhaps worth noting that while we have collaborated throughout the book, each of us assumed primary responsibility for particular chapters. Chapters 1, 2, 3 and 6 were primarily authored by Pepper, while McCrisken was the primary author of Chapters 4, 5 and 7. The collaborative nature of the project brought with it many challenges, some of which were rather daunting. Coming from different disciplinary backgrounds, we did not always find ourselves in agreement on how to analyse the relationship between film and history or indeed how to interpret both the nature of American power in the post-Cold War era and the structural changes in the Hollywood film industry. Ultimately our productive disagreements, although perhaps not entirely reconciled, enabled us to bring to bear on our analysis a wide range of critical, theoretical, methodological and disciplinary perspectives that we hope makes a modest contribution to the task of pushing forward the terms of film and history criticism.

INTRODUCTION

Hollywood has not typically enjoyed a good reputation as a purveyor of history. American filmmakers are frequently condemned for rewriting history, for providing an 'arrogant distortion of the historical record' or even for the 'rape of US history'.[1] Films made about particular episodes or events from America's past are often accused of providing a disturbingly falsified picture of 'what really happened'; they consistently privilege action and drama over historical accuracy; they simplify the complexities and contingencies of the past by attempting to impose clear-cut resolutions on the 'mess' of history; and their aim is to entertain audiences and make money for their producers rather than to represent the past in a fresh light or encourage audiences to critically reflect on this past in new ways. As Robert Brent Toplin puts it, critics of historical feature films would seem to hold the unshakeable view that: 'To learn about history, go to a book, not to a movie'.[2]

Since at least the 1970s, however, many historians have been increasingly willing to recognise the value of Hollywood films as both tools for teaching and as resources for helping to interpret American history.[3] A small library of books on the subject of historical films and regular articles and forums in major journals such as *American Historical Review* and the *Journal of American History* attest to the seriousness with which many historians now treat feature films that focus on historical events or characters. Despite this acknowledgement, however, no real consensus has emerged as to the status of historical feature films as a pedagogical tool. Most banal has been the response of critics like Robert Gregg and Ernest Giglio, who argue that the pedagogical role of film should only ever be a secondary or exemplary one. Giglio asserts that 'film should not become a substitute for reading texts and researching primary resources' and Gregg argues that 'films can never be a primary source in this quest for knowledge'.[4] More intriguingly, however, Robert Burgoyne, Robert

1

Brent Toplin and Robert Rosenstone have all contended that since we can no longer trust 'History – with a capital H'[5] – that is, the idea that historical truths exist, at least in any pure, unmediated forms – opportunities are created to consider the ways in which Hollywood films engage with history in more complex ways than their detractors will allow.

Taking this assumption as our starting point, it is our ambition in this book to develop an argument about contemporary Hollywood film and American history along three critical lines. The first asks us to think about films as texts that can help us to engage with questions and issues about history and to consider what we might be able to learn about the past from such films. In other words, which films constitute 'good' history and why? What can such films reveal to us about the nature of historical characters and events? How can they help us interpret and make sense of the past? Second, we plan to think about film not as a transparent 'window through which we observe a world that replicates our own.'[6] Rather, we conceive of film as a complex cultural and ideological construction that not only reveals 'something of the dreams, desires, displacements, and, in some cases, social and political issues confronting American society'[7] but also moulds 'the self-image of the nation in pervasive and explicit ways.'[8] As Debbie Lisle puts it, 'Critical approaches in Film and Cultural Studies provide a more . . . complex understanding of representation that allows us to understand that film not only reflects reality but also produces it.'[9] We ask, therefore, what do historical films reveal about the social, political and cultural concerns of the time in which they are made? This, then, points to our third critical line of inquiry, which considers the ways in which Hollywood films are centrally preoccupied with 'America' and American history; that is, how and whether they attempt to revise 'official' understandings of American history and what this engagement reveals about both the contested status of historical truth and the needs and preoccupations of the United States in our own post-Cold War moment.

There is now a general consensus that Hollywood films are complex cultural documents which speak either implicitly or explicitly to the concerns and preoccupations of their own moment of production. However, the question of whether films based on historical events, characters or periods are capable of presenting 'good' history has caused much greater controversy and disagreement. Professional historians and other critics often accuse historical films of 'manipulation, invention, distortion, misrepresentation, and simplification.'[10] As such, they are usually not grounded in the same rigorous archival and documentary research that underpins written histories, and often take dramatic license with events, characters, timelines and dialogue. As Cameron concludes, even 'good' historical films are 'thin in context and narrow in subject. Few embody questions; most are assertions. Few take account of alternatives. . . Most celebrate or fictionalise; they do not analyze.'[11]

While Hollywood films will always disappoint those looking for a definitive, explanatory text of an historical event or period, however, such views do not necessarily need to set the limit for our own critical thinking. As Robert Brent Toplin observes:

> Historians now better recognize that a film is not a book or an article. It cannot 'cover' every topic they wish to see addressed; it will not introduce complexity and multiple causes to the degree that history in print does; and it is less effective than print in providing abstract analysis. Furthermore, film-based history demonstrates a greater tendency to portray the past through appeals to the emotions and attention to personalities.[12]

Furthermore, while history in film is constrained by narrative conventions, commercial concerns, the need for dramatic impact, and other structural elements, written histories also face similar constraints that require 'selectivity' and even 'creative imagination.'[13] Academic historians often collapse historical time, or emphasise some events and people while de-emphasising others, in order to further their argument or provide a particular focus or interpretation. 'Practically speaking,' Cameron argues, 'compression [has] to be made whether in film or in written history.'[14] Rosenstone, meanwhile, simply makes the point that 'everyone who deals with historical evidence must make personal judgements. They have to shape disparate evidence into an interpretation.'[15]

While we share the concerns of critics and academics who accuse many Hollywood historical films of bias and misrepresentation, such views also run the risk of problematically insisting upon history and the historical record as fixed, inviolate and unchanging. After all, historians who berate Hollywood films for falsification should perhaps ask whether the historical record that they are using as an evaluative yardstick is necessarily as secure and uncontested as they imagine.

The point, as Burgoyne puts it, is that 'historical writing delivers not the "real" of the historical past but rather a mental conception of it, a system of discursive representations, in which speculation, hypothesis, and dramatic ordering and shaping closely inform the work of historical reconstruction and analysis.'[16] Hayden White makes a similar point:

> No history, visual or verbal, "mirrors" all or even the greater parts of the events or scenes of which it purports to be account, and this is true of even the most restricted "micro history." Every written history is the product of processes of condensation, displacement, symbolization, and qualification exactly like those used in the production of filmic representation.[17]

Most historians accept that empirical facts exist, but the writing of history is all about interpreting those facts. There are almost as many versions of 'historical truth' as there are historians since all 'facts' are open to interpretation and their meanings are infinitely debatable. 'Knowledge' and 'truth' are contingent on perspective, methodology, intent and ideology. As Laclau and Mouffe argue: 'There is not an in-itself of history but rather a multiple refraction of it, depending on the traditions from which it is interrogated.'[18] We begin from the assumption that history is never settled, clear-cut or wholly knowable; it is forever open to differing, often conflicting interpretations, all of which are invested with certain theoretical, ideological, theological or other assumptions. Nonetheless it would be wrong to assume that this questioning of historical truths should necessarily lead us into the arms of a bland relativism where all versions of history automatically assume equal status. Some versions of history are more convincing or persuasive than others and can be assessed for their 'worth' as history. The way such judgements are made is, of course, influenced by theoretical and/or ideological standpoints but the authority of particular historical accounts can also be assessed, to some extent, by their methodology and the ways in which evidence is found and presented. As Rosenstone argues: 'The "truth" of history resides not in the verifiability of individual pieces of data but in the overall narrative of the past and in how well that narrative engages the discourse of history – the already existing body of data and arguments on a topic.'[19]

At stake here, then, is the question of how we make judgements about Hollywood films made about particular episodes or events from America's past. What constitutes 'good history' on film? Many critics of historical films complain about factual errors or the failure of filmmakers to use the appropriate props, costumes or settings for the events they are portraying. Such criticisms, however, often amount to little more than nit-picking. Indeed, even a film that has great attention to detail in its recreation of the past will not necessarily be a good work of history or for that matter more 'authentic' in its distillation of the past. As Custen points out, 'To address history from the point of view of "accuracy" alone is to accept that such a condition exists.'[20] Cameron, meanwhile, argues that westerns made in the 1970s, such as *The Long Riders*, that attempted to 'look' more real by using more authentic costuming 'did not become more accurate by trying to become more realistic; they simply became different – bad history in a different way.'[21]

Our point is that we cannot make discriminations about historical films based upon problematic claims to accuracy. Rather, such films must be judged both in formal terms or, as Rosenstone puts it, 'at the level of argument, metaphor, symbol,'[22] and in thematic terms, as political and historical texts. Accordingly the problematic relationship between historical events and their representation by what Sklar calls 'a cinema of affirmation'[23] lies at the heart of this book. The issue is not that Hollywood films have always constructed 'bad' histories by compressing, reducing and simplifying past events in order to fit particular patterns whereby personalities are collapsed into representative types and a collective drama is filtered through the exploits of a single, usually heroic figure. Nor is it that false claims to historical authenticity made by some Hollywood films are rendered plausible by a formal style whereby 'camera position, continuity editing, lighting, acting'[24] all give the impression that what appears on the screen is somehow 'real'. Our point is simply that the question of whether particular films make 'good' or 'bad' history requires us to develop or appropriate a critical idiom that considers these issues of genre and style in the context of broader concerns about the relationship between pedagogy and representation.

Cameron similarly contends that a good historical film 'must allow for argument, or at least for alternatives. It must, like a well-reasoned article, admit its opposite. It must prove, or at least persuasively present, its own idea.'[25] Essentially, then, for a film to be successful as a work of history it must challenge its viewer to *think* about how the events being portrayed can be interpreted. It should not be an open and shut assertion of a viewpoint but raise questions, not all of which are answered during the film. Narrative conventions in most Hollywood films demand 'closure' by the time of a film's end but since history remains open to further interpretation, a good historical film should leave the viewer wanting to know more, to dig deeper and question the validity of the film's viewpoint and think about possible alternatives. When we assess Hollywood's recent portrayals of American history, therefore, we shall not simply be looking at the 'authenticity' of what is presented on the screen. We will consider what kind of questions, if any, the films raise about the meaning and significance of the events and characters they portray. How much historical contextualisation do these films provide? What historical questions do they engage with? How do they interpret the past? What messages and conclusions are they sending to the audience? Do they provoke the viewer to think about the many ways in which the events being portrayed can be understood or do they simply assert a closed viewpoint? Is there an argument about the past being made in the film? How well does it make that argument and does it indicate why it is important? Do any distortions or uses of fiction in the films undermine our ability to interpret history or can they, perhaps paradoxically, actually strengthen the argument being made and add to the viewer's ability to learn something about the historical period in question?

In this respect, we start by acknowledging the work carried out by Robert Rosenstone theorising the relationship between film and history and our book is an attempt to build upon his ideas and apply them in a more specific way to the question of how and why filmmakers working in Hollywood since the end of the Cold War have sought to engage with and represent American history. We draw on a number of criteria that Rosenstone has suggested the 'best historical films' meet. Such films show 'not just what happened in the past' but also what the past 'means to us'. They 'interrogate the past for the sake of the present' because 'historians are working for the living, not for the dead'. They create 'a historical world complex enough so that it overflows with meaning; so that its meanings are always multiple; so that its meanings cannot be contained or easily expressed in words'. They 'ruminate on the possible meanings of historical events or eras, such as disparities of cultures and sense of time in the modern world'. They 'analyze and question the images of the historical realities we think we know most clearly'. Perhaps most controversially, historical films can also create 'a spectacle' that carries 'a particular feeling' of what the 'past means'.[26] On this last point, for example, *Apocalypse Now*, while being a work of almost total fiction, is often praised for conveying a sense of the confusion, madness and contested purpose of the Vietnam War. Ultimately, Rosenstone argues, a good historical film will both 'contest' and 'revision' the past. It will 'provide [an] interpretation that runs against traditional [historical] wisdoms', perhaps showing us the past in 'new and unexpected' ways by 'utilizing an aesthetic that violates the traditional, realistic ways of telling the past . . . challenges a normal dramatic structure [and] mixes genres and modes'.[27]

In applying these ideas to the specific moment of post-Cold War Hollywood's engagement with American history, one of the central questions that we address in this book is whether or to what extent the resultant films service and legitimise an affirmative and quite traditional version of nation and national identity. American history has long been dominated by a liberal perspective that draws upon an essentially liberal ideology of national exceptionalism and progress. The dominant 'official' view of American history is thus the 'benign meta-narrative' which sees the US as a leading force for forwarding human progress. Historians of the US either challenge or affirm this view, using the meta-narrative and its mainstream acceptance in the US as a starting point for critically analysing how and for what ends American public history is constructed. In recent years, for example, the idea of the US as a progressive force acting in the 'universal' interest has come under increasing attack. Such attacks have explored the ways in which differences of race, gender, class, and other factors, have unsettled traditional understandings of the United States and American history and have demanded that greater consideration be paid to such factors and to the 'internationalisation' of America by placing US narratives in a wider trans-national history. Hollywood film, therefore, plays a crucial role in the construction and revision of this public history or 'benign meta-narrative'. As our starting point, therefore, we consider how and why a range of post-Cold War Hollywood historical films have contributed to this process; that is to say, whether or to what extent Hollywood filmmakers have become more self-conscious about their role as public historians and how they have sought to engage with complex questions about what constitutes America domestically and internationally in the post-Cold War world. As such, we are also interested in how the historical films we address engage with their own social, historical, political and cultural moment. What issues about the contemporary post-Cold War world – about identity politics and US foreign relations, for example – are expressed, promoted or challenged through these films? And do these films represent a new departure in the way in which Hollywood filmmakers have approached and represented American history? Do they either explicitly or implicitly draw attention to ways in which the modes and practices of filmmaking have altered and thus to structural changes in the film industry itself?

Our aim, then, is to situate our discussions of film-as-effective-history in the context of a more careful examination of the relationship between power, identity and representation. This is, to reiterate, that historical films should not be seen as transparent windows onto the past but as ideologically contradictory, textual mediations whose forms and representational strategies produce, and are produced by, ever shifting relations of power. Accordingly, the question of popular film as a pedagogical tool is transformed and what matters, to use Snead's distinction, is not 'seeing' films in an uncritical and unselfconscious manner but 'seeing through films'.[28] As Henry A. Giroux explains, the point is to develop 'the critical skills to engage how the ideological and the affective work in combination to offer up particular ways of viewing the world in ways that come to matter to individuals and groups'.[29]

This task of 'seeing through' films is especially important since the ideological commitments and preoccupations of Hollywood films in general achieve their power because they are often invisible. Viewers do not immediately recognise the ways in which they are being positioned by particular modes of representation. As Ryan and Kellner observe:

> The formal conventions – narrative closure, image continuity, nonreflexive camera, voyeuristic observation, sequential editing, causal logic, dramatic motivation, shot centering, frame balance, realistic intelligibility etc. – help to instil ideology by creating an illusion that what happens on the screen is a neutral recording of objective events, rather than a construct operating from a certain point of view.[30]

Robert Kolker, meanwhile, explicitly identifies such a practice with American filmmaking: 'American film, from its beginnings, has attempted to hide itself, to make invisible the telling of its stories, and to downplay or deny the ways in which it supports, reinforces, and even sometimes subverts the major cultural, political and social attitudes that surround and penetrate it.'[31] Seeing through films, therefore, requires us to develop an appropriately sophisticated critical lens and idiom whose goal is not just, in formal terms, to render the invisible visible but also to uncover how such practices conceal a film's ideological commitments. Nonetheless this task is made even more difficult because the techniques and strategies of filmmaking identified by Ryan and Kellner are themselves undergoing changes. The scale and scope of contemporary 'blockbuster' films may not be completely new. Jeanine Basinger makes the point that just because Hollywood epics from earlier eras did not have digital effects does not mean that audiences (and critics) were not equally if not more affected by the spectacle they provided.[32] Nonetheless, it would be hard to argue that 'blockbusters' like *Pearl Harbor* do not constitute some kind of new variation for Hollywood, if only in terms of their relentless privileging of aesthetics, spectacle and sensation over and above more traditional preoccupations with cinematic 'realism'. As Stam and Miller argue, 'the old critiques of dominant cinema in terms of linear narrative, eyeline matches and invisible editing no longer quite "work" since recent blockbuster cinema . . . is less interested in verisimilitude and spatio-temporal integrity than in pure sensation'.[33]

We do not want to insist upon blanket or generalised claims about Hollywood filmmaking per se; that recent Hollywood films, for example, constitute some kind of dramatic break with their forerunners. Far from it. Some recent films like *Pearl Harbor* and *The Patriot* constitute, in part, a throwback to classic Hollywood films in so far as they set about securing and reaffirming what we might tentatively call the dominant ideology. Others, like *Ride with the Devil* and *The Thin Red Line*, are more representative of a type of formally innovative and thematically subversive cinema that enjoyed its ascendancy in the late sixties and early seventies, and unsettle culturally dominant understandings of the US. What we do suggest, however, is that Rosenstone's description of the 'best' historical films account for a relatively small percentage of Hollywood's post-Cold War output. In other words, films which open up rather than close off debates about what constitutes history, which foreground the inherent complexities of particular episodes and events, which require audiences to reflect upon what they are watching and encourage them to simultaneously hold on to alternative perspectives and versions of the 'truth', and which violate traditional ways of telling history, are, from our point of view, to be celebrated, but they do not constitute the norm in contemporary Hollywood. Rather, many recent historical films (*The Patriot, Amistad, U-571, Pearl Harbor*, and so on) are characterised by their trite, simplified representations of the past, by their formal conventionality, and by their tendency to close off rather than open up historical debates and obscure rather than foreground what Ryan and Kellner call 'signs of cinematic artificiality'.[34]

As such we are less much optimistic than Burgoyne's *Film Nation* about the ability of mainstream Hollywood films to necessarily 'rearticulate the cultural narrative that defines the American nation'.[35] Certainly we agree that the sheer number of films being made in Hollywood since the end of the Cold War about particular episodes and events from American history, and the increasingly self-conscious ways in which filmmakers themselves have theorised their role as public historians, make this an important area of study. That is to say, in so far as 'the most visible manifestations of this changing narrative of nation' has been 'the resurgence of films that take the American past as their subject,'[36] the relationship between Hollywood films and American history does require greater critical scrutiny. But, while we acknowledge that American history has become an increasingly 'contested domain' and that the national narrative has undergone sustained challenge from 'stories that explore the meaning of nation "from below"',[37] we draw back from Burgoyne's assertion that contemporary historical films, in general, have a critical rather than a recuperative agenda; that they seek 'to recover a different meaning from the past, a message that will validate the increasingly hybrid and poly-cultural reality of American life'.[38] Rather, we argue that despite the growing presence of historical films which give voice to perspectives 'from below' (for example, *Malcolm X, Ali*), and acknowledging that many recent films have sought to contest or at least question the benign meta-narrative of American history (for example, *JFK, Nixon, Ride with the Devil, Three Kings*), many films are, and remain, preoccupied with constructing and securing some kind of imaginary consensus whereby everyone's point of view is duly noted and assimilated into ultimately affirmative narratives of national and global reconciliation (that is, *The Patriot, Amistad, Pearl Harbor*). In other words, it would be folly to ignore the contention that filmmakers must be 'very attentive to popular attitudes' if they want to secure a substantial audience for their product;[39] or that films are products of what is now a vast global entertainment industry; or that 'affirmative' and 'optimistic' films tend, in the current climate, to have greater mass appeal than 'complex' or 'difficult' ones. Moreover, as Stam argues, we should be especially careful about lauding the subversive potential of Hollywood films, whether this potential is embedded within texts or articulated at the moment of consumption, 'at a time when most alternative productions . . . are being frozen out by blockbuster films and media mega-conglomerates'.[40]

These blockbuster films are as successful at the international box office as they are at the domestic US box office, and are made for a global rather than for an *exclusively* American audience. This is not to suggest that films like *Pearl Harbor* or *Black Hawk Down* no longer end up celebrating and legitimising a quite traditional version of nation and national identity. Rather, we are suggesting that in so far as American values are promoted as universal in their application, these universal values are shaped not just by the demands and preoccupations of nation but also by a more nebulous and universalising preference for tolerance, inclusion, multiculturalism, professionalism, order, management and putting everything into its proper place. In short, they speak to the political and economic logic of free-market neo-liberalism currently in the global ascendancy. Though these positions may not actually be in opposition with one another, we try to differentiate between those films which seek, first and foremost, to re-affirm, in a quite straightforward way, the privileged status of the US and American national identity in the global realm (*Saving Private Ryan*), and those films which strive to conceive of traditionally 'American' values such as 'freedom' and 'liberty' in more diffuse and amorphous ways (*The Patriot*). Moreover, while we argue throughout that 'good' historical films are those which compel us through particular formal and thematic strategies to critically engage with their representations of the past, 'bad' historical films tend to be those ones which combine a preference for spectacular action and predilection to excite, stimulate, console and stupefy audiences – encourage them to feel rather than to think – with a falsely or problematically inclusive desire to represent everyone's point of view. In other words, this kind of need or desire to acknowledge diversity and celebrate tolerance is false or problematic because it effectively conceals the ways in which newer, friendlier and more diffuse strategies of domination are manifesting themselves both in films and in the political world.

While acknowledging the claims that Hollywood films can make on America's and the world's collective imagination, we would not want to suggest that audiences and critics are, in any way, helpless in the face of what some might see as the ideological juggernaut that is contemporary Hollywood filmmaking. One cannot escape the fact that the entertainment industry in the US, as Giroux notes, is 'the second largest export – second only to military aircraft' and that the film industry is 'controlled by a very limited number of corporations that exercise enormous power in all major factors of movie-making – production, distribution and circulation in the United States and abroad'[41] but it would be quite wrong to identify the films made in this system merely as the product of their corporate sponsors or indeed to assume that audiences in the US and throughout the world respond to Hollywood films in any uniform or straightforward way. The fact that successful films, according to Giroux, are 'seen by 10,000,000 people in theaters [in the US] and millions more when it is aired on cable and exported to foreign markets'[42] is testament both to their mass appeal and the effectiveness of American-dominated marketing practices and distribution networks. However, one should not automatically bemoan this state of affairs or, in the case of Hollywood's engagement with American history, assume that its films serve no useful pedagogical function or that their function in the classroom can only ever be a secondary or illustrative one. Rather, we should be asking how or indeed whether these films afford us opportunities to consider how the past is represented, why and for what purposes; that is, to see historical events as they are mediated by some films not as straightforward, fixed and unchanging but as complex, contested and contingent. By acknowledging film's ability to engage mass interest and provoke pedagogical debates, this book is an attempt to foster this kind of critical intellectual enquiry. As Giroux concludes, 'Film, in this instance, registers a public dialogue and set of experiences that offer the opportunity to revitalize those democratic public spheres in which the popular intersects with the pedagogical and the political in ways that suggest that film cannot be dismissed simply as a commodity but now becomes crucial to expanding democratic relations, ideologies, and identities.'[43]

NOTES

1 Joan Hoff, '*Nixon* film review', *American Historical Review*, Vol. 101, No. 4, October 1996, pp. 1173–74.
2 Robert Brent Toplin, ed., *Oliver Stone's USA: Film, History and Controversy* (Lawrence, KS: University of Kansas Press, 2000), p. 6.
3 See John E. O'Connor and Martin A. Jackson, eds, *American History/American Film* (New York: Frederick Ungar, 1979).
4 Ernest Giglio, 'Using film to teach political concepts', *European Political Science*, Vol. 1, No. 2, Spring 2002, p. 53; Robert W. Gregg, *International Relations on Film* (Boulder, CO: Lynne Rienner, 1998), p. 1.
5 Robert Rosenstone, 'The Future of the Past', in Vivian Sobchak, ed., *The Persistence of History: Cinema, Television and the Modern Event* (London and New York: Routledge, 1996), p. 202.
6 Robert A. Rosenstone, ed., *Revisioning History: Film and the Construction of a New Past* (Princeton: Princeton University Press, 1995), p. 11.
7 Leonard Quart and Albert Auster, *American Film and Society Since 1945*, 2nd ed., (Westport, CT: Praeger, 1991), p. 2.
8 Robert Burgoyne, *Film Nation: Hollywood Looks at US History* (Minneapolis: University of Minnesota Press, 1997), p. 6.
9 Debbie Lisle, 'Screening Global Politics', *International Feminist Journal of Politics*, Vol. 5, No. 1, March 2003, pp. 135–6.
10 Robert Brent Toplin, 'The Historian and Film: Challenges Ahead', *Perspectives Online*, April 1996, http://www.theaha.org/perspectives /issues/1996/9604/9604FIL.CFM (1/7/02).
11 Kenneth Cameron, *America on Film: Hollywood and American History* (New York: Continuum, 1997), p. 233.
12 Toplin, 'The Historian and Film'.
13 Ibid.
14 Cameron, *America on Film*, p. 238.
15 Rosenstone in 'Introduction', Toplin, *Oliver Stone's USA*, p. 7.
16 Burgoyne, *Film Nation*, p. 5.
17 Hayden White in George F. Custen, *Bio/Pics: How Hollywood Constructed Public History* (New Jersey: Rutgers University Press, 1992), p. 11.
18 Ernesto Laclau and Chantal Mouffe, 'Post Marxism without Apologies', *New Left Review* (166), Nov/Dec 1987, p. 99.
19 Robert Rosenstone, 'Oliver Stone as Historian', in Toplin, *Oliver Stone's USA*, p. 28.
20 Custen, *Bio/Pics*, p. 11.
21 Cameron, *America on Film*, p. 235.
22 Rosenstone, 'Oliver Stone as Historian', p. 34; emphasis removed.
23 Robert Sklar, *Movie-Made America: A Social History of American Movies* (New York: Random House, 1975), p. 197.

24 Rosenstone, *Revisioning History*, p. 11.
25 Cameron, *America on Film*, p. 236.
26 Robert A. Rosenstone, *Visions of the Past: Challenge of Film to Our Idea of History* (Cambridge, MA: Harvard University Press, 1995), pp. 238–9.
27 Rosenstone, 'Oliver Stone as Historian,' pp. 35–6.
28 James Snead in Henry A. Giroux, *Breaking In To Movies: Film and the Culture of Politics* (Malden, MA and Oxford: Blackwell, 2002), p. 9.
29 Giroux, *Breaking In To Movies*, p. 9.
30 Michael Ryan and Douglas Kellner, *Camera Politica: The Politics and Ideology of Contemporary Hollywood Film* (Bloomington: Indiana University Press, 1990) p. 1.
31 Robert Kolker, *A Cinema of Loneliness: Penn, Stone, Kubrick, Scorsese, Spielberg, Altman*, 3rd ed., (Oxford and New York: Oxford University Press, 2000), p. 11.
32 Jeanine Basinger, *The World War II Combat Film: Anatomy of a Genre* (Middletown, CT: Wesleyan University Press, 2003) pp. 255–6.
33 Robert Stam and Toby Miller, eds., *Film and Theory: An Anthology* (Oxford: Blackwell, 2000), p. 228.
34 Ryan and Kellner, *Camera Politica*, p. 1.
35 Burgoyne, *Film Nation*, p. 2.
36 Ibid., p. 1.
37 Ibid.
38 Ibid., p. 2.
39 Robert Brent Toplin, ed., *Hollywood as Mirror: Changing Views of 'Outsiders' and 'Enemies' in American Movies* (Westport, CT: Greenwood Press, 1993), pp. ix–x.
40 Robert Stam, *Film Theory* (Oxford: Blackwell, 2000), p. 229.
41 Giroux, *Breaking In To Movies*, p. 11.
42 Ibid., p. 11.
43 Ibid., p. 15.

Chapter 1

LESSONS FROM HOLLYWOOD'S AMERICAN REVOLUTION

There are a number of points of departure for this chapter, and this book as a whole. The first relates to the vexed question of historical accuracy and the now familiar complaint that Hollywood films deliberately falsify the historical record, as though that record itself is somehow inviolate and unchanging. As we argued in the Introduction, we begin from the assumption that what should concern us when considering how the past is represented is not so much the issue of how accurately films represent history but rather what they can reveal to us about the ways in which history is told and how film's engagement with history has been shaped by the material conditions under which filmmakers construct their narratives and audiences watch and make sense of them. We are interested primarily in the ways in which filmmakers have used, and are using, American history as a way of engaging with the question of what 'America' stands for, culturally and politically, in the post-Cold War world. In this particular chapter, what interests us, therefore, is how an event as sanctified as the American Revolution – one that continues to occupy a privileged position in the benign meta-narrative of American history – is used and transformed by filmmakers both to reveal something about the event itself and to shed some light on our own cultural and political moment. What is at stake here is not only the question of how or indeed whether Hollywood's role as public historian has changed. We are also interested in whether Hollywood itself has changed in ways that affect what films get made and how they are made. In other words, attempts by contemporary filmmakers to represent particular events and incidents that took place in America between 1775 and 1781 may end up shedding some new light on such events, place them in an appropriate context, explain why they might have happened, or give audiences some sense of what the past might have looked like. However, the *way*

15

in which history has been shaped and packaged – by filmmakers, by film studios, by multinational corporations, by the demands of narrative, genre and audiences – reveals just as much about the contemporary concerns and preoccupations of a far from homogenous 'America' and of what is an increasingly diffuse filmmaking industry.

Given the apparent centrality of the American Revolution to the benign meta-narrative of American history, it perhaps comes as something of a surprise that, unlike World War II or the Civil War or even Vietnam, the events of 1775 and thereafter have been largely overlooked by Hollywood as a subject for its films. In fact, since the United States celebrated its Bicentennial in 1976, just two films have been made or part-financed by Hollywood which feature the Revolution in any meaningful way: Hugh Hudson's ill-fated *Revolution* (1985), a film whose abject box office performance effectively bankrupted its British production company Goldcrest, and *The Patriot* (2000), a big-budget 'blockbuster' film starring Mel Gibson and made by the production team also responsible for *Independence Day* (1996) and *Godzilla* (1998). In this chapter we look at both films, even though *Revolution* falls outside the post-Cold War timeframe of our study, since this earlier film acts as a useful counterpoint for thinking about *The Patriot*. Explanations for the relative lack of cinematic interest in the American Revolution remain speculative; most daringly, Michael Ventura has argued that Hollywood has tended to shy away from the Revolution for the same reasons that most US television networks refused to air a dramatised reading of the Declaration of Independence during the 1976 Bicentennial: because to do so would be to remind people of the document's incendiary, subversive principles and hence how far 'America' had fallen from its original promise.[1] Certainly filmmakers tackling the Revolution as a subject inevitably find themselves caught between a rock and hard place. Represent it as far-reaching and genuinely revolutionary and you run the risk of exposing the ever-growing gap between the rhetorical claims of the Declaration of Independence and what Gregory Jay calls 'the stubborn realities of particularity and exclusion'[2] associated with the United States from its inception. Yet suggest that the break with Britain was somehow limited in its scope and impact and you implicitly undermine a strongly-held belief in American exceptionalism and, in turn, an idea that has inexorably permeated throughout American cinema from its inception.

The story of the founding of the nation may not have featured in many Hollywood films but its trace – virtuous rebels overcoming tyrannical colonial oppressor – haunts all national myths. Indeed, in so far as Hollywood has typically sought to contain and resolve contradictions between competing values and mythologies through a strategy of displacement (displacing contradictions arising from the 'real' into melodrama as a means of resolving them), then this mythologised trace of the revolutionary story has found its way into films as diverse as *My Darling Clementine* (1946) and *Star Wars* (1977). If cultural myths, as John Hellmann contends, 'enable a nation to cohere by reconciling, in the ambiguous relations of narrative, conflicts that its people cannot solve in the sharply delineated realm of analytical thought',[3] then we should perhaps see their assimilation into Hollywood films as a form of ideology as much as an expression of national preoccupations. Slotkin, for example, argues that myth does not 'argue its ideology' but rather 'exemplifies' it. 'It projects models of good and bad behaviour that reinforce the values of ideology, and affirm as good the distribution of authority and power that ideology rationalizes.'[4] The displacement of the historically 'real' into myth, therefore, is part of a wider process whereby cultural forms avail themselves to the task of reinscribing the status quo. The question that lies at the heart of this chapter is how or whether the displacement of the historically 'real' into narrative forms which themselves borrow heavily from myth impacts upon their contradictory status as vehicles of ideology and pedagogically useful texts; that is, texts which can help contemporary audiences better understand what might have happened in the past and why. It has always been the case that history which purports to be the 'ultimate reality and source of truth' in fact 'manifests itself in narrative constructs' or 'stories designed to yield meaning through narrative ordering'.[5] The question that concerns us is how this process is affected or intensified by its translation into a type of narrative – the Hollywood movie – typically known for its affirmative vision of American life. Of course, we need to be careful about conceiving of the 'Hollywood movie' as a standardised, homogenous product, just as we also need to be aware that the practices and processes of making films – and financing and distributing them – have changed significantly throughout the twentieth century. Still, if the term Hollywood now more than ever is shorthand for a type of spectacular, often banal, ideologically conservative, star-studded and special effects-driven filmmaking, then the question of how such changes might have influenced Hollywood's role as American historian does require our attention.

REVOLUTION: HISTORY, MYTH AND SUBVERSION

If it is unfair to berate Hollywood filmmakers for the fact that they rewrite history – for history itself is by no means a pure, unmediated account of the past – then one should perhaps ask how films like *Revolution* or *The Patriot* can help us to better understand the complexities and contingencies of particular historical episodes or events; that is to say, help us see history as both product and process. Here, *Revolution*, a film which focuses on the struggle between the colonial armies and the forces of the British Crown initially in New York and ultimately at Yorktown, constitutes both a success and failure. Certainly there is little in the film to explain what might have motivated the rebellion against Britain, aside from the rambling sentiments of Al Pacino's Tom Dobb, who talks wistfully to his injured son about 'making a place for ourselves' where 'there ain't no kings or queens' to 'tell us what to do'. Nonetheless the film skilfully elucidates the ambivalence of those who, like Dobb, found themselves thrust into battle on the side of the Continental Army without explicitly believing in the cause for which they were fighting. It also highlights, albeit heavy-handedly via a schism between archetypal patriot Daisy McConnahay (Natassja Kinski) and her loyalist family, the way in which the wider conflict split families and communities. Furthermore, just as John Shy claims that the war itself was revolutionary in so far as the act of mobilising against the British had a transforming effect on the colonial population,[6] it is only once Dobb has suffered at the hands of the enemy that, evoking the spirit of Thomas Paine's *Common Sense*, he talks of wanting 'to make a place for ourselves' where 'there ain't no one to bow down to' and 'where there ain't no lord or lady better than you'.

Even more significantly, the film, like Ray Raphael's study of the American Revolution,[7] starts to explore or at least open up the class divisions created by the conflict. Though the men who enlist for the newly formed Continental Army are promised 150 acres of land and Dobb, whose fishing boat is requisitioned for the cause, is promised $200 in addition, at the end of the film the same people are told that land and money owing to them has been sold by Congress to pay for the war debt. The resulting disturbances may be muted but the point

is well made; the poor go to the wall while McConnahay, a specula-
tor who initially supported the Crown but who subsequently
changed sides, benefits financially and politically in this new
America. As a powerless Dobb is jostled from the centre of the frame
by an unruly mob, the visual imagery evokes disarray rather than
consensus and unity of purpose. Behind the veneer of a newly
created national 'sameness' lies a myriad of competing, potentially
explosive class claims and differences.

At stake here is not the issue of how 'accurately' *Revolution* recreates particular episodes and events from the American Revolution
but rather how, or how far, this process is shaped by a desire to offer
a particular reading or interpretation of the past, by the narrative convention of Hollywood cinema, or indeed by the cultural and political
imperatives informing the film's moment of production. We are
interested in not only how historical films can help us to 'vision' the
past,[8] but also whether they challenge received and apparently
settled versions of history, or how they open up rather than close off
interpretative possibilities, and force us to think for ourselves about
the contested nature of historical 'truth'. Moreover, in so far as our
expectations of how America's past might have been or what it
'looked like' are inevitably tied up with the production of cinematic
images and narratives, the question also becomes one of how far
these films disrupt the formal and thematic conventions of
Hollywood cinema.

Traditionally, then, the western has tended to set the limits of
Hollywood's engagement with history, or rather Hollywood has
sought to narrate the growing pains of the nation through the
mythologised exploits of a single, heroic figure. As Slotkin puts it,
'When history is translated into myth, the complexities of social and
historical experiences are simplified and compressed into the actions
of representative individuals or "heroes."'[9] So what of Tom Dobb
and *Revolution* in general? Does he slide comfortably into the outlaw
hero's cowboy boots and does the film reduce and simplify the complexities of 'real' history? Certainly it would be fair to say that the
film's attempts at historical revisionism take place through the lens
of generic revisionism; that is to say, its means of telling the 'truth'
about history is to summon up the slower, darker, more contemplative mood of westerns such as *McCabe and Mrs Miller* (1971); films
which were not necessarily any more 'realistic' than their earlier
counterparts but which self-consciously sought to challenge myths

about the viability of individual heroism or the ability of such figures to shape and order the chaotic 'mess' of public history.

From the beginning, Dobb struggles to assert himself. In fact, he is dwarfed by his surroundings, by the sheer physicality of a New York in turmoil. The film's mis-en-scene here is revealing. As the moving camera attempts to follow him through the teeming streets, Dobb is jostled from the centre of the frame, disorientating both him and the viewer. A little later, as the conscripts leave the city by boat, the camera pulls back slowly to reveal Dobb in a sea of equally blank-looking faces. Visually, as with the earlier street scenes, the effect is to situate him in a context where the collective is privileged over the individual, in a situation over which he has no control. Of course the classic western often began this way, with the outlaw hero reluctant to sacrifice his independence in order to help the wider community achieve some kind of desirable collective goal.[10] In *Revolution*, Dobb reluctantly agrees to join the war effort in order to protect his son and eventually to 'make a place for ourselves' but his efforts make little or no difference to the collective cause. Underlining this point, in a scene that self-consciously evokes the climax of John Ford's *Stagecoach* (1939), British dragoons – stand-ins for Ford's Apaches – pursue and attack a coach driven by Daisy McConnahay, the woman that Dobb loves. Rapid editing between close-ups of the pursuers, the galloping horses and the stagecoach itself intensify the connection. But whereas Ford's hero, the Ringo Kid (John Wayne), is instrumental in repelling the Apaches, Dobb can only watch from a distance as the British attack and upend the stagecoach. His decision to chase after it on foot strikes one not as heroic but as the desperate response of a man who is all too aware of his own limitations.

Many of Ford's films strive to integrate the outlaw into a positive, enabling community. Though the dictates of the outlaw code precludes permanent engagement, the solidarity that is fostered through some kind of encounter with a hostile, external force is genuinely uplifting, and even where the outlaw's anti-social tendencies threatens to undermine this solidarity – as in *The Searchers* (1956) – the communal goal of settling the land cannot be achieved without his help. *Revolution* works to an altogether different end: the isolation and entrapment of individuals who, as Kolker puts it, 'though part of a large organisation, are forced to be alone'.[11] Alienated both from the Patriot army which he grudgingly serves and his son who interprets his self-interest as cowardice, Dobb veers between action and passivity. Occasional successes, such as his rescue of his son from a heavily fortified British army camp, are punctuated by long periods of introspection and melancholy. Failure, or rather ambivalence, is Dobb's leitmotif. As the film lurches towards its climax – the last stand of the British at Yorktown – it flirts with conventionality in so far as the wider conflict is displaced into a stand-off between Dobb and Peasy (Donald Sutherland), a British soldier who has previously captured and beaten Dobb's son. Still, even here, the film's willingness to flout convention is evidenced. Dobb wounds Peasy and has the opportunity to kill him but, at the behest of his son, decides not to, allowing Peasy to make his escape.

There are three ways to read this sense of ambivalence. The first is to frame it in terms of artistic failure; that is, to interpret the film's slow, contemplative pace, its willed incoherence and its dramatic confusion as a failure on the part of its makers. The film's abject performance at the American and British box offices, and its mauling at the hands of some film critics, lends a certain amount of credibility to this argument. *Time's* Richard Corliss, for example, described it as a 'chaotic two hour and four minute mess' and claimed that preview audiences had 'giggled derisively through it'.[12] Pauline Kael, in *The New Yorker*, believed the film was so bad 'it puts you in a state of shock' and said of the disjointed introductory sequence: 'this is the American Revolution as you might expect to see it on MTV'.[13]

For us, the more pressing issue is how we might begin to read or make sense of this confusion and ambivalence not in aesthetic terms but as a work of historical revisionism. It would certainly be fair to suggest that the film cannot work out what to do with Pacino's character, or how to make sense of his twin role as conscientious objector and standard-bearer for the emerging nation. To some extent, attempts to wrap him up in the Stars and Stripes, as the film's trailer sets out to do, reflect a traditional preoccupation with celebrating an uncomplicated 'American-ness'. His ambivalence, meanwhile, speaks to, and about, a more subversive desire to unsettle straightforward notions of what constitutes an 'American' identity. More to the point, this incoherence or tension must be situated quite explicitly in the context of 1980s America; that is to say, one might think about how the contradictory ideologies informing the production of the film shape the way in which the film represents history. For a start, there is something unconvincing about the film's flirtation with a celebratory vision of America and American national identity – a vision that was central to

Ronald Reagan's presidency.[14] To be sure, in the climate of a Reagan-inspired attempt to resuscitate a positive sense of American national identity from the trauma of defeat in Vietnam and the so-called 'crisis of confidence' that paralysed Carter's administration, the decision to wrap Pacino in the American flag in the film's trailer makes perfect box-office sense. Simultaneously, however, the film is ultimately uninterested in occupying the patriotic territory claimed by movies like *Rambo: First Blood Part II* (1985). Rather, *Revolution* is curious in that it wants to explore the legacy of America's 'crisis of confidence'. To put it another way, if the critical cinema of the 1970s – inspired by both Vietnam and Watergate – was essentially one of anxiety and ambiguity, then *Revolution* is intrigued by this legacy without ever fully committing itself to continuing it. The film embraces and recoils from representing an ambiguous national identity, knowing that a film about failure and vulnerability might not play well to audiences in the thrall of Reagan's can-do boosterism. As Adrian Turner notes, 'Al Pacino is not John Wayne as David Crockett defending democracy and dying at the Alamo; nor is he John Rambo, a one-man task force regaining for America a whimsical self-respect and national pride after the humiliations of Vietnam and Iran . . . *Revolution* subverts this image of heroism.'[15]

The film's engagement with the legacy of the 1970s manifests itself most obviously in its willed incoherence and formal disjointedness, as though part of Hudson's desire is not to make a 'bad' film but rather a difficult film, one that requires audiences to work at eliciting meaning. Building upon this starting point, we want to argue that what is being evoked here is not the confused ideological undercurrents of the mid-1980s but an alternative, even subversive way of 'seeing' history. If American cinema has tended to treat history as popular myth – that is to say, to displace the complexities, discontinuities and contingencies of the 'real' into a simplified form where such contradictions can be resolved – then what we see in *Revolution* represents a different approach to history, one in which the sweep of public events takes precedence over the private exploits of individuals and where neatly packaged answers and clear visual and narrative signposts are not provided.

For all its flaws, therefore, the film's determination to unsettle our expectations, to withhold clues about how to read character and motivation, to disempower its protagonist and show war to be dirty, brutal and shorn of heroic aura, serves to throw into relief the more general relationship between cinema and history. Accordingly, *Revolution* may not be 'true' in the sense that it sets out to dispassionately and objectively record what really happened, but, as Robert Rosenstone argues, the idea that 'truth' and 'accuracy' are necessarily synonymous is itself problematic. As he explains, 'The historical film will always include images that are, at once, invented and, at best, true . . . true in the sense they symbolize, condense, or summarize larger amounts of data; or true in that they impart an overall meaning of the past.'[16] What we see in *Revolution*, then, is a fictional recreation of the 'real' as seen through the eyes of an invented figure, Tom Dobb, but one that is 'true' in so far as it imparts 'an overall meaning of the past' or at least one that shows what it might have been like to have lived in or through the events of the revolution. When we see Tom Dobb being caught up in circumstances over which he has no control, what we are actually witnessing is the surrender of the private or individual to the collective. As Michael Ventura points out:

> Hudson's subject is the emotional context of a rebellion. How it swings in wild extremes, both brutal and lyrical. Here everyone and everything is dirty and confused and bold and contradictory and desperate and sweet and unkempt . . . [The film's characters] only have a story in so far as they're swept up into the flow of the rebellion, and to be swept up is, by definition, not to have a story of one's own. To be part of such movements is to surrender one's private story to the collective story.[17]

The film's failure at the box office can be explained by its willed ambivalence and its refusal to jump onboard a populist patriotic bandwagon, and perhaps too by its narrative incoherence and its weak characterisation, theatrical dialogue and wooden acting. But we would like to propose an additional reason for its failure; one that relates to the political project of rebellion and the attendant anxieties produced when social and political hierarchies are questioned by mainstream cinema. If Ventura's point that American filmmakers 'haven't dared to portray the American Revolution' because 'there's no way to do it without being at least incendiary if not downright subversive' is true, then it perhaps explains the small number of films made about the event. Certainly, as he concludes, however the 'revolutionaries' are represented, 'you've still got the most articulate principles of rebellion ever spoken; the invention . . . of modern guerrilla war; and the application of political terrorism'.[18] *Revolution* may not be entirely successful in articulating these principles and imperatives, but in so far as it exposes the chaos and upheaval associated with radical change, the class divisions opened up, and the gap between utopian rhetoric and lived reality, then it makes for viewing that is by no means comfortable and reassuring. Moreover, the film challenges a patriotic, benign reading of the American Revolution which posits it as a landmark in human progress and suggests that the revolution, *in spite* of its incendiary rhetoric, was essentially a conservative one or at least a struggle which ended up securing the interests of the landed class. Certainly when Dobb arrives back in New York at the end of the film, little or nothing has changed: land and money promised to him has gone to pay off the war debt, speculators and businessmen have assumed control of the city and the streets throng with the injured and dispossessed. The lasting images of the film, meanwhile, are the grim, impressively staged battle scenes which impress, in the final analysis, not simply because they reveal war to be brutal, dirty and shorn of any heroic aura, but also because they allow audiences the time and space to reflect on the damage wrought on individuals and groups. As Dilys Powell concluded, 'I can think of no film which with such amplitude of vision offers a more powerful impression of an old, simple war and the heartless annihilators of warfare.'[19]

THE PATRIOT: HISTORY AND THE POLITICS OF AUTHENTICITY

The first thing that strikes a viewer of Roland Emmerich's *The Patriot*, after watching *Revolution*, is the pleasantness of it all. Gone is the dour, grimy, washed-out look of Hudson's film and in its place we are treated to an altogether softer, gentler vision. The first scenes are indicative. Cue a shot of mist-clad rolling hills, lush tobacco and millet fields bathed in hues of rich, golden sunlight, verdant trees draped in Spanish moss, and Benjamin Martin (Mel Gibson) idling happily on the porch of his pristine homestead with young daughter. Cue, too, a shot of 'lovely' Charleston, South Carolina. Not the crowded, noisy and disorientating city of *Revolution* but rather a lantern-lit, tree-lined space inhabited by stately ante-bellum buildings and populated by high-spirited but well-behaved rebels firing their guns politely into the air. This is Disneyland's Main Street nostalgically posing as the historically 'real' or rather history as make-over. Everything, it seems, has been painstakingly recreated not merely to look 'authentic' but rather to seem somehow more real, as though representing history is primarily a matter of fulfilling people's expectations of how the past was supposed to have looked. So just as the film's 'official' companion book tells us how the green jackets of the Crown's Green Dragoons were changed to red coats in order to facilitate audience recognition – 'so that [audiences] knew they were British'[20] – it also describes how one of the set's terracotta, brown, yellow and pale green buildings was 'reflected in the ward-robe of the extras who filled the adjacent courtyard'.[21] The past, it seems, must not only seem 'authentic' but also be visually attractive. The official companion also describes how the production team filled another building with 'beautiful, pastel-hued hoop skirts and ornate hats and jewelry worn by the female extras . . . [while] British officers provided splashes of scarlet in their trademark red coats, easily spotted against the twilight sky and green lawns'.[22]

Such claims to authenticity are founded upon the assumption that representations of history must somehow conform to certain expecta-tions or preconceptions that people have about historical periods; in the case of the American Revolution, that the British must wear 'red-coats' and be suitably tyrannical and that the American rebels look suitably earthy and possess noble values. Of course, these expecta-tions or preconceptions have themselves been shaped by certain nar-rative or generic conventions. In the case of a critically-minded film like *Revolution*, the fact that it seeks to contest the myth of the individ-ualist hero does not mean that it is not still centrally preoccupied with that myth. In the case of a more conservative film like *The Patriot*, its attempts to simultaneously make history look 'authentic' and yet dis-place the complexities and contingencies of history into a narrative form whose resolution is determined by a single heroic figure seems eminently typical and perhaps therefore comforting for audiences who have grown to expect such practices. In other words, rather than marking some kind of new departure in the way in which Hollywood films engage with American history, *The Patriot* would seem to conform to a set of quite familiar conventions: what Robert Ray describes as 'the reluctant hero' story, in which an 'exceptional' figure is somehow persuaded by the needs of the larger community to tem-porarily sacrifice his hard-earned independence in order to further some politically or socially significant collective cause.[23]

In the case of *The Patriot*, this requires Mel Gibson's Benjamin Martin, a widowed homesteader, to come out of hard-earned retirement – like all gunfighters he has a reputation for, and a history of, violence – and commit himself to the cause of fighting against the British and those colonists loyal to the Crown. In the light of this distinction, it would perhaps be unfair to suggest that the film reveals nothing to us about the strains and tensions within American colonial communities in the early years of the fighting. For example, a scene depicting the debate in the Charleston Assembly indicates that its representatives in 1776 were by no means agreed upon which path to follow, whether to fight for independence or remain loyal to the Crown. That said, what could potentially turn into a sophisticated argument about the nature of power, or, as Richard B. Morris explores, how or even whether the social, political and economic disruption caused by the war generated fundamental changes in the institutional structures of government,[24] quickly becomes one that is addressed and resolved in the context of Martin's private affairs. Though, as we find out, he is opposed to 'taxation without representation' and believes in 'self-government' he is unwilling to commit himself to the cause because he feels he can better protect his family by remaining at home; especially, as he remarks, because 'the war will be fought not on some distant battlefield but amongst us'. In other words, the whole question of whether it is appropriate for the colonists to take up arms against the Crown ultimately boils down to the issue of Martin's desire to protect his family. From the way the scene is filmed, the viewer is encouraged to believe that the Patriot cause, even before the fighting has started, is a lost one without him. Whereas *Revolution* demanded the surrender of the individual to the collective, *The Patriot*'s view of history is dependent on the opposite, on the surrender of the collective to the individual. The result is predictable – the utter lack of the former film's ambivalence and ambiguity. Everything in *The Patriot* is explained and explainable. For example, why does Martin eventually join the cause? Because his home is attacked by British soldiers and one of his sons is killed. This particular scene is indicative of the film's process of simplification. From the moment when Colonel Tavington (Jason Isaacs) arrives at Martin's home on horseback and rejects Martin's pleas for clemency, choosing to demonstrate 'something of the rules of war' by shooting dead one of Martin's sons, a highly complex, multi-faceted conflict between the British and

Americans, loyalists and patriots, and coloniser and colonised, boils down to a personal feud between two men.

If there is something typical about the way in which *The Patriot*, to paraphrase Slotkin, simplifies or compresses 'the complexities of social and historical experiences' into 'the action of representative heroes',[25] then we perhaps should not be too surprised that the view of history we are given in the film is, to say the least, a skewed one. This is not to say that the film entirely botches its history or that its representation of particular characters and incidents has no basis in other, perhaps more carefully documented historical accounts. According to the film's production notes and 'official companion', for example, Martin's character is loosely based on a number of 'real' figures who waged a guerrilla war against the Crown across the Carolinas. 'Martin's slippery elusiveness', we are told, 'is reminiscent of [Francis] Marion, who would attack the British and retreat into the swamps, earning him the sobriquet "The Swamp Fox"', but at the same time Martin's 'independent spirit, his talent for recruiting men to join his militia, and his effective guerrilla campaign reflect [Thomas] Sumter' as well as Andrew Pickens and Daniel Morgan, whose '1000-strong force of light infantry, riflemen, regular army and militia led the crucial colonial victory at the Battle of Cowpens' which is represented in the film'.[26] Whether such claims lend *The Patriot's* attempts at representing history any credibility is open to question but one could perhaps argue that it does support John Shy's assertion that the British force under Banastre Tarleton – Colonel Tavington in the film – 'acquired in the course of its operations a reputation for inhumanity that drove apathetic citizens towards the rebels for protection'.[27] To demonstrate this, the film focuses on Tavington's brutal campaign of terror against the population of the Carolinas, culminating in his burning down of a church with women, children and old people locked up inside. But while this scene may have been 'true' in the sense that Tarleton, by some accounts, 'enthusiastically burnt the farms of suspected Patriots and summarily executed suspected guerillas', there is little evidence to suggest that he 'committed the atrocities of the sort depicted in *The Patriot*'.[28]

It is not difficult to find evidence the accounts of historians that contradict many of the film's historical claims. For example, while Shy maintains that the rebel militia was 'poorly trained, badly led . . . and seldom comprised of the deadly marksmen dear to American legend',[29] *The Patriot* suggests that the militia, once organised and trained by Martin, is a potent weapon in the war against the Crown forces. And whereas Shy's point is that the militia's crucial function was a non-military one – politicising the rural population and thus embodying 'sand in the gears of the pacification machine'[30] – the film indicates that the militia, with Martin at its helm, was absolutely instrumental in driving the British army not just out of the Carolinas but also out of America. Indeed, just prior to the final battle, when Martin appears on horseback carrying the Stars and Stripes – unlikely, to say the least, because the Continental Army had not adopted the flag as early as 1781 – one is left in no doubt as to his talismanic presence. As if to underline the displacement of the 'real' into the melodramatic, Martin picks up the fallen American flag and drives the sharp end of the pole into Tavington's oncoming horse, before finishing him off in a desperate hand-to-hand fight with a knife and tomahawk. As he does so, General Cornwallis (Tom Wilkinson), who is watching the struggle from a distance, is heard to mutter, 'How could it come to this, an army of *peasants*? Everything will change. Everything has changed.' Because the instant that Martin kills Tavington, independence from the Crown is realised.

Our point here, however, is that an excessive focus on the question of historical (in)accuracy ultimately manifests itself in a banal list-making of a film's failings, itself a critical dead-end because, inevitably, the historical record against which a film is evaluated is by no means secure and beyond challenge. To this end, when thinking about the significance of Martin's unlikely appropriation of the Stars and Stripes and about *The Patriot*'s representation of the American Revolution, what should concern us is not whether this could have happened but rather what message it might convey to audiences about the meaning of the American Revolution in our own hybridised, globalised, post-Cold War world. Our first point is that the film, on one level, wants to affirm a quite traditional, benign, patriotic reading of the American Revolution. It is not interested, as *Revolution* was, in showing the fighting as dirty and dispiriting, or in suggesting that the passage from colonialism to independence threatened to unravel into social anarchy, or even that the war itself utterly transformed the fabric of life in the ex-colonies. Rather, with its emphasis on an American perspective and insistence that the principles being fought for by the Patriots primarily centered upon an amorphous notion of 'freedom', the film would have us believe that the American Revolution was some kind of heroic landmark for human progress –

a revolution for all humankind. However, in so far as the values that are constituted in the film as American (that is, freedom, choice, diversity) are also universal ones, and given that the drive to export these supposedly American values to a global marketplace now constitutes an important part of America's cultural, political and economic foreign policy, one wonders how far a film like *The Patriot*'s attempts at representing history are not motivated by a desire to help us to better understand the complex 'realities' of the Revolution itself but rather to reinforce some contemporary ideas about what the United States can apparently offer the world (that is, freedom, democracy, hope, and so on). In this scenario, then, the film ends up securing an ultimately conventional version of national identity whereby American values are aggressively foregrounded as beneficial to everyone. Still, the fact that *The Patriot* is not made exclusively for an American audience,[31] or with exclusively American finance, and that as a result it exists within and has been shaped by a set of power networks which inevitably transcend the sovereign boundaries of 'America' itself, opens up the possibility of reading it in an alternative way: that is, as expressing the concerns and ambitions not of an imagined America but of global corporations like Fox and Sony, which may or may not be the same thing. In this scenario, the usurping of the nation-state by global corporations is by no means inevitable, particularly given the continuing political, economic and cultural domination of the United States; but the question of how realignments in the relationship between nation-states, even ones as powerful as the United States, and multinational conglomerates impacts upon the role that films play in either securing or contesting national ideologies requires further examination. In the case of *The Patriot*, we might ask whether the film's relentless privileging of style or spectacle over politics (or over developing a coherent political and/or historical viewpoint) and its excessive reliance on the 'star' presence of Mel Gibson speaks about important changes in the ways in which contemporary films are made, distributed and watched – and consequently the way in which history is represented.

One can detect a hint of this influence in *The Patriot*'s treatment of domestic relationships between white settlers and freed or escaped African-American slaves. According to the film's makers, its depiction of both groups and the relationships between them is scrupulously handled. Calling upon the expertise of the Smithsonian National Museum of American History in Washington DC, the film's makers sought to recreate an 'authentic' Gullah village on the Carolina shores of the Atlantic Ocean, populated by runaway and freed slaves originating from Angola, Congo and the Ivory Coast. *The Smithsonian* magazine referred enthusiastically to the role that the institution's staff had played in getting the attention to detail right. 'The scene at the Gullah village', an on-set Lucinda Moore observed approvingly, 'is of thatched-roof huts, men on horseback and women in African head-wraps along a narrow strip of land bordered by a wooded swamp, a tidal pool filled with docked canoes, and the Atlantic crashing and foaming behind it.'[32]

But the question of whether the film accurately portrayed the constitution of the village wattle-and-daub huts, or equipped the villagers with the 'correct' cooking utensils, obscures the far more important question of why the Gullah village is represented at all in the film, particularly as it is not vital to the narrative as a whole, and how the depiction of African-Americans in general might owe less to the demands of history than to the imperatives of a twenty-first-century cultural and political logic. The film's careful elision of any references to slavery – those who work on Martin's farm do so under their own volition and for a fair wage – certainly moved Spike Lee to anger. In an open letter to the *Hollywood Reporter*, he described the film as 'pure, blatant American Hollywood propaganda' and said that when 'talking about the history of this great country, one can never forget [it] was built upon the genocide of the Native Americans and the enslavement of African people' and that to imply otherwise, as *The Patriot* seeks to do, was nothing short of 'criminal'.[33]

While the polemic intent of Lee's argument is useful for political mobilisation against racism, such an analysis fails to notice that *The Patriot*'s racial politics are working in more complex and diffuse ways than Lee allows. *The Patriot* is not simply 'pure, blatant American Hollywood propaganda', nor is it a naive return to *Gone with the Wind*-style plantation movies, with their emphasis on an absolute racial difference. Instead, *The Patriot* seems intent on eradicating racial differences either by pretending they have no profound social or political consequences, or by insisting upon a cultural equivalence and relativity that seems to be of our own contemporary making rather than the product of eighteenth-century North America.

Hence the Gullah villagers, with their own indigenous culture and language, are entirely free, in the context of the film, to do whatever they choose, unbounded by the strictures of white authority. Martin's farmhands, meanwhile, may not be able to own land themselves, hence they have to work for him, but they are not his property and are treated with affection, tolerance and respect. Yet this freedom is something of a chimera: it speaks to a contemporary cultural and political logic. African-Americans in *The Patriot* may be 'free' in one sense but only in so far as they are permitted to occupy particular carefully demarcated spaces and given certain unchallenging tasks to perform. In this sense, a shift away from absolute racial difference does not signal the arrival of some kind of race-less, multicultural utopia, but rather indicates merely that differences are to be celebrated, managed and incorporated into new social and political hierarchies. What we see in *The Patriot*, therefore, reflects not so much the historical 'reality' of America in the 1770s, but rather the logic of our contemporary moment in which differences are initially disregarded and then celebrated and finally arranged and managed in a complex, diffuse organisational system.[34]

Accordingly, the scene in which Martin's eldest son Gabriel (Heath Ledger) marries local sweetheart Anne (Lisa Brenner) in the 'safe' confines of the Gullah village is an instructive one. The question of security is an important one, since Gabriel and his father are, by this stage in the film, being actively pursued by the British. As the camera slowly zooms in on Gabriel and Anne, the onlookers from the village, who are literally outside of the tent, are erased from the frame. The villagers might be 'hosting' the wedding but their role is a marginal one; as night falls, we are shown shots of maracas and a xylophone and hear the unmistakable sounds of what is now commonly referred to as 'world music'. In other words, despite the hybrid possibilities inherent in the way in which the scene insists upon incorporating and mixing white colonial and 'maroon' cultures, the freed and escaped slaves are ultimately little more than a colourful backdrop to the wedding celebrations, or rather they are incorporated into a hierarchy or chain of command with Martin, and his family, at its helm. Indeed, this applies not just to racial differences but also to class ones, for however much the film wants to pretend that the rhetoric of the Declaration of Independence is binding, once British rule is brought to an end, it is instructive that the first act performed by the militia who served under Martin, once the war has been won, is to rebuild his burnt-out home. Explaining this, Hardwick, an ex-slave who has earned his freedom by fighting in the militia, says to

Martin, '[Your son] said if we won the war we could build a whole new world. Just figured we'd get started right away with your home.' Hardwick is standing next to another militiaman, a white man, who admitted, earlier in the film, that he didn't 'like the idea of giving muskets to slaves'. The fact that he has changed his opinion speaks to, and about, this 'new world' where 'all men are created equal under God'. In other words, what these scenes do is impose a bogus contemporary 'reality' on a historical moment altogether more complicated.

While *Revolution* hinted at the possibility that the chaos and anarchy of war might lead to radical social and political change, and presented that reimposition of class hierarchies at the end of the film as a loss, *The Patriot* seems to suggest that the only thing wrong with North America by the late 1770s was the presence of the British and that once removed everything can proceed as normal. This might, of course, be a sly reference to the essentially conservative nature of the Revolution itself – that the ambition of those leading the struggle was not to destroy the social and political order but to reconfigure the balance of power within pre-existing agencies and institutions – but it speaks just as forcefully about our own 'depoliticising' moment. The fact that the film ends not with the chaos and upheaval seen in *Revolution* but with a group of poor whites and freed slaves volunteering to rebuild Martin's homestead is indicative. Such a vision is so seductive precisely because it appears to be both inclusive and informed by common sense (and hence free of ideology).[35]

The more important question, therefore, is not whether the cooking utensils used by the Gullah villagers are authentic, but who or what is determining a politics of representation that seeks to conceal its own particularity and masquerade as a universal consensus. It is worthwhile, here, to consider that the makers of *The Patriot* were also responsible for *Independence Day* (1996), the global blockbuster which features a poster-perfect alliance of multi-ethnic Americans battling aliens and making America and then the rest of the world safe. The most obvious reading of the film is that a form of old-fashioned American imperialism underpins the film's universal liberalism, a reading supported by the content and tone of President Whitmore's (Bill Pullman) climactic speech in which he declares: 'We are reminded not of our petty differences but of our common interests . . . From this day forth, the Fourth of July will no longer be remembered as an American holiday but as the day that the world declared in voice that we will not go quietly into the night.' In other words, *Independence Day*'s appeal to an imaginary universal is at once conceived as an American celebration and as the manifestation of a triumphant America bestriding a world – and a new world order – apparently formed in its own image. But, as Gregory Jay notes, the crucial point is that this new global/American order secures its power through the manufacturing of universal consent rather than through the reaffirmation of imperialist structures of power or through acts of military coercion:

> With the Americans in the lead, the whole earth prepares to be reborn on the Fourth of July. It is as if scapegoating the extraterrestrial will vanquish the legacy of imperialism and make the Third World grateful once more for the superior power of the West... Any doubt about the racism of the film is resolved when, to illustrate victory, the camera pans an African savannah where traditionally dressed tribesmen wave spears in jubilation at the sight of the downed alien craft. The actuality of the postcolonial condition . . . is erased by a visual narrative that returns the happy primitives to their place in the world.[36]

A similar point could be made about *The Patriot*, in so far as the freedom being articulated by Gibson's Martin in eighteenth-century North America is identical to the freedom being demanded by another Gibson characterisation, William Wallace in thirteenth-century Scotland in *Braveheart* (1995), or for that matter by Whitmore in *Independence Day*. Exactly what this freedom constitutes is never explicitly explained, though this tendency towards abstraction is probably not coincidental because it allows us to read it either as a universal right in itself or as a universal right conceived in the image of an imagined America. On this occasion, the ambivalence is reductive rather than provocative because it doesn't require us to discriminate between competing perspectives or arguments or ask questions about the nature of historical inquiry. Rather, it is informed by a lazy relativism whereby all opinions and views are nominally judged to be of equal value and all versions of history are equally affirmed. In one view, America stands for, and guarantees, a set of particular values (that is, freedom from British colonial tyranny) and as such the film's representation of the American Revolution underscores an uncomplicated American exceptionalism and affirms the benign meta-narrative of American history. In another view, apparently 'American' values are subsumed into a larger universal category and hence lose their particular distinctiveness and as such the film's representation of the American Revolution serves simply to articulate a freedom that is so undifferentiated that it means almost nothing. To put this another way, *The Patriot* is depoliticising, first of all because it does not require us and does not want us to think about history as a contested entity. In other words, rather than self-consciously acknowledging its own partiality, that it represents a particular view, it problematically seeks to convince us it is everyone's story because everyone's view is apparently taken into account. More than this, however, it is depoliticising because this inclusionism is handcuffed to a visual style based upon the privileging of spectacle and sensation over more traditional preoccupations with realism. A film like *The Patriot*, despite its claims to historical authenticity, is depoliticising because it is ultimately less concerned with cinematic verisimilitude and an attendant sense of history as both 'real' and constructed than with bombarding audiences with a series of empty signifiers: images of spectacular excess that serve to gratify more than to disturb or challenge.

To illustrate this point, the closing remarks of this chapter will be addressed to a particular scene from *The Patriot*. The scene in question takes place after Gibson's Martin has witnessed the murder of one of his sons by Tavington and the capture of another. Taking his two youngest sons, he ambushes the platoon that is transporting Gabriel to their camp and proceeds to attack them. The scene takes place after the last Crown soldier drops his weapon and starts to run away. Martin removes his tomahawk, steadies himself and plants it squarely in the man's back. The scene cuts to a shot of the youngest sons freeing Gabriel. Out of the frame, we hear Martin grunt. It cuts back to Martin, who is kneeling over the dead soldier, disembowelling him with his tomahawk, and then to a close-up of his bloody face. The scene cuts back to his three children, who stare at him, ashen-faced. Finally, it returns to Martin, who turns to face them, his hair, face and clothes covered in fresh blood.

Initially shocking, what is excessive about the scene and what threatens to unravel the film – the unsanctioned brutality, the cold-blooded slaying of a soldier who had dropped his weapon, and the sheer scale of the violence – is quickly mitigated by subsequent reaction. The attack is reported to the British high command not as a horrific slaughter but as a morale-boosting victory for the Patriot cause, while any guilt that Martin might have felt is assuaged shortly afterwards by one of the sons who claims to be 'satisfied' with the killing. Even the son who is most repulsed by the violence relents and offers Martin a reconciliatory hug. On reflection, what is most striking about the way in which the scene is constructed is that Martin's children witness the slaughter in order to replicate how the film asks that we, as viewers, watch it. Their gaze, as Antonia Quirke argues about this particular scene, 'mitigates – sanctifies, even – their father's behavior by presenting the whole thing to us as a familial rite of passage'.[37]

In other words, Martin's violence is justified because it serves as implicit support of the white, middle-class family. Moreover, precisely because of the gratifying scale of the 'spectacle' (which of course transcends all national and linguistic boundaries) and the solace we receive immediately following it (where we are reassured the everything is all right), the scene ends up evoking *Braveheart*, or for that matter *Lethal Weapon* and *Independence Day*, more than *Revolution*. Even more so because its perpetrator is not Benjamin Martin but Mel Gibson; that is to say, the potential for reading this scene in ambiguous ways is nullified because its perpetrator is Gibson, because his 'star' image all but guarantees that our identification with him will never be broken. The result, as Miller says about much contemporary Hollywood filmmaking, ends up being 'a spectacle that has been meticulously engineered to "gratify" at every single moment . . . [and whose] images are designed to keep us happy, thereby composing a heavy atmosphere of . . . easy shocks along with constant solace, flattery and affirmation'.[38]

The fact that a film ostensibly about a foundational moment in the history of the American nation took as much money at the international box office as the domestic US box office speaks simultaneously about the international popularity of action films, the 'star' appeal of Gibson and the effects of American-dominated distribution networks. But it could also be argued that such 'success' owes something to its anodyne attempts to excite, stimulate, comfort and gratify audiences through spectacular action sequences and easy explanations rather than engage them in any thoughtful or challenging way. *The Patriot*'s history, then, is a digitally remastered version of the past whose 'high concept' style, to use Justin Wyatt's term, speaks to important structural changes in the film industry and 'can be described most productively . . . as one strain of contemporary American cinema whose style has a direct economic motive'.[39] To put this another way, if high concept films are founded upon the availability of an exploitable presence – something which 'can motivate moments which are excessive in the film'[40] – then Gibson himself is such a presence and the function of his excessive behaviour is not to engage with the messiness of history but rather to thrill and titillate audiences reared on unthinkingly violent action films and expecting Gibson to do as he has done throughout the *Lethal Weapon* series: kill 'bad' people in the name of an unquestioned 'good'. More particularly, *The Patriot*'s version of the past, of an American past, is aimed at an audience that is no longer exclusively or even predominantly American. The point, here, is not whether non-American audiences are actually seduced by such images but that Hollywood directors like *The Patriot*'s Roland Emmerich are having to think about questions like, 'How can I construct this film in order to maximise revenue not just in America but also in Europe, the Far East, and so on?' As Frederick Wasser concludes, 'The trend line is not absolute but the economic circumstances of current production demands that fewer and fewer films will address a specific community or national audience in a profound way.'[41]

NOTES

1 Michael Ventura, 'A Revolution Worth Having', *LA Weekly*, 27 December 1985–January 2 1986, p. 21.
2 Gregory J. Jay, *American Literature and the Culture Wars* (Ithaca: Cornell University Press, 1997), p. 79.
3 John Hellmann, *American Myth and the Legacy of Vietnam* (New York: Columbia University Press, 1986), p. 218.
4 Richard Slotkin, *The Fatal Environment: The Myth of the Frontier in the Age of Industrialization* (Norman, OK: University of Oklahoma Press, 1998), p. 19.
5 See Jonathan Culler in Tony Bennett, 'Outside literature: Texts in History', in Keith Jeffries, ed., *The Postmodern History Reader* (Routledge: London and New York: 1997), p. 219.
6 John Shy, 'The Military Conflict as a Revolutionary War', in Michael Penman, ed., *Perspectives on the American Past Vol. 1: To 1877* (Chicago: Heath, 1996), p. 135.
7 Ray Raphael, *A People's History of the American Revolution* (New York: Harper Perennial, 2002).
8 Robert Rosenstone, 'Oliver Stone as Historian', in Robert Brent Toplin,

ed., *Oliver Stone's USA* (Lawrence, KS: University Press of Kansas, 2000), p. 35.

9 Richard Slotkin, *Gunfighter Nation: The Frontier Myth in Twentieth Century America* (New York: Athenum, 1992), p. 13.

10 See Robert Ray, *A Certain Tendency of Hollywood Cinema 1930–1980* (Princeton: Princeton University Press, 1985).

11 Robert Kolker, *A Cinema of Loneliness: Penn, Stone, Kubrick, Scorsese, Spielberg, Altman*, 3rd ed. (Oxford and New York: Oxford University Press, 2000), p. 109.

12 Richard Corliss, 'Losing Battle', *Time*, 6 January 1986, p. 55.

13 Pauline Kael, 'Revolution', *The New Yorker*, 13 January 1986, p. 67.

14 See Lou Cannon, *President Reagan: The Role of a Lifetime* (New York: Touchstone, 1991); Robert Dallek, *Ronald Reagan: The Politics of Symbolism*, revised ed. (Cambridge, MA: Harvard University Press, 1999).

15 Adrian Turner, 'Rambo's Revenge', *Guardian*, 6 February 1986, p. 13.

16 Rosenstone, 'Oliver Stone as Historian', p. 7.

17 Ventura, *LA Weekly*, p. 21.

18 Ibid.

19 Dilys Powell, 'Yankee Doodles', *Punch*, 5 February 1986, p. 84.

20 Suzanne Fritz and Rachel Aberly, *The Patriot: The Official Companion* (London: Carlton, 2000), p. 59.

21 Ibid., pp. 76–7.

22 Ibid., p. 77.

23 Ray, *A Certain Tendency of Hollywood*, p. 90

24 Richard B. Morris, 'A People's Revolution', in Michael Penman, ed., *Perspectives on the American Past Vol. 1: To 1877* (Chicago: Heath, 1996), pp. 118–27.

25 Slotkin, *Gunfighter Nation*, p. 13.

26 Fritz, *The Patriot*, p. 25.

27 Shy, *Perspectives*, p. 135.

28 William Ross St George Jr, 'Movie Review: The Patriot', *Journal of American History* Vol. 87, No. 3, December 2000, http://www.history cooperative.org/journal/jah/87.3/mr_2.html (20/02/04).

29 Shy, *Perspectives*, p. 138.

30 Ibid.

31 *The Patriot* earned $102.0 million at the international box office and $113.3 million at the domestic US box office; see http://www.boxoffice guru.com/intlarch4.htm (20/02/04).

32 Lucinda Moore, 'America's Fight for Freedom', *Smithsonian*, Vol. 31 No. 4, July 2000, p. 52.

33 See Duncan Campbell, 'Film director Lee spikes Patriot guns', *The Guardian*, 8 July 2000, p. 16.

34 This thesis about the inclusion and management of differences within newly emerging apparatuses of rule and networks of power is best articulated by Hardt and Negri; what they call 'Empire' (a structure of rule that both privileges American interests but that is decentered and deterritorialising; that is, without conventional boundaries) 'does not create divisions but rather recognizes existing or potential differences, celebrates them, and manages them within a general economy of command' (Michael Hardt and Antonio Negri, *Empire*, Cambridge, MA and London: Harvard University Press, 2000, pp. 200–1).

35 This position is best described by Slavoj Zizek: 'In post-politics . . . via the process of negotiation of interests, a compromise is reached in the guise of a more or less universal consensus. Post-politics thus emphasizes the need to leave old ideological divisions behind and confront new issues, armed with the necessary expert knowledge and free deliberation that takes people's concrete needs and demands into account.' (*The Ticklish Subject*, London and New York: Verso, 1999, p. 198)

36 Jay, *American Literature and the Culture Wars*, p. 63.

37 Antonia Quirke, 'Old leatherface gets blood on his hands', *Independent on Sunday*, Culture, 16 July 2000, p. 3.

38 Mark Crispen Miller, ed., 'Introduction', *Seeing Through Movies* (New York: Pantheon, 1990), p. 233.

39 Justin Wyatt, *High Concept: Movies and Marketing in Hollywood* (Austin, TX: University of Texas Press, 1994), p. 8.

40 Ibid., p. 31.

41 Frederick Wasser, 'Hollywood Goes Global: The Internationalization of American Cinema', in Steven R. Ross, ed., *Movies and American Society* (New York and Oxford: Blackwell, 2002), p. 358.

Chapter 2

RATTLING THE CHAINS OF HISTORY: STEVEN SPIELBERG'S *AMISTAD* AND 'TELLING EVERYONE'S STORY'

If the American Revolution is a brilliant mirror for the nation's dominant ideologies, an event whose image encapsulates all that its boosters imagine or desire 'America' to be, then slavery is its unpalatable alter ego; an indelible stain on the collective consciousness, a system or institution whose impact is both invisible and yet impossible to ignore and, like a ghost in the machine, whose presence continues to be felt in all areas of American life. Nowhere, one might add, is this ambivalence felt more acutely than in Hollywood. The cultural moment for *Gone with the Wind*-style representations of slavery as domestic idyll and 'Uncle Toms' contentedly serving their white 'massas' has long since passed but what, if anything, to replace them with remains a contentious subject. The dilemma, at least, is a simple one. Portray the slave plantation as anything less than a blood-soaked prison camp, a regime founded upon the systematic brutalisation of African descendents, and a multitude of protesting voices are all but guaranteed. But represent the slave plantation in its full, unremitting grimness and you run the risk of alienating audiences – black and white – who are either unwilling or unable to deal with such images, though for different reasons. If silence and obfuscation mark contemporary attitudes towards slavery *across* the racial spectrum, Tara Mack makes a useful distinction: whereas white Americans have used this silence 'to distance themselves from the guilt and responsibility', black Americans have used it 'to distance themselves from the shame'.[1]

It should not come as too much of a surprise that Hollywood's engagement with a subject as difficult as slavery has been limited. That is, especially since Hollywood's contribution to American culture, as Robert Sklar argues, has 'essentially [been] one of affirmation'.[2] The upshot of which has been the virtual eradication of explicit references to slavery in Hollywood films, at least since the demise of 'blaxploitation' films like *Mandingo* in the mid-1970s, coupled with a displacement of related anxieties about race and racism into other genres or types of film.

Therefore, the release of Steven Spielberg's *Amistad* (1997) constitutes something of a new direction in Hollywood's attitude towards both slavery and its role as public historian. Indeed, the two are related. Henry A. Giroux makes the important point that to view film simply as 'textual practice' makes it hard to talk about it as a 'public pedagogy' or think about 'how film relates to public life' – a scenario that is 'all the more problematic, especially since film has become so prevalent in popular and global culture as a medium through which people communicate to each other'.[3] We will return to questions of audiences, film reception and the relationship between film and public pedagogy later in the chapter but our argument in the book as a whole is that Hollywood filmmakers have become more self-conscious about their role in the shaping of public history; that is to say, a growing number of filmmakers have taken it upon themselves to use historical films in order to critically engage with complicated questions about what constitutes 'America' domestically and internationally in the post-Cold War world. A renewed interest on the part of some filmmakers in tackling 'difficult' subjects might, then, relate to this preoccupation, particularly in the light of contemporary debates raging on Capitol Hill and elsewhere about the vexed question of reparations for slavery. Nonetheless, whether one film constitutes a 'critical intervention' on the part of Hollywood in general is questionable, and one could just as easily argue that the film was only given the green light by studio executives on the basis that one of the most powerful players in Hollywood, Steven Spielberg, was attached to it. In the production notes, Debbie Allen, one of *Amistad*'s producers, makes it clear that the project had been 'stonewalled' until Spielberg showed an interest. As she puts it, 'Here was a filmmaker who could understand and embrace this project and help me to get it done.'[4]

Accordingly, the question of whether this shift or intervention marks a new epoch in the representation of slavery remains to be seen. At best, a growing awareness of the fluid and unstable currencies of nation, race, gender and class, and the multiple ways in which identities are produced and consumed in contemporary culture, has compelled mainstream filmmakers to abandon the kind of narratives in which ethnically diverse characters implicitly measured themselves against the 'essential' norms of a white, patriarchal Americanness. As Davies and Smith argue, 'While liberal 1980s films invested in a model of integration to smooth over difference – and, wittingly or not, re-inscribed white patriarchal power – more recent films have employed more complex and overlapping constructions of identity.'[5] Robert Burgoyne, too, is optimistic that the emergence of questions of national, racial and cultural identity as a central topic of debate in the United States has encouraged filmmakers to articulate 'a counternarrative of American history' as a means of validating what he sees as 'the increasingly hybrid and poly-cultural reality of American life'.[6] 'Even within mainstream Hollywood filmmaking,' Burgoyne asserts, 'the foundational narratives of nation are being contested by films that open up the locked doors of the national past and that emphasize the histories forgotten or excluded from dominant accounts.'[7]

But it is difficult for us to share Burgoyne's enthusiasm wholeheartedly. At worst, the type of identity politics or liberal multiculturalism that has underpinned this 'new' respect for the Other is something of a political chimera. Most self-evidently, one might argue that Hollywood filmmakers tackling the subject of slavery, irrespective of their 'good' intentions, run the risk of caving into a bland political relativism whereby albeit worthy efforts to represent the inherent goodness and humanity of black slaves are married to a contradictory but pragmatic need to rescue some aspect of what constitutes 'America' in the eyes of the audience. To this end, one of the triumphs of what we might call neo-liberalism and attendant discourses of political correctness has been the virtual eradication of traditional methods employed by the dominant culture to silence other voices, but this has not necessarily led to the creation of a freer, fairer, more democratic society. Rather, older strategies of domination and control have simply mutated into newer, shinier, 'friendlier'[8] versions, and practices such as inference, coding and symbolism have replaced segregation, exclusion and crude racial stereotyping. Apparently enlightened thinking, then, may well pose a challenge to what Hardt and Negri describe as 'the binary logic of Self and Other that stands behind modern colonialist, sexist and racist connotations',[9] but are we to assume that strategies of domination do not change themselves in response to new circumstances? Or, as Hardt and Negri put it, what happens when power no longer 'poses hierarchy exclusively through essential identities, binary divisions and stable oppositions'?[10] One of the key arguments of this chapter is that contemporary formations of power – or at least as they manifest themselves in post-Cold War historical films – cannot be understood in straightforward terms. Simply put, Hollywood films do not, nor can they any longer, reflect the bald logic of an unreconstructed racism. Instead, power, as it acts on and through contemporary films, needs to be understood in more diffuse, networked, mobile terms; that is to say, in relation to, and as part of, a myriad of newly emerging political and economic institutions and cultural formations. In the case of a film like *Amistad*, what we need to consider is whether or to what extent discussions about the production and reception of images of chattel slavery need to be situated in the context of newly emerging political, economic and cultural trends and patterns. Our point here, as we shall demonstrate later in this chapter, is that *Amistad*'s effectiveness in reinscribing American hegemony is predicated not on any kind of heavy-handed, top-down racism, but precisely on its ability to preach and privilege tolerance, acceptance and cultural diversity. In doing so, the film implicitly speaks about the changed and changing nature of cultural and economic power and requires us to develop a new critical idiom to come to terms with concepts such as race, racism, national identity and multiculturalism.

At stake is less the question of what images of black and white people mean or represent but rather what kind of overlapping and conflicting processes impinge on their construction. Accordingly, the kind of progressive rearticulation of narratives of nation proposed by Burgoyne need to be interrogated in the light of what Omi and Winant call the fast-narrowing gap between neo-liberal and neo-conservative racial rhetoric and indeed of the ever closer links between cultural productions and the vast, globally-focused corporate webs of which they are part.[11] In the context of films which address the subject of slavery, one needs to remain vigilant to the multiple ways in which these webs co-opt and render harmless critical voices and reinscribe an ideology that is both universal and satiated in a white, capitalist, patriarchal logic. It is a testament to the power of our contemporary consumer culture that an historical event as grim as slavery could itself be turned into a commodity whose function is not simply to instruct and/or entertain audiences but also to shore up the unsteady foundations of a system by no means free of the same racial and economic imperatives which informed slavery. It is here that the practice of mainstream Hollywood filmmaking and the recently raised question of reparations for slavery are joined. As Paul Gilroy puts it, 'This is what a consumer culture does: makes financial transactions and commodities out of injustices.'[12]

PLANTATION BLUES AND *ROOTS* RIFFS

Ed Guerrero identifies three distinct stages of black American involvement in, and with, Hollywood: black accommodation and submissiveness, marked most emphatically by the crude racial stereotyping of the 'plantation' movie; the 'blaxploitation' era of resistance and co-option, in which the framing of icons of black power and liberation took place within a cinematic form or genre financed, and hence ultimately determined, by the imperatives of white studio executives; and finally the emergence of what Guerrero calls 'a liberated black cinema', a necessarily independent – that is, independent to Hollywood – group of black filmmakers making low budget but formally interesting, thematically subversive movies.[13] By the same logic, black and white filmmakers operating inside Hollywood's perimeter fences cannot help but allow the system's repressive racial ideologies to infect their films. Guerrero acknowledges that such ideologies are not imaginary loaded weapons and argues that attempts to frame blackness in ways that end up affirming existing racial hierarchies are perpetually being contested. Nonetheless his thesis ultimately indicates that the possibilities of making a film which challenges the racial norms of a system and culture where a nominal rhetoric of inclusiveness masks a more painful reality of segregation and discrimination are slim.[14]

Certainly the case of *Roots*, a television mini-series first shown in the United States in January 1977, demonstrates the applicability of Guerrero's remarks; that is, it shows how a subject as harrowing as chattel slavery could be assimilated into the notoriously conservative world of network television and made to appeal even to white, middle-class viewers. Based on Alex Haley's book of the same name, the television mini-series told the story of Kunta Kinte and his passage from his Gambian home to his enforced removal and resettlement in the American South, and eventually to his, and his family's, freedom. In short, it appears to privilege a black, rather than white, perspective, at least in so far as it focuses on the violence inflicted on black people by whites and presupposes an ineradicable black/white difference. Somewhat surprisingly, then, the series, when it was shown in the US by the ABC network over consecutive nights (because the network's Program Executive did not feel the series had a strong enough appeal to carry its white audience over the usual twelve weeks)[15] became a national television sensation. It is estimated that 130 million viewers watched some or all of the series (out of a total population of 215 million), a figure which represented 85 per cent of all households that owned a television set.[16] 'If it is possible for a nation of 215 million to have a communal experience,' James Monaco comments, '*Roots* week was it.'[17]

The popularity of *Roots* across different viewing communities speaks to, and about, the ability of mainstream cultural institutions like the US television networks to take a potentially grim subject (that is, slavery) and, in so far as the show was promoted as entertainment rather than factual 'docudrama', turn it into popular viewing. Nonetheless, as Karen Ross argues, it perhaps more pertinently invites 'a critical enquiry about precisely who this rags-to-riches story is for'[18] and, by implication, how the not necessarily overlapping concerns of the network, its advertisers and the viewers shaped the programme's content and racial imagery. An article by Tucker and Shah offers a persuasive account of how Haley's richly textured, sensitive and multi-faceted story about slavery, told from a black perspective, was transformed into a television series produced, written and directed by whites and watched by a predominantly white audience, and how this process both fundamentally altered the show's political and cultural complexion and diluted 'the horrors, complexities, and seriousness of slave holding'.[19]

According to Tucker and Shah, the primary task of the production team was to make the series more palatable to its white viewers. This was achieved in a number of ways. First, the visibility and attractiveness of the white characters was enhanced. As one of ABC's executives admitted, 'Our concern was to put a lot of white people in the promos. Otherwise we felt the program would be a turnoff.' Another just said, 'We made certain to use white [actors] viewers had seen a hundred times before so they would feel comfortable.'[20] In addition, a concerted effort was made by the writers to treat the white characters with more sympathy than Haley had done. As one of them remarked, 'it was equally unwise, we thought, to do four hours of television without showing a white person with whom we could identify.'[21] Tucker and Shah also argue that the programme's makers strove to dilute, or ignore, the richness of Haley's carefully drawn portrait of slave culture in America and make the point that they were less interested in developing Kunta Kinte's African heritage than they were in demonstrating his assimilation into mainstream American life. In short, their representation of Africa as an exotic, mystical land was, in classic Orientalist terms, framed by a white (colonial) imagination and, as such, was more indicative of, say, an 'exhibition at the Smithsonian Institute than the living, breathing, thriving community Haley describes'.[22]

Accordingly, both Karen Ross and Tucker and Shah acknowledge that the broad appeal of *Roots* lay in the way in which the programme makers managed to universalise the experiences of the African slaves and their tortuous passage from indigenous natives to hyphenated Americans; a fact that perhaps explains the popularity of the series in Britain and elsewhere. In their hands, the individual and collective experiences of African-Americans are ultimately situated in the context of the ubiquitous rags-to-riches immigrant 'success' story. This has two important effects. First, it dilutes the distinctiveness of those experiences and implicitly suggests that African-Americans' struggle for freedom was only qualitatively rather than quantitatively different from the struggle facing other immigrant groups; in other words, that chattel slavery and racial discrimination were, at worst, obstacles that could be surmounted through perseverance and hard work. Second, by shifting the focus of attention from public to private, from institutional impediments to social, political and economic advancement, to familial and individual strategies for survival and gain, its makers, wittingly or not, were playing a cunning and quite reactionary double game. On the one hand, they sought to assuage white guilt by implicitly suggesting that, in so far as black social, political and economic progress was attainable within existing but slightly modified institutional structures, the work of the Civil Rights movement had been completed. On the other hand, their message, particularly to black viewers, was ultimately this: 'Do not look to political movements for liberation but instead to yourself and your family to achieve personal success.'[23] In both instances, further changes to the system were deemed unnecessary, with appeasement and assimilation, inevitably, triumphing over divisiveness and separation.

PUBLIC PEDAGOGY V. HISTORICAL AUTHENTICITY

To move seamlessly from a discussion of *Roots*, first shown on US television in 1977, to Steven Spielberg's *Amistad*, released some twenty years later, constitutes something of a critical leap. Indeed, such a critical move provokes certain questions: what has happened in the interim? Has *Amistad* 'moved on' from *Roots* or is it driven by similar imperatives? And what narratives of racism and slavery are now influential? Certainly the fact that mainstream filmmakers have steered clear of what has always been perceived of as a 'difficult' subject does not mean that the 'peculiar institution' and attendant debates about its nature and effects have somehow dropped off the public radar. Arguably, with the question of reparations for slavery becoming a 'hot' political issue, slavery and its effects have remained at the forefront of the public imagination. In part, then, *Amistad* constitutes an important moment in this resurgent interest, a critical intervention by a well-known director at the height of his fame making an 'event' film about slavery. Nonetheless, whether such an intervention marks a new or defining moment in the way in which slavery has been represented is another question. Actually, the representational strategies employed by *Amistad's* makers suggest that the type of apparently benign but ultimately quite reactionary practices adopted by the makers of *Roots* has, if anything, intensified and assumed newer, slicker forms.

In our critical treatment of *Amistad*, it should not be forgotten that a movie which brings to light a little known (in mainstream circles) incident about a slave revolt onboard a Spanish slave ship sailing out of Havana in 1839 and the subsequent capture, and trial, of the slaves in the United States, can and does serve an important pedagogical function. Howard Jones, author of one of the film's historical source materials, *Mutiny on the Amistad: The Saga of a Slave Revolt and Its Impact on American Abolition, Law, and Diplomacy* (1987), certainly felt so, arguing (albeit before he saw the completed film) that its makers had a great opportunity to 'expose the evils of the African slave trade and slavery itself' and to 'bridge the gulf between historians and the general reader by making history both interesting and accessible on a wide scale'.[24] Visiting the film set, he reportedly said to Spielberg, 'Because of your work, the story will finally make its way into the history books where it belongs'[25] and on one level it is hard to dispute his claim. Certainly Jones himself found that interest in his book rocketed as a result of the film. As he explains:

Oxford University Press issued a revised version of my book . . . and assigned a senior publicist to its marketing campaign. [The publicist] arranged a tour of New England that included TV and radio interviews (one of which was the Joan Rivers show), lectures, and book signings. In the meantime the editors at *American History* magazine invited me to write an article on the subject, and *Mutiny on the Amistad* became a December selection of the Book-of-the-Month Club, History Book Club and Quality Paperback Book Club. In one of those rare moments, history and Hollywood had proved warmly compatible, perhaps even encouraging a wider reading about the *Amistad* . . . The impact of the 'Spielberg touch' is phenomenal.[26]

On the one hand, then, the film's – and Steven Spielberg's – ability to generate widespread interest in a largely overlooked instance of black resistance and agency should not be dismissed as worthless or necessarily dangerous, particularly in the light of Jones' comments. Additionally, one could argue that in so far as the film asks us to think about the human cost and suffering associated with slavery and (albeit simplistically) about a range of claims for slavery's continuance, it provides some kind of contextual insight into the type of long-standing arguments about human and property rights that would culminate in the Confederate secession and subsequently the Civil War.

Nonetheless, whether *Amistad* actually constituted 'one of the rare moments' where history and Hollywood proved to be 'warmly compatible' is open to question. Many commentators and historians were uneasy about the film's claims to historical veracity and about the 'gratuitous liberties' it takes 'with the historical record'.[27] The combined list that Sally Hadden and Adam Rothman, for example, compile is a damning one: the Africans' lawyer, Roger Baldwin (Matthew McConaughey), was a well-known abolitionist when the trial began and would not have seen the issue simply as a matter of property rights as the film implies; the film overlooks the role played by New York abolitionists, particularly Lewis Tappin (who in one particular scene is seen to play some kind of Machiavellian game in which the Africans are treated by him as bargaining chips) in securing the Africans' freedom; the film suggests that John Quincy Adams (Anthony Hopkins), who represented the Africans in the US Supreme Court, struck up a friendship with Cinque (Djimon

Hounsou), the leader of the slave revolt, when it appears they never met, and that Cinque played a key role in his own defence even though there is no 'evidence' to support this claim. In addition, Rothman claims that the film 'caricatures almost all the leading politicians who enter the story, especially John Quincy Adams and Martin Van Buren, whose careers with respect to slavery were vastly more complicated than *Amistad* indicates' and finally that 'it exaggerates the significance of the Supreme Court's action in the *Amistad* case, which was decided on rather narrow, technical grounds and did not free any person legally held as a slave in the United States'.[28]

To the chagrin of many historians, this situation was made considerably worse by the distribution of a study guide or learning kit to American high schools. Eric Foner, writing in *The New York Times*, indignantly pointed out the 'dangers' of such practice:

> The study guide erases the distinction between fact and fabrication, urging students, for example, to study the film's composite character (an anti-slavery printer played by Morgan Freeman) rather than the real African-Americans on whom he is based . . . The learning kit [also] claims that the Supreme Court's decision to free the Africans aboard the Amistad was a 'turning point in the United States in the struggle to end slavery in the United States.' The truth is that the Amistad case revolved around the Atlantic slave trade . . . and had nothing to do with slavery in this country. In the study guide, students are not told that in the 19th century it was perfectly possible to condemn the importation of slaves from Africa while simultaneously defending slavery . . . in America.[29]

Foner's arguments are not to be dismissed lightly but to criticise a learning kit that asks us to treat any film as historically accurate, as George Custen points out, is to problematically assume 'that such a condition exists and that it is disinterested, rather than ideologically motivated'.[30] Or, to quote Michael Wood, 'Clearly it is good to get things right but people who complain about inaccuracies normally have an agenda. They argue "facts speaks for themselves" but those tend to be conservative claims, the facts are conservative until proved otherwise.'[31] Our point is neither to condemn films that tamper with the 'historical record' nor to promote them, without reservation, as teaching or classroom aids. Rather, it is to suggest that films, *Amistad* included, can serve a useful pedagogical function if the way in which they are taught draws attention, say, to disjunctures between a film's narrative and what Rosenstone calls the discourse of history – 'the already existing body of data and arguments on a topic'[32] – and asks us to read or make sense of them in the context of the present and contemporary ideological and discursive formations. As Ken Loach puts it, 'The only reason to make a historical film is because it illuminates the present.'[33] What we need to discuss, then, is not whether a film like *Amistad* is 'historically accurate' but rather why it sets out to represent the past as it does, what it omits, what it includes, why it was made and for whom, and why it is important to situate our discussions of it in the context of present day debates about race, identity politics and the emergence of new formations of global power. In other words, the fact that Spielberg chose to make a mainstream film in which the prime movers in the global slave trade are Spanish rather than American needs to be discussed in the context of (a) Spielberg's position and status in Hollywood; (b) the role and function of Hollywood films more generally in American and global culture and politics; and (c) the neo-liberal agenda which has shaped the film's and arguably Spielberg's imagination.

There are two scenes in *Amistad* that allude to, without entirely laying bare, the film's ideological ambitions. Before we indicate why this is, some summarisation is required. The first scene occurs half an hour into the film. Theodore Joadson (Morgan Freeman), a freed slave and abolitionist printer, approaches Anthony Hopkins' John Quincy Adams on the steps of Capitol Hill and reminds the former President of their collective responsibilities to the ongoing project of nation-building. 'I know you and your presidency as well as any man, and your father's,' he tells Adams. 'You were a child at his side when he helped invent America and you, in turn, have dedicated your life to refining that noble invention. There remains but one task undone, one vital task the Founding Fathers left to their sons before the thirteen colonies could precisely be called the United States, and that task, as you well know sir, is crushing slavery.' The second scene occurs as part of the film's climax, when Adams is petitioning the Supreme Court on behalf of the fifty-three African slaves to secure their freedom. Silhouetted by a helated light, Adams (whose address, according to the court records, actually lasted eight hours and was largely based on the legality of the Atlantic slave trade) summons forth the rhetorical power of the Declaration of Independence and uses it to issue a powerful warning to the assembled Justices. 'Give us the courage to do what is right,' he declares, 'and if it means Civil War then let it come and when it does, let it finally be the last battle of the American Revolution.'

One obvious claim that we could make is that the film in general and these scenes in particular are heavily invested in the task of nation-building or securing the benign meta-narrative of America's emergence as a nation-state. This much is clear from the deeply problematic claims made by these scenes; that the task of nation-building in the early Republic was mostly dependent upon crushing the institution of slavery; that the Founding Fathers were aware of this fact and had the best interests of the slaves in mind when they drafted the Declaration of Independence and later the US Constitution; that the business of refining the noble invention of 'America' was a patriarchal one, passed on from father to son; and that the Civil War was essentially an extension of the American Revolution, an opportunity for the combatants in the later conflict to deal with the unfinished business of the earlier one with regards to the question of slavery.

However, to argue this position is to slightly miss the point because *Amistad*'s concerns are not exclusively tied up with attempts to explain and contextualise a significant but only slightly known incident relating to the treatment of African slaves in the context both of the Atlantic slave trade and domestic US legislation and culture in the late 1830s. Rather, as we shall see, the film's engagement with the historical past also needs to be understood as an intervention in contemporary debates about what constitutes American culture and identity in the context of a racially diverse, multi-ethnic present and about what characterises America's relationship with the rest of the world. But in order to understand *how* the film does this, how it tries to convince us of its own 'rightness', we should give some thought to the relationship between form and content; that is, how the ideological ambitions of a film like *Amistad* and a filmmaker like Spielberg are embedded not just in the content of the story but rather how that story is broken down, organised, filmed, edited and put back together. As a starting point, Robert Kolker's analysis of Spielberg's 'appeal' is instructive:

> Spielberg's films are obviously well-crafted . . . dependent on cinematic effects, and at the same time determinedly realistic and manipulative – realistic because they are manipulative. His

work brings to the fore the central problem of the illusory form, the power of American cinema to create itself as an unquestioning site of belief. Let's recover a bit of ground: the way in which Spielberg's films so happily and energetically foreground their narrative and cinematic devices makes them readily accessible to formal analysis, while at the same time creating a sense of ongoing story into which we are deeply drawn . . . But despite all these elements, he disallows distance and objectivity. He tightens his films like a trap, so that the viewer is unable to see beyond the image content and remains immediately unaware as to why there is no escape. From the outside, the camouflage is difficult to penetrate.[34]

Formally, Spielberg's style is both invisible and excessively deterministic. It is invisible in so far as the technical aspects of filmmaking – editing, camerawork, frame composition – are skilfully subsumed into, and are subordinate to, the demands of narrative and the seamless or closed practice of giving audiences the optimum vantage point to view the film's unfolding story. It is excessively deterministic in so far as the manner in which Spielberg puts his films together all but guarantees that his audiences will respond to them in 'appropriate' ways. Formally, therefore, Spielberg's films work through camouflage and thematically they work through displacement – displacing the contingencies, contradictions and complexities of the 'real' into melodrama as a means of resolving otherwise troublesome tensions and conflicts, such as race, class and gender. To put it another way, the spectacular nature of his subject matter – dinosaurs, UFOs, aliens and killer sharks, for example – and the invisibility of his films' technical aspects work to secure audience passivity and acceptance, particularly since his narratives 'speak about a way of being in the world . . . that viewers find more than just comfortable, but desirable and – within his films – available'.[35] However, the question of whether this assent is achieved when the subject is not merely spectacular but 'real' or historical is a vexed one. On the one hand, watching the sequence in *Saving Private Ryan* (1998) where the D-Day landings are restaged, for example, it is not easy to resist the implicit logic that the scene is closer to 'reality' than previous attempts at re-enactment. On the other hand, and this applies particularly to the film bookends where a D-Day veteran and his family return to the beach where the landing took place, Spielberg's ideologically motivated practice of displacing the 'real' into melodrama, quite simply, cannot go unnoticed. What is invisible therefore becomes all too visible, and just like the moment when you see the strings which control a puppet's actions, the desired-for 'verisimilitude' is threatened.

What should concern us when thinking about Spielberg's historical films is whether or to what extent audiences are willing to accede to their narrative and ideological demands. The success of *Saving Private Ryan* (see Chapter 4) and *Schindler's List* (1993) at the US and the global box offices suggests one answer while the relative failure of *Amistad* suggests another.[36] Accordingly, Spielberg's celebrated Holocaust film offers a useful point of comparison for our discussion of *Amistad*. The dilemma facing Spielberg when making *Schindler's List* and *Amistad* would not perhaps have been so different; namely how to effectively do justice to the unremitting grimness and alienating horror of both historical moments while simultaneously maintaining some level of audience interest and identification. In the case of the former, Kolker argues that the figure of Schindler (Liam Neeson) himself was pivotal:

> Spielberg wants us to understand the heroism of one German who saved some Jews. At the same time he wants the viewer to see the huge, disgusting canvas of the slaughter. He cannot only do the latter, because the film would be like a documentary and, without a drama, would not draw a large audience. He cannot make the drama too complex, because that would endanger the emotional bond that Spielberg must build between audience and film.[37]

Kolker argues that the exchanges between Schindler and Amon Goeth (Ralph Fiennes), the sadistic SS camp commander, offer simple confrontations of a banal, mindless evil versus a sophisticated, compassionate intelligence, thus fitting a template perfected by Spielberg in which a battle between good and evil all but guarantees that audiences will identify with the former's inevitable triumph.[38] Schindler's developing conscience, in the final third of the film, functions as an emotional safe haven for audiences, a residue of goodness in an otherwise bleak moral landscape where the appalling spectre of Auschwitz hovers intractably over the film's horizons. If Hayden White's claim that events like the Holocaust 'can only find their appropriate tenuous representation in the "de-realization" effected by modernist forms such as collage and fragmentation'[39] is upheld, then Spielberg's preference for conventional narrative forms renders it a failure. But, arguing against this position, Janet Staiger suggests that we should be more concerned with textual effects than textual forms and that, as a result, the film's willingness to show the liquidation of Jewish ghettoes by SS stormtroopers using grainy black and white images, for example, creates *some* kind of emotional distance from which audiences can contemplate the moment's attendant horrors.[40] Certainly we would argue that audiences *are* given an insight into the mechanistic working of Nazi bureaucracy, where being included or excluded from lists equates to either life or death. The greatest threat to life facing Spielberg's Jews therefore comes not from bad men like Goeth with guns but from bureaucrats with pens and desks, and what promises to emerge from the film is a riveting and muted portrait of the banality of evil.

It is difficult to determine precisely why *Schindler's List* was a commercial success and *Amistad*, in relative terms, was a commercial failure, though it could relate to two interlinked factors. By jettisoning the style of filmmaking he used in *Schindler's List*, Spielberg in *Amistad* allows us less distance or space from which to 'see' the events of the film. Our assent, as Kolker would argue, is implicitly and unambiguously demanded by the more conventional style of filmmaking that he perfected in films like *Jaws*, *E.T.* and *Raiders of the Lost Ark*. The problem is that we cannot give this assent in the same way because the subject matter will not allow it. That is to say, we cannot simply accept images of torture and brutality in the same way that we can images of familial harmony. But where Spielberg could be more daring in *Schindler's List* and show the horror of the death camps without having to redeem the Nazi perpetrators in the eyes of the audience, in the case of *Amistad*, those responsible for establishing and upholding the institution of slavery in the US also constituted the film's core audience (that is, white Americans). Hence Spielberg's desire not only to show the horrors of slavery but also to frame these in the context of white institutional benevolence, an almost impossible task even for a director as adept as Spielberg at smuggling meanings into his films under the pretence of merely telling a story. *Amistad* cannot deal with the question of chattel slavery in the American South head-on because to do so would be to draw attention to the way in which US institutions like the Supreme

Court were responsible not just for setting slaves free (as the film shows) but also for maintaining their enforced slavery and subjugation. The main problem with the film is not that Spielberg has tampered with the historical record (though he has done exactly this) but that he wants us to be simultaneously moved by the courage and agency of the black slaves and also by the virtuosity of the system of rule established by the Founding Fathers. Since this, quite simply, is not possible, even or in spite of the ideological potency of the medium that Spielberg is using and is so familiar with, the film itself crumbles in his hands. In wanting to be all things to all people, as we shall see, the logic of the film expresses a neo-liberal preference for inclusion, tolerance and acceptance. The implied eradication of barriers and the unequivocal acceptance of difference does not herald the arrival of some kind of raceless, classless utopia in which old strategies of domination–subordination have simply been swept away. Rather, the eradication of traditional barriers and boundaries presupposes the emergence of alternative structures of rule in which power functions in newer, more diffuse ways.[41]

TWO VIEWS OF RACIAL DIFFERENCE

The film's opening image is a shot of a glistening black male face, followed by a close-up of his eyes, his nose and fingers, which have successfully loosened the bolt that keeps in place his shackles. It anticipates another image of the man, who we later find out is Cinque, after he has led his fellow slaves in revolt against their Spanish captors. It is a powerful but troubling image. From below his feet the camera pulls upwards into the darkness and pouring rain, slowly taking in Cinque's muscled, semi-naked torso, his bloody hands and his contorted, enraged expression, a visceral cocktail of long repressed anger and sanctified relief. It is a powerful image because it establishes black agency as a significant force in the film and it is a troubling one because it fetishises black masculinity; that is, aside from the unlikely notion that Cinque could have emerged in such remarkable physical shape from the hardships of the Middle Passage, it evacuates all the politics out of black power or resistance and transforms it into an issue of bodily strength. Likening the scene to a Robert Mapplethorpe photograph, Caryl Phillips claimed in *The Times*, that he had to ask himself whether the film 'was a serious, dramatic recreation of slavery or a black, gay porno flick' and made the point that 'there's something vaguely obscene about the way in which Spielberg's camera exoticises the black male form'.[42]

This may well be true but initially it is also a troubling image because, and this is why it is unusual or even daring for a filmmaker like Spielberg, there is no guidance in terms of how to read it. To see it as a fetishisation of the black male form makes perfect sense in the wider context of the film but in these opening moments, its effect is disorientating. What is the intent and effect? Does such an image celebrate black resistance or for that matter constitute some kind of implicit attempt to force particularly white audiences to investigate their own prejudices about a pathologised blackness? This possibility is left open by what is arguably the most effective scene of the film, one in which, having take control of the slave ship, the Africans near land not knowing where they have ended up or rather where the Spaniards have guided them. Another ship inhabited by wealthy white party-goers glides past them. The scene cuts between images that privilege the gaze of the Africans as they look on, uncomprehending, at the rituals and costumes of an alien culture and ones taken from behind the white party-goers as they stare with bemusement at the black faces as they pass them. It is a moment where difference is established but not managed or made hierarchical, where whiteness *and* blackness are both defamiliarised, made to seem strange.

But the film cannot, or does not want to, maintain the ambiguity of this moment. Though it nominally seeks to achieve balance by dividing its attention between the Africans as they attempt to come to terms with their captivity in New Haven and subsequent legal manoeuvering to secure their freedom and the various white figures involved in this process, it soon becomes clear that the film's weighting in this respect is by no means equal. If there is anything interesting or refreshing about being given access to the Africans' conversations through subtitling, or indeed in that they are allowed to speak their own language, one has to ask why we were denied subtitles until they were safely incarcerated in an American prison. Similarly, one has to wonder whether the film's unwillingness to develop a portrait of the Africans beyond their status as emblems of a noble, unchanging blackness speaks far more about the racial politics of the film's creators than it does about the Africans themselves. So when screenwriter David Franzoni remarks, about Cinque, 'He doesn't bend, he doesn't equivocate . . . and because he has that kind of power, that absolutely unswerving drive, he becomes – even while in prison – the freest man on earth'[43] he is actually speaking not about Cinque but about the relative proximity of conservative and liberal rhetoric on race and racial difference.

In the context of the US, a conservative position on race might conceive racial difference as a threat to the common culture and the ideological and bodily purity of a sanctified, and largely mythic, white America. In this scenario, racial difference is tolerated only in so far as it is the first step of a process of assimilation into the dominant (white) American culture.[44] Meanwhile, a liberal position on race might emphasise difference in enabling terms; that is, such a position might stress the immutability of difference, and call forth a pluralist vision of the United States where no one group or culture takes precedence over the other.[45] If, as Omi and Winant argue, '[t]here is a continuous temptation to think of race as an essence, as something fixed, concrete and objective [and] there is also an opposite temptation: to imagine race as a mere illusion, a purely ideological construct which some ideal non-racist social order would eliminate',[46] then the film works hard to integrate and reconcile both positions and thereby ignore the extent to which both are false.

In conservative terms, the film sets about trying to remake the Africans not as Americans per se but rather as 'universal' or cosmopolitan citizens; we hesitate to use the term African-Americans because of its associations with chattel slavery in the American South, a subject which the film, as we have discussed elsewhere, does not to want to want to address head-on. The transformation of the Africans during their stay in the United States from noble savages to politically engaged freedom fighters also speaks to a neo-colonial discourse of 'civilisation' and it is instructive that the Bible plays some kind of role in this process. In a notable scene, Yamba, one of the Africans, reading from an illustrated Bible, learns about the Jews and the story of Jesus. He says about the former: 'Their people suffered more than ours, their lives were full of suffering.' Aside from the heavy-handedness of Spielberg's efforts here to link Jewish and black suffering, and overlooking for a moment the issue of whether someone who had endured the Middle Passage would make such a claim, our point is that the Africans' conversion into cosmopolitan citizens requires tacit acknowledgement that suffering and redemption through some kind of undifferentiated Christian/Judaic faith constitutes a universal 'truth' (and is hence unrelated to specific material conditions). In other words, if what goes wrong with the scene, according to Kolker, 'is the sentimentalizing of characters who "naturally" discover the rightness of the Christ story', then 'it is almost as if Spielberg were aware of and parodying Althusser's definition of how ideologies work, insinuating that the obviousness of white Christian culture will "hail" everyone into its obviousness'.[47] What is missing from Kolker's analysis, here, is some sense of how the scene itself functions to conflate Jewish and African-American suffering even if, as David Theo Goldberg notes, 'the sense of Jewish enslavement depends on a more distant, more metaphorical experience than African-American slavery'.[48] That said, Kolker's remarks usefully draw attention to the way in which Spielberg's film works to secure a hegemonic consensus, in this instance problematically reconciling the lived experiences of Jews, Africans and white Christians into one amorphous entity.

In liberal terms, meanwhile, the film sets out to protect or even sanctify racial difference. Rather than insisting upon the assimilation and allegiance to a common identity and culture, this position argues that whereas essential or biological differences may be false, cultural ones which draw upon a separate-but-equal political logic should be emphasised and even celebrated. In this sense, the film's desire to construct America's political institutions and American culture in benign, uplifting terms is matched by a need to affirm the vitality and authenticity of an unspecified indigenous African cultural tradition. In one scene, Baldwin, the lawyer, asks Cinque to describe whereabouts he has come from. Cinque walks to the furthest point in the room in order to underline the racial and cultural chasm that separates them. But it is a prison cell and not merely a room, a fact that unwittingly alludes to what is missing from this kind of cross-cultural dialogue: namely the question of power. To put it another way, what is missing from liberal and conservative conceptions of racial difference and hence what is missing from the film is any sense of the way in which power – or rather the *unequal* distribution of political and economic power – frames the construction of social identities. In this sense a liberal desire to sanctify difference and a conservative desire to assimilate difference are joined in so far as both speak problematically about race, to quote Omi and Winant, as something 'fixed, concrete and objective' and also as 'a mere illusion, a purely ideological construct which some ideal, non-racist social order would eliminate'. A conservative desire to assimilate racial difference into a fixed and unitary model of national identity (conceived in the image of the dominant white culture) and a liberal desire to 'respect' differences to the point where everything and everyone is the same are *both* satisfied. Instead of trying to 'understand race as an unstable and "decentered" complex of social meanings constantly being transformed by political struggle' or think beyond both 'the utopian framework which sees race as an illusion . . . and also the essentialist formulation which sees race as something objective and fixed',[49] Spielberg's film unproblematically conflates two views of racial difference in an attempt to 'tell everyone's story'.

There is one extended sequence in the film that unsettles this reading: the re-creation of the Middle Passage, and the harrowing conditions endured by African slaves during their journey aboard ships travelling from the west coast of Africa to the New World. In this sequence, which makes for grim and remarkable viewing, the brutal practices adopted by slaveholders and their representatives in order to maintain their power are all too visible. Whether or not it is 'accurate' or 'authentic' is not the point; by showing us a version of events in which slaves are chained together and pulled overboard to their deaths by lead weights because there is insufficient food to feed them, we are given some kind of insight into the mindset and logic of a system and institution predicated upon the commodification of life, the insistence that the lives of slaves only have value in so far as they can be exchanged for money and profit.

But the positioning of this particular sequence in the film is significant. This disturbing film-within-a-film is assimilated into the wider narrative that frames and contains it. How this happens needs to be carefully unpacked because it alludes to the film's ideological ambitions. This sequence does not prefigure the revolt aboard the slave ship but rather is narrated retrospectively by Cinque to the New Haven courthouse in response to Adams' insistence that the Africans tell their own story. In other words, the social function of stories becomes central to our understanding of the film. Stories, Alan Sinfield reminds us, are not just things we read or hear about but are carriers of ideology that make plausible systems and concepts in order to explain how the world works and what our place in it is. Like ideology, stories are produced everywhere and do not necessarily collude with accepted ways of seeing the world, but Sinfield insists that because certain 'institutions – by definition those that usually corroborate the prevailing power arrangements – are vastly more powerful than others', 'the stories they endorse are more difficult to challenge, even to disbelieve'.[50] Initial viewing suggests that Cinque's story is one of those that is harder to challenge or disbelieve and hence that telling his story secures for him a more central position or voice in the film. But the fact that he is telling his story to an *American* judiciary suggests Cinque's catharsis once he has told his story in court and the benevolence and fairness of those American institutional structures are linked. In other words, the film uses the peerless status of Cinque's story to verify the truthfulness of another story about the inherent goodness of American institutions, even as those same institutions in the historical moment of the film were turning a blind eye to the plight of millions of African-Americans trapped in a system every bit as inhuman as the one which Cinque has described.

It is significant too that the Africans are not merely granted their freedom by the US Supreme Court but are also somehow changed by their experiences in America and their exposure to its legal system. Indeed, their departure at the end of the film for Africa dressed in fine linen robes – designer cool meets tribal chic – means that the troublesome issue of their status in pre-Emancipation America is conveniently avoided, and we are left with the sense that they are going back to wherever they came from, not as Americans perhaps, but certainly as better or improved versions of who they were before. The fact that the ship taking them back to Africa sails under the American flag would confirm this notion. With an image of Cinque shaking hands with Baldwin against the backdrop of the court still resonant in our mind, one can only ask whether this ending and its attendant reconciliatory message speaks more about 1990s neo-liberalism and Clintonian multilateralism than it does about pre-Emancipation racial politics. One could even make the point that, in so far as it is a US court which frees the slaves and a British navy commander who, in the end, liberates the West African slave fortress from where the Africans originated, the film's politics are not too far removed from a contemporary neo-liberal insistence that the 'enlightened' world (that is, the US and its junior partner Britain) must and does act in the interests of some kind of manufactured universal consensus.

The US, as Goldberg argues, has 'begun to realise [that racial purity is a thing of the past] but continues to deny the deep implications this realisation has for the racialising project'.[51] One could say the same thing about Spielberg, on the evidence of *Amistad*, at least in so far as the film strives to celebrate difference while simultaneously eliding the profound social, economic and political consequences of racial discrimination. The business of manufacturing consensus makes most sense in this context and it is significant, as such, that for Spielberg, *Amistad* is a particular story about slavery, black agency and resistance, as well as both an American story and a universal one. Indeed, such a view is self-consciously mapped out by Spielberg himself. To Caryl Phillips, Spielberg said, 'None of my children and none of their friends know about it', referring to the *Amistad* incident (Phillips notes that two of Spielberg's six children are African-American), adding, 'I'm interested in history, I'm interested in recording the growing pains inside of America.'[52] To Nigel Farndale, meanwhile, Spielberg gave a slightly different reason for making the film. 'I felt everyone had to share in the pride of an American Supreme Court which except for one dissenting voice turned these people back to the freedom they were born with. I felt a wave of patriotism at that.'[53] So *Amistad* is both an African-American story and an American story but what about a 'universal' story? Again Spielberg stated that: 'While I was making this film, I never felt I was telling someone else's story. I felt like I was telling everyone's story. This is a story that people of all nationalities and races should know.'[54] But in attempting to address or speak to and for everyone it could be argued that Spielberg ends up speaking to and for no one, or rather that the message of the film becomes so watered down or confused that it ultimately fails to engage the interest either of black and white Americans or for that matter the rest of the world whom Spielberg wants to remake in his own image. To this end, Spielberg's film speaks quite interestingly both about the failure of neo-liberalism rather than its triumph and about the desire of such a political logic to falsely reconcile liberal and conservative views of racial difference. What we do not see is any attempt to conceive of race either as 'an element of social structure rather than an irregularity within it' or 'a dimension of human representation rather than illusion'.[55] Race does still matter, to paraphrase Cornel West, but not in the slick, relativist way that Spielberg imagines.[56]

NOTES

1 Tara Mack, 'Payback Time', *Guardian Unlimited*, http://www.guardian.co.uk/Archive/Article/0,4273,4236219,00.html (24/2/04).

2 Robert Sklar, *Movie-Made America: A Social History of American Movies* (New York: Random House, 1975), pp. 196–7.

3 Henry A. Giroux, *Breaking In To Movies: Film and the Culture of Politics* (Malden, MA and Oxford: Blackwell, 2002), p. 6.

4 See *Amistad*, Production Notes, p. 3.

5 Jude Davies and Carol R. Smith, *Gender, Ethnicity and Sexuality in Contemporary American Film* (Edinburgh: Edinburgh University Press, 2001), p. 9.

6 Robert Burgoyne, *Film Nation: Hollywood Looks at US History* (Minneapolis: University of Minneapolis Press, 1997), p. 2.

7 Ibid., p. 7.

8 See Henry A. Giroux, 'Living Dangerously: Identity Politics and the New Cultural Racism', in Giroux and Peter McLaren, eds., *Between Borders: Pedagogy and the Politics of Cultural Studies* (London and New York: Routledge, 1994).

9 Michael Hardt and Antonio Negri, *Empire* (Cambridge, MA and London: Harvard University Press, 2000), p. 139.

10 Ibid., p. 142.

11 Michael Omi and Howard Winant, *Racial Formation in the United States: From the 1960s to the 1990s*, 2nd ed., (New York and London: Routledge, 1994).

12 Paul Gilroy in Ed Vulliamy, 'Black leaders divided over reparations for slavery', *The Observer*, 26 August 2001, p. 18.

13 See Ed Guerrero, *Framing Blackness: The African-American Image in Film* (Philadelphia: Temple University Press, 1993), pp. 3–4 for full explanation of these three stages.

14 For a fuller account of Guerrero's arguments, see *Framing Blackness* ('Introduction', pp. 1–7); 'Be Black and Buy', in Jim Hillier, ed., *American Independent Cinema* (London: BFI, 2001), pp. 69–73; and 'A Circus of Dreams and Lies: The Black Film Wave at Middle Age', in Jon Lewis, ed., *The New American Cinema* (Durham and London: Duke University Press, 1998), pp. 328–42.

15 See James Monaco, 'Roots and Angels', *Sight and Sound*, Vol. 46 No. 3, Summer 1977, p. 161.

16 Karen Ross, *Black Images in Popular Film and Television* (Cambridge: Polity, 1996), p. 97.

17 Monaco, *Sight and Sound*, p. 161.

18 Ross, *Black Images*, p. xii.

19 Lauren R. Tucker and Hemant Shah, 'Race and the Transformation of Culture: The Making of the Television Miniseries *Roots*', *Critical Studies in Mass Communication*, 9, 1992, p. 325.

20 Ibid., p. 328.

21 Ibid., p. 329.

22 Ibid., p. 332.
23 Ross, *Black Images*, p. 97.
24 See Howard Jones, 'A Historian Goes to Hollywood: The Spielberg Touch', *American Historical Association – Perspectives Online*, http://www.theaha.org/perspectives/issues/1997/9712/9712FIL.CFM (24/2/04).
25 Ibid.
26 Ibid.
27 See Adam Rothman, 'A Fine New Book', *American Historical Association – Perspectives Online*, http://www.theaha.org/perspectives/issues/2001/0109/0109fil2.cfm (24/02/04).
28 For a fuller account of the apparent historical 'inaccuracies' in *Amistad*, see Sally Hadden, 'Amistad: An Internet Review of Merit', *Film and History*, Vol. 28 No. 1–2, 1998, pp. 62–8; Adam Rothman, 'A Fine New Book'; Helen Halyard, 'Amistad: Some historical considerations', http://www.wsws.org/arts/1998/feb1998/amist.shtml (24/2/04).
29 Eric Foner in Stuart Jeffries and Simon Hattenstone, 'In the Light of History', *The Guardian*, G2, 6 February 1998, p. 3.
30 George Custen, *Bio/Pics: How Hollywood Constructed Public History* (New Jersey: Rutgers University Press, 1992), p. 11.
31 Michael Wood quoted in Jeffries and Hattenstone, *Guardian*, p. 3.
32 Robert Rosenstone in Robert Brent Toplin, ed., *Oliver Stone's USA: Film, History and Controversy* (Lawrence, KS: University Press of Kansas, 2000), p. 28.
33 Ken Loach in Jeffries and Hattenstone, *Guardian*, p. 4.
34 Robert Kolker, *A Cinema of Loneliness: Penn, Stone, Kubrick, Scorsese, Spielberg, Altman*, 3rd ed., (Oxford and New York: Oxford University Press, 2000), p. 256.
35 Ibid., pp. 256–7.
36 According to figures, whereas *Amistad* earned $29.8 million at the international box office and $44.2 million at the domestic US box office, *Saving Private Ryan* earned $268.8 million internationally and $216.3 million domestically and *Schindler's List* took $225.1 million internationally and $96.1 million domestically (http://www.boxofficeguru.com/intl.htm) (24/2/04).
37 Kolker, *A Cinema of Loneliness*, p. 321.
38 Ibid., pp. 320–1.
39 See Vivian Sobchak, 'History Happens', in Sobchak, ed., *The Persistence of History: Cinema, Television and the Modern Event* (London and New York: Routledge, 1996), p. 8.
40 Ibid.
41 For a fuller explanation of the ways in which power has become deterritorialised and decentered, see Michael Hardt and Antonio Negri, *Empire*.

'In contrast to imperialism,' they argue, 'Empire establishes no territorial center of power and does not rely on fixed boundaries or barriers' (p. xii).

42 Caryl Phillips, 'Slaves in Spielberg's manacles', *The Times*, 28 February 1998, p. 22.

43 See *Amistad*, Production Notes, p. 4.

44 See, for example, Arthur Schlesinger, *The Disuniting of America* (New York: Norton, 1992).

45 See, for example, Lawrence Fuchs, *The Ethnic Kaleidoscope: Race, Ethnicity and Civic Culture* (Hanover, NH: University of New England Press, 1990).

46 Omi and Winant, *Racial Formation in the United States*, p. 54.

47 Kolker, *A Cinema of Loneliness*, p. 317.

48 David Theo Goldberg, *Racial Subjects: Writing on Race in America* (London and New York: Routledge, 1997), p. 137.

49 Omi and Winant, *Racial Formation in the United States*, p. 55.

50 Alan Sinfield, 'Cultural Materialism, *Othello* and the Politics of Plausibility', in Julie Rivkin and Michael Ryan, eds, *Literary Theory: An Anthology* (Oxford and Malden, MA, 1998), p. 807.

51 Goldberg, *Racial Subjects*, p. 59.

52 Steven Spielberg in Caryl Phillips, 'Double life of a director', *The Guardian*, G2, 16 September 1997, p. 3.

53 Steven Spielberg in Nigel Farndale, 'The History Man', *Sunday Telegraph*, magazine, 22 February 1998, p. 13.

54 Steven Spielberg in Adam Bresnick, 'Telling everyone's story', *Times Literary Supplement*, 20 February 1998, p. 18.

55 Omi and Winant, *Racial Formation in the United States*, p. 55.

56 See Cornel West, *Race Matters* (Boston: Beacon Press, 1993).

Chapter 3

HOLLYWOOD'S CIVIL WAR DILEMMA: TO
IMAGINE OR UNRAVEL THE NATION?

The unpopularity of slavery as a subject for Hollywood is underlined by the significantly larger proportion of films made about the American Civil War. The Civil War has traditionally occupied a hallowed place in the benign meta-narrative of American history, one in which the bloody divisions between North and South are incorporated into a larger story of nation in which the sacrifice, suffering and bravery of both sides are equally celebrated. As such, Hollywood, one of the key 'players' in shaping the nature and ideological content of American public history, has played an important role in transforming the Civil War, to use David Thelen's words, from a 'story of bitter, irreconcilable conflict between two societies and between two sets of values' into one of 'human courage and bravery exhibited by all'.[1] This chapter focuses on the ways in which a range of post-Cold War films about the Civil War – *Glory* (1989), *Gettsyburg* (1993), *Ride with the Devil* (1999) and *Cold Mountain* (2003) – have engaged with this benign meta-narrative; that is, whether or to what extent they have challenged or reinforced an affirmative notion of national identity and how their engagement with such concerns speaks about the numerous, complex ways in which 'America' is being re-constituted domestically and internationally in the post-Cold War world.

At stake here is the significance of Hollywood's interest in the Civil War and the role that films about the subject have tended to play in the task of reconciling competing versions of what constitutes the United States, socially, culturally and politically. Indeed, the relative success of this task can be seen in the fact that, according to Stephen Bates, this bloodiest, costliest and most divisive of all American conflicts is now widely regarded 'as a curiously blame-free experience'.[2] Bates' point is not that the war left no trace of bitterness and resentment on the part of its winners and losers; the Civil War certainly continues to cast a shadow over North–South relations in the US. His point is, rather, that the *perception* that the experience was 'blame-free' needs to be understood in relation to the ideological task, subsequently undertaken by storytellers and historians throughout the nineteenth and twentieth centuries, of fortifying and securing the nation by creating narratives of the Civil War that would appeal to North and South alike. The jettisoning of blame and elevation of an elite of Great Men from the North and South onto the same overcrowded moral high ground is one of the features of *Gettysburg*. This four-hour epic is devoted entirely to the restaging of the pivotal battle that turned the tide of the Civil War against the South and claimed the lives of over 40,000 soldiers on both sides. For the director, Robert F. Maxwell, *Gettysburg* constitutes a new departure for American cinema's engagement with the subject of war:

> The evolution of American cinema has been where the bad guys were the Indians, the Japs or the Germans. Later, because of the Vietnam experience, we went through a period when we were the bad guys and the others were the good guys; . . . but the American Civil War was not so simple . . . So it's disturbing for the audience to see *Gettysburg* where suddenly you find yourself in an excruciating dilemma, where you are feeling for, and identifying with, both sides.[3]

Maxwell's analysis may allude, correctly or otherwise, to a certain tendency of Hollywood to simplify the experience of war into one where 'good' lines up against 'bad', even if his reading of Vietnam films whereby the Vietnamese are transformed into 'the good guys' is entirely erroneous. Nonetheless it fails to identify a related tendency in his own film. *Gettysburg*'s desire to make every soldier on the battlefield sympathetic by emphasising their manly courage and moral reserve ends up obscuring the complex reasons and motivations that underpin the conflict in the first place. Such an approach, moreover, is entirely representative of a certain tendency characteristic of historians and filmmakers when tackling the subject of the Civil War to constitute both North and South as heroic embodiments of contrasting and yet related strains of the same American character.

RACE, REVISIONISM AND RECUPERATION IN *GLORY*

Glory, an account of the exploits of a regiment of black soldiers in the Civil War, made during the last days of the Reagan presidency and released in 1989, might not seem particularly fertile territory for developing an argument about the emergence of a new political and aesthetic sensibility in contemporary Hollywood's engagement with American history. If anything, most critics who reviewed the film on its release commented on its traditional qualities and passed judgement depending on whether they felt this apparent iconoclasm to be a 'good' or 'bad' thing. *Time*'s Richard Schickel's enthusiasm for the film seemed, for example, to be based on the film's single-handed reinvention of the large-scale historical/Civil War epic and its 'gumption in flinging [this type of film] in the face of movie audience's indifference to the pretelevised past'.[4] Conversely, Mark Cooper, of *The Face*, an avant-garde style magazine attracting a centre-left readership, was disturbed by the film's 'unflinching assertion of traditional military values'[5] – particularly in the context of the profound ambivalence towards American militarism displayed by a generation of post-Vietnam filmmakers. Where critics did comment on the film's revisionist tendencies, the remarks were largely favourable and centered on its willingness to recover what Kurt Jacobsen in *The Guardian* referred to as 'the outrageously ignored'[6] saga of black military heroism and sacrifice for a contemporary audience. Meanwhile, although some critics were attuned to the film's liberal politics and saw it as part of a liberal project to assimilate black history into a national historical narrative, few took the opportunity to critique this liberalism as anything more than 'ponderous' and insipidly 'honourable'.[7] Only Nelson George, in *The Village Voice*, remarked on the way in which black history and historical figures have been appropriated by dominant discursive formations in order to secure their power. For George, then, *Glory* made him 'flash on the image' of Colin Powell, 'the highest-ranking African-American in the nation's history', and of Powell himself, George remarked, 'there's no denying that our post-slavery progress has created a crew of well-oiled cogs in the machinery of white world domination'.[8]

If this constitutes the genesis of our critique of *Glory*, the way in which an apparently well-meaning historical film ends up underscoring a contemporary vision of national reconciliation and of racial difference, then the critical moves which have brought us to this conclusion require further elucidation. It perhaps goes without saying that black Americans, for most of the twentieth century, were excluded from the Civil War's story of national reconciliation and that its unfolding logic, at least until the emergence of the Civil Rights movement in the post-World War II period, did not extend as far as integrating black and white America into this mutually affirming narrative. As such, *Glory* should be applauded for its positive contribution to the ongoing project of recovering previously marginalised black histories and for recognising the sacrifice made by 180,000 African-American soldiers during the Civil War. In this respect, its usefulness as a pedagogical tool is self-evident. These issues are not unrelated, as much of the critical attention surrounding *Glory* has centered on its status as 'historical truth' and hence its appropriateness as an educational text. That is, as a film either to be applauded for showing contemporary audiences that black Americans suffered and sacrificed alongside white soldiers to secure their freedom and the Union, or critiqued, like other Hollywood films, for once again tampering with the 'historical record'.

Our point is neither to deny the film's potential effectiveness as a teaching tool nor to condemn it for its wanton disregard of history but rather to ask how we might situate a discussion of 'film-as-history' in the context of a more careful examination of the relationship between power, identity and representation. What should concern us when thinking about *Glory* is not the fact that, for example, the drill sergeant is represented as Irish and not as African-American but rather how this disjuncture needs to be understood as the manifestation of particular discursive and ideological strategies. At stake here is the question of how, or to what extent, the film operates in progressive terms to offer a corrective to the benign meta-narrative of American history and revise a sense of national belonging 'from below' or through the atomising lens of contemporary identity politics. For Burgoyne, and Davies and Smith, *Glory* does exactly this; it departs from the themes of many Civil War films (which 'typically focus on the emancipation of the slaves and the rebirth of national ideals of community and equality'[9]) to explore the complex, contingent ways in which belonging and identity are constructed via the competing and overlapping demands placed on individuals by imperatives of nation, race, ethnicity, gender and region. Neither account is prepared to argue that *Glory* manages, or even wants, to entirely unsettle what Burgoyne calls the master 'narrative of American history'[10] but, as Davies and Smith put it, 'there are signs that the film *is* intended to engage with race, history and representation in more complex ways than the direct telling of historical "truths" or the production of "positive images"'.[11] In other words, it effectively unsettles this master narrative by successfully displacing the white gaze as the film's dominant 'look'; by reconfiguring black and white identities in history through the contemporary lens of debates about race and ethnicity; by contesting stereotypical images of black masculinity which have remained popular in Hollywood throughout the twentieth century; and by situating black American experiences much more centrally in the national consciousness.[12]

As we argued in Chapter 2, however, the essential optimism of such claims is a little misplaced. We acknowledge that a film like *Glory* – or for that matter *Amistad* – can offer us fresh insights into little-known historical episodes. We also accept that, in so far as such films privilege particular perspectives on the past that may once have been marginalised or discounted, they can compel us to think about how history is produced, why, and for whom. It would be at best optimistic and at worst naive, however, to assume that *Glory* was made simply for revisionist purposes or to correct past mistakes or to radically contest the benign meta-narrative of American history. The film's status as a useful or even compelling historical exploration needs to be questioned because, although it jettisons an old-fashioned racial politics based upon 'essential identities, binary divisions and stable oppositions', it then embraces the type of diffuse, slippery racial politics that we also associated with *Amistad*, whereby racial differences are affirmed, tolerated and managed.[13] 'Good' historical films require us to think about the contested nature of historical 'truths'; raise questions about the status of particular versions of historical accounts; compel us to critically evaluate our own responses to what appears on the screen; or at the very least give us some sense of what a particular historical moment might have 'looked' like. On the basis of these criteria, *Glory* is both a success and a failure. It nominally critiques the implicit ethnocentrism of the benign meta-narrative of American history and challenges our received understandings about the significance of racial differences in Civil War America. It perhaps even encourages us to think about the relationship between racial politics, an ideology of nation, and the production of historical truths. However, *Glory* also works hard to contain those really divisive racial divisions and reconcile 'black' and 'white' characters into a quite sophisticated story of national healing in which racial differences and different historical perspectives are initially emphasised, then tolerated and then managed in a complex hierarchy of command.[14]

Placing *Glory* alongside the traditionally accepted version of events, there are three or four significant omissions and deviations that initially require our attention. The first involves the letters written by Robert Gould Shaw (Matthew Broderick), white commander of the black 54th Massachusetts Volunteer Regiment featured in the film, which are used as the basis for passages of narrative 'voiceover' that from time to time punctuate the film. The letters highlight perceived differences and similarities between Shaw and the black soldiers under his command but significantly exclude references and comments which might constitute him as racist from a contemporary perspective. The second relates to the fictionalisation of key black figures within the regiment; while Shaw and other white military figures including Colonel Montgomery (Cliff de Young) are imported into the film as characters, the four black soldiers around whom much of the film revolves – Trip (Denzel Washington), Rawlins (Morgan Freeman), Searles (Andre Braugher) and Sharts (Jihmi Kennedy) – are all fictional creations. The third and related discrepancy involves Frederick Douglass and his sons, one of whom not only served in the 54th but also acquired the role of drill sergeant. Though Douglass, by some accounts, played a key role in setting up the regiment and saw the use of black troops in the conflict as a way of furthering the political and economic claims of black Americans, the film represents him as an all-but-mute figure who contributes little or nothing to discussions about the constitution of the new regiment. In addition, the drill sergeant in *Glory* is not one of his sons, as was the case, but a fictional Irish character, Sergeant Mulcahy (John Finn).

The most common explanation for such discrepancies is that revisions are made in order to accommodate dramatic possibilities or encourage audience identification with particular characters; that is, as Bill Nichols puts it, fictional films, unlike non-fiction films, are subject to the pull of erotics rather than ethics or 'a centrifugal pull on elements of authenticity away from their historical referent and toward their relevance to plot and story'.[15] In the cases highlighted above, whether such an argument is relevant is open to question. Certainly one could claim that the inclusion of potentially racist remarks made by Shaw in his letters may have alienated particular viewers or groups of viewers. Whether Shaw was in fact racist or not is less important than the way in which extracts from Shaw's letters have been edited and packaged, and how this process of shaping could be read as a manifestation of a much more contemporary cultural and political logic.

The letters themselves function to underline the film's apparent historical authenticity, a fact that is supported by the film's opening titles which inform us that they 'are collected in the Houghton Library of Harvard University'. But their inclusion also underscores Shaw's privileged position in the film, the fact that his perspective is given more significance than that of other characters, notably other black characters in the film. Therefore, while the film appears to offer a range of historical perspectives and positions from which to see the events which culminate in the assault on Fort Wagner in 1863, these positions have been carefully organised into a hierarchy of authority with Shaw at its apex. The film's attempts to tell and shape history cannot be explained by references to Hollywood's usual practice of subsuming 'reality' into 'drama'. The decision to use fictional 'types' instead of actual historical figures to depict the exploits and achievements of the black members of the 54th does little to further the film's dramatic claims. Rather, in the context of Shaw's privileged position in the film, this decision contributes to the leaking of authority *away* from the black soldiers even as their centrality is apparently being emphasised. Since Shaw is the only one of the main characters who was 'actually there', the assumption must be that his voice is somehow the most trustworthy or 'accurate'. The virtual silencing of Frederick Douglass, and the decision to depict the drill sergeant as Irish rather than one of Douglass's sons, simply reinforce the logic of this particular manoeuvre. Though the film makes claims to the effect that it is recovering a previously overlooked incident in American Civil War and African-American history, it is simply incorporating a version of that history into a larger narrative that privileges and celebrate Shaw's vision and courage.

The racial politics of *Glory* are a good deal more sophisticated than this makes it sound and we would not want to suggest that the film replicates what has traditionally been the preferred Hollywood strategy of differentiating black and white characters into rigid binary castes. Burgoyne, and Davies and Smith, are right to draw attention to the numerous ways in which the film challenges the binary logic of a system of rule rooted in nineteenth- and early twentieth-century imperialism, one in which the boundaries between 'us' and 'them', 'white' and 'black' and 'inside' and 'outside' must be vigilantly monitored and policed. Our point is that the mutation of binary divisions into more diffuse taxonomies of authority signals the emergence of alternative ways of incorporating and managing difference. In *Glory*, differences are initially disregarded, then celebrated and finally incorporated into a variegated hierarchy of interests.[16] Though the film purports to be a historically accurate depiction of the establishment and development of an all-black regiment culminating in the attack on Fort Wagner, what we see up on the screen is beholden less to the demands of historical authenticity than to a contemporary logic where American hegemony is asserted but within an newly emergent neo-liberal order that is continually being remade. To put it another way, the subversive possibilities suggested by the film's unconventional racial politics dissolve in the face of a relentless quest towards order and management whereby everyone is assigned a clear role and has the opportunity to assert their voice but where nothing changes, or is ever likely to change, because consensus is always achieved and achievable.[17]

The film opens with sentiments that underscore both its conventionality and its apparently inclusionary racial politics. Voiced as extracts from letters written by Shaw to his mother, his thoughts appear to bind the collective fates and ambitions of all Americans into some kind of national imaginary:

> How great it is to meet the men from all of the States, east and west, ready to fight for their country, as the old fellows in the Revolution, but this time we must make it a whole country for all who live here, so that all can speak. Before the war began, many of my regiment had never seen a Negro; now the roads are choked with the dispossessed. We fight for men and women whose poetry is not yet written but which shall be as enviable and renown as any.

In part, therefore, Shaw is speaking to the logic of national unity, one rooted in the historical period that the film is representing. Significantly, of course, Shaw is extending that logic to include African-Americans, though such thinking would not have been uncommon in someone brought up in an educated, liberal, Northern environment in the pre-Civil War United States. As with *Amistad*, though, racial differences are both underlined and initially discounted. To some extent, the film's engagement with the 'real' past requires that attitudes expressed by its characters are rooted in the logic of its own historical moment. Moreover, the implicit imperative that it 'accurately' reflect the hierarchies of power and position appropriate to the Federal Army in 1863 means that Shaw's place at the head of the 54th Regiment, and the subordinate status of the black soldiers who serve in it, is all but guaranteed. Procedures and rules that separate and secure these boundaries are rigidly adhered to. Within the regiment, mixing between soldiers of different rank and status (and hence racial identity) is forbidden. Though Searle, one of the recruits, is a childhood friend who shares his appreciation of Emerson and other American literary stalwarts, Shaw refuses to address him as anything but an enlisted soldier, and from the moment that he squares up to the assembled regiment on horseback, telling them, 'I am your commanding officer', we are left in no doubt as to where power in the regiment, and in the film, resides.

Such hierarchies may have been insurmountable in the context of nineteenth-century America, but what about mid-nineteenth-century America seen through the lens of late twentieth-century Hollywood cinema? One of the film's intentions, announced by Shaw's opening monologue, is the *eradication* of difference and the creation of 'a whole country for all who live here, so that all can speak'. All very well but how is such a vision to be achieved, given the imperatives of 'historical truth' demand that hierarchies of rank, and hence race, within the regiment at least be drawn as fixed? One answer would be that we are encouraged to believe that the situation outside of the regiment, one that is rarely glimpsed in the film, *is* different. The fact that Shaw and Searle are shown to be good friends and equals before they enter the regiment implies that it is only the regulations of the Federal army that require such divisions. Outside the regiment, they can be friends. The logic of this position extends to the film's treatment of North and South. Unlike most Civil War films, *Glory* explores a division within the Federal army whose primary characteristic would seem to be racial. Soldiers of the 54th are treated as second- or third-class citizens by army top brass; they are the last to receive guns, the last to receive ammunition, the last to receive uniforms and boots, and the last to be ordered into combat. Indeed, whenever white Federal soldiers come into contact with their black counterparts, insults are exchanged and the mood turns sour.

But this is *inside* the army. Outside, the only glimpse of the North we are given is that of genteel Boston society, where figures like Searle, and Frederick Douglass, though silenced by the film, can move with impunity and can help shape public policy. The other glimpse of the North that we see exists as a reflection of the liberated South. As if to underline the possibilities implicit in the rhetoric of Northern boosterism, Rawlins tells a black child, 'It ain't no dream', when the regiment lands in South Carolina. 'We left as runaway slaves and return as fighting men.' As if the point needs reinforcing, we are then shown a group of black school children singing 'Let Freedom Reign' under the watchful eye of their Northern liberators.

But the film is not content simply to draw attention to the 'superior' racial politics of the civilian North. Rather, what it strives to do is indicate how enlightened thinking can transform the way in which differences are negotiated throughout society and, as such, like *Amistad*, how it attempts to reconcile a conservative and liberal view of race whereby racial hierarchies are both concretised and potentially unstable. Indeed, though Shaw's privileged position in the film and the regiment is underscored from the outset, *Glory* is not content to sanctify this difference in absolutist terms. For example, when Trip learns that the regiment will be paid three dollars less a month than its white counterparts, and urges everyone to tear up their pay slips, Shaw seizes the opportunity to underline their sameness rather than their difference by telling the gathered regiment, 'If you men will take no pay, none of us will.' Meanwhile, when Shaw's military commanders refuse to grant his regiment the same privileges as they would to white regiments, or when he encounters explicit racism expressed in the attitudes of his superiors – Colonel Montgomery, for example, refers to the black soldiers in his regiment as 'little monkey children' – Shaw is resolute in his efforts to 'correct' their attitudes. It is Shaw, too, who insists on his regiment's readiness to fight and who secures the opportunity to lead the assault on Fort Wagner. When he leads the regiment into battle through a phalanx of assembled white soldiers, their cheers of affirmation and support constitute the fulfilment of his liberal vision.

In certain respects, *Glory* is a quite traditional war film, at least in so far as differences between the soldiers are ultimately subsumed into a larger, unifying quest or struggle. As such, the transformation of the film's black recruits into soldiers must, as Davies and Smith argue, be understood as a masculine rites-of-passage story in which the imperatives of war create the conditions for male camaraderie to take root and therefore to transcend differences of class, race, religion and so on.[18] Searle, the educated, effeminate Bostonian, must learn how to fight and kill; Sharts, the illiterate, simple-minded Southerner, must develop a mental and physical toughness; Rawlins, the Uncle Tom character, must learn to stand up to his white superiors; and Trip, the miltitant escaped slave, must learn to curb his racially-motivated anger and get behind the emancipatory cause. 'We're going to have to ante-up and kick in like men. *Like men,*' Rawlins shouts at Trip. 'Dying is what these white boys have been doing for nigh on three years, dying in their thousands, dying for you.' To repay this debt, the men of the 54th must die, too, and during the assault on Fort Wagner in the film's climax they do so in their hundreds, and through death, fulfil their potential as men and soldiers, transcend their racial 'difference' and in the process secure a quite traditional version of nationhood.

However, whereas discourses of nineteenth-century nationalism tended to conceive of the state and national identity in racially homo-geneous terms – that is, to construct an absolute racial difference against which a homogeneous national identity might be forged – *Glory* seems to want to argue for a version of national identity in which racial differences are conceived of not in absolutist or biologi-cal terms but rather as culturally contingent. As such, it is able to affirm the viability of a common cause and culture whose goal, as Shaw states, is creating a 'whole country for all who live here'. Such a vision also celebrates cultural differences and draws attention, in liberal, enabling terms, to the distinctive backgrounds and traditions from which Shaw, on the one hand, and Trip, Rawlins and Searle on the other, come from. As such, the black recruits are not simply the same as white ones but, as Shaw states in a letter written to his mother, different and potentially even better:

> The men learn very quickly, faster than white troops, it seems to me. They are almost grave and sedate under instruction and they restrain themselves. But the moment they are dismissed from drill every tongue is relaxed and every ivory tooth is visible and you would not know from the sound of it that this is an army camp. They must have had to learn this from long hours of meaningless and inhuman work, to set their minds free so quickly. It gives them great energy and there is no doubt that we will leave this state as fine a regiment as any that has marched.

Initially, what seem to be quite traditional views expressing an Orientalist preoccupation with the Other as exotic, on closer reflection assumes an altogether less crude complexion. Shaw's efforts to distinguish himself from the soldiers serving under him may be clumsy but the fact that he chooses to do so not in biological or physiological terms but rather via reference to their music and culture is significant. Difference in this sense is not destructive, something that points towards the fragmentation and Balkanisation of the emerging nation-state into ineradicable racial essences. Rather, difference is enabling because, in cultural terms, it explains why the soldiers are 'as fine a regiment as any that has marched'. If the end result of such a process is the assimilation of all voices and perspectives into the same cultural and political field or order, one consequence is the virtual eradication of any meaningful opposition: how can you oppose a political order where everyone is nominally on the same side and working towards the same ends? Only Trip seems to be aware of this dilemma; that is, only Trip seems to be aware that everyone is not on the same side or working towards the same ends and that, for him at least, being identified and identifying himself as black rather than white has some very profound social, political and economic consequences. For him, then, Shaw is not an enlightened saviour but a 'weak, white boy' who exercises power over him not because he is 'superior' but simply because his 'mummy and daddy fixed it'. And the fact that this situation is itself the product of slavery and its legacy is underlined when Shaw's punishment of Trip for apparently 'deserting' the regiment is a brutal whipping.

This particular scene is the most arresting of the film. The cutting and editing between close-ups of the two men's faces as the whipping takes place both unsettles the dominance of Shaw's (white, male) gaze and forges an emotional connection between him and Trip. What the film must do is find a way to build upon this emotional connection and re-affirm Shaw's status and privileged position in a way that both acknowledges the rightness of Trip's grievances and rescues Shaw's credentials as enlightened. For Shaw, the chance to do so arises when he learns from Rawlins that Trip's 'desertion' was merely an attempt to find new boots. Taking this opportunity, he attempts to reason with Trip and persuade him of the rightness of their mission as soldiers. The fact that Trip refuses the 'honour' of carrying the regiment's colours into battle and tells Shaw, 'I ain't fighting the war for you, sir', threatens to undo the wider project of the film but his stance is noticeably softer and his refusal is tainted with ambiguity. Trip, too, must change, and though this does not materialise until the climax of the film, when in the heat of battle he grabs the fallen colours and is killed in the process, it is nevertheless sufficient to fulfil the film's ambitions. If Shaw's transformation depends on his recognition of Trip's suffering and by implication that of African-Americans in general, then Trip's requires him to learn the virtues of knowing one's place and sacrifice. Ultimately, the image of Shaw's corpse being tossed into a mass open grave and ending up next to Trip suggests they have both learnt their lessons. Any sense that death brings equality and flattens out racial difference, however, is undone by the image of the Robert Gould Shaw 54th Regiment Memorial as the credits roll. Indeed, the fact that the memorial bears only Shaw's name, and privileges Shaw's contribution by placing him on horseback while the faceless African-American soldiers march under him, suggests the entrenchment and not the erosion of racial differences. But, by eliding or concealing these differences, the film would implicitly have us believe that different versions of history (that is, history from the 'top down' and history from 'the bottom up') have somehow been incorporated into a single coherent narrative of racial reconciliation where everyone's perspectives and arguments have been given due attention and weight.

CONTINGENCY, AMBIVALENCE, HISTORY: *RIDE WITH THE DEVIL* AND *COLD MOUNTAIN*

Glory constitutes an apparently worthy but ultimately quite reactionary attempt to recover and celebrate the exploits of a black regiment in the Civil War. In its heavy-handed efforts to assimilate the narratives of black soldiers into a larger story of universal sacrifice and white liberal virtuosity, the film speaks to a particular moment in the cultural politics of the nation; that is, it is informed by a desire to acknowledge and celebrate the diverse experiences of America's multi-racial population while at the same time reconstituting and ordering those experiences according to a more diffusely calibrated system of rank and privilege. Celebrating diversity does not, in this context, mean advocating equality. As such, *Glory* is the product of its own moment: a time in the late 1980s and early 1990s when an enthusiasm for what became known as identity politics swept through the academy and the cultural arena. For whereas *Glory* in

particular and identity politics more generally threatened to transform and complicate the ways in which many Americans conceived
of their own and their national identity, their largely celebratory tone
meant that insufficient critical energies were directed towards scru-
tinising the structural, institutional, cultural and psychological barriers faced by many seeking to 'advance' themselves in the social,
economic and political realm. The fact that two more recent films
about the Civil War, *Ride with the Devil* (1999) and *Cold Mountain*
(2003), are centrally concerned with mutual incommensurability –
that is, with antagonisms and hatreds that cannot easily be assimilated into some kind of benign meta-narrative – speaks to the bitter
divisions opened up by the conflict itself and the failure of a particular kind of identity politics to address questions of racial, ethnic, class
and gender differences in anything more than a nominal way.
Certainly there is a harder edge to both films. *Ride with the Devil* is a
rich, lyrical, violent film about bitter, partisan skirmishes between
irregulars across the Kansas–Missouri border during the Civil War
and as such contests, if not entirely unravels, efforts to explain and
justify the brutality of the conflict in straightforward terms. *Cold
Mountain*, a more conventional, handsomely staged and polite film,
draws back from insisting that the consequences and scars of the conflict can be healed in any obvious way. But, as we shall see, its tendency to subsume the particular contexts informing the fighting into
a self-consciously 'universal' story of suffering and redemption, and
its attempts to reconstitute an alternative form of female-centered
family as central to any process of rebuilding war-savaged communities, make it a less nuanced and interesting film than *Ride with the
Devil*. In fact, while *Ride with the Devil* underlines the awful, disinterested, contingent nature of violent conflict (where nothing can be
taken for granted and everyone is subject to circumstances over
which they have no control), *Cold Mountain*'s very structuring
premise – an embittered Confederate soldier returning home to his
loved one – gives the film a reassuring teleology that protects that
soldier from the radical uncertainties of the conflict that he is seeking
to leave behind him.

The dramatic climax of *Ride with the Devil*, and the film's pivotal
sequence in terms of its re-staging of history, is the infamous sacking
of Lawrence, Kansas, by a band of pro-Southern Missouri 'bushwackers'. On 21 August 1863, these men rode across the state border into
Kansas and killed 150 Lawrence abolitionists in cold blood. Edward

Countryman describes the raid as 'the most frightful atrocity of the Civil War' and describes how some 450 guerillas led by the notorious William Quantrill 'burst upon the sleeping town, massacring its male inhabitants [alternatively called 'defenseless civilians'] and burning down most of its buildings'.[19] Shelby Foote offers a much fuller account of the raid, including some contextual materials that help to throw some light on the motives of the attackers. Prior to the raid, Northern 'jayhawkers' had captured and imprisoned a group of Missourian women in a 'dilapidated three-storey brick-affair' in Kansas City, which promptly collapsed, killing four of the women. Outraged at this contravention of an implicitly agreed 'hands-off' attitude towards women and children, the Southern bushwackers under Quantrill planned the raid on Lawrence. The town was a place where, as he told his bloody-minded cohorts, 'we can get more revenge and more money there than anywhere else in the state of Kansas'. Ordering the killing of 'every man big enough to carry a gun' and issuing a so-called 'vengeance list' beforehand outlining all of those who were to be murdered, there followed 'a three hour orgy of killing interspersed with drinks in commandeered saloons and exhibitions of fancy riding'. In between 'men were chased and shot down as they ran; others were dragged from their homes and murdered in front of their wives and children; still others were smothered or roasted alive when the houses in which they hid were set afire'. While some of the 'less blood-thirsty' members of the raiding party 'managed to protect a few of the fugitives', the carnage was nonetheless devastating; the bushwackers headed back towards the Missouri border leaving '80 new widows and 250 fatherless children weeping in the ruins of the town'.[20]

It is a daring move to place such a notorious incident at the centre of a feature film. It is even more daring to make a film whose subjects are not the 'innocents' of Lawrence but rather members of the 'bloody-minded' raiding party: no effort is made to gloss over the awfulness of the event and the scene's murdering and pillaging take place much as Foote describes them in his account. Quantrill's (John Ales) pre-raid speech refers to their own 'sisters and mothers' who died in a Kansas City jail and thus emphasises the pre-programmed, retributive nature of the violence that ensues: death lists are handed out and orders are given that no one is to be spared. Nor are we, as viewers, spared from the bloody nature of the raid; scenes in which Federal soldiers are slaughtered in their tents by marauding bushwackers are followed by images of unarmed citizens being dragged from their homes and shot in the head at point-blank range, and businesses and shops being ransacked and set ablaze. This is not to suggest that the film re-stages the raid exactly as it happened. As we have argued throughout this book, such a task is an impossible one. Rather, in so far as Rosenstone argues that, 'What happens on screen is at best a distant approximation of what was said and done in the past, a series of visual metaphors that do not depict but rather point to the events of the past',[21] *Ride with the Devil* is less interested in showing us the past, at least in any straightforward, apparently detached way, than in contesting some prevailing assumptions about the meaning of particular historical events by exploring the ways in which personal animosities and irrational hatreds shape and inform the broader 'sweep' of history.

Based on Daniel Woodrell's novel *Woe to Live On* (1995), *Ride with the Devil* comments on and raises issues about the past by representing the raid on Lawrence not as an 'objective' or universal history but rather as witnessed by two centrally involved fictionalised characters, Jake 'Dutchie' Roedel (Tobey Maguire) and Daniel Holt (Jeffrey Wright). What influences their view of and their participation in the attack is neither a bloody thirst for vengeance nor an unswerving loyalty to the Southern cause but rather a deep-seated ambivalence. During the raid itself, Holt and Roedel do not fire their own weapons in anger but neither do they intervene, except in one particular case, to save any of the citizens of Lawrence from being massacred. As they witness the slaughter, Roedel simply mutters, 'It's just bad-luck citizens finding out how bad luck can be.' Choosing instead to eat breakfast in the town's only hotel, they step in belatedly to prevent one of the more sadistic bushwackers, Pitt Mackeson (Jonathan Rhys Meyers), from dragging the elderly proprietor outside and shooting him. As they retreat, one of the raid's planners, Black John (James Caviezel), rides up along side Roedel and asks him if he is a 'betrayer' and says: 'You spared, boy. I told you not to spare'. Later, during a skirmish with pursuing Federal forces, Roedel is fired upon not by the advancing Federals but from behind by Pitt Mackeson. In Rosenstone's terms, this is a version of the past which explores the myriad of overlapping and conflicting regional, class and racial identifications at play in a war fought not between professional armies but between neighbours and across shifting, porous boundaries. It is a film which attempts to make sense of a war fought by a disparate group of farmers, peasants, idealists, outlaws and psychopaths for a multitude of reasons: not simply to defend the institution of slavery but also to show loyalty to kin and friends, to safeguard their distinctively Southern existence, to exact vengeance or, indeed, to repel the encroachment of what many Missourians in the film take to be the Northerner's alien cultural and political philosophy.

Roedel is at the heart of the film. He is a second-generation immigrant brought up on the Kansas–Missouri border by his Unionist German father and by the plantation-owning parents of his long-standing friend Jack 'Bull' Chiles (Skeet Ulrich), who raised Jake and their son as 'Southern'. Liberal on the issue of slavery, Roedel and Jack Bull join the cause out of loyalty to the Confederacy and for vengeance, having witnessed the murder of Jack Bull's parents by Northern jayhawkers. To this extent, Roedel is caught in a liminal space between North and South, between Kansas and Missouri, and between his father's pro-Unionist immigrant community and Jack Bull's Southern heritage. As such, he must negotiate a treacherous path through the snake-pit of competing claims on his loyalty. Opting for the South as opposed to the North does not mean that he cares nothing for his birth father nor does it mean that he is automatically accepted by his Southern compatriots: some come to respect his bravery and his abilities as a soldier, others distrust him because of his ancestry, his superior education and his links with the hated Union. In this internecine war between neighbours, Roedel identifies a captured Unionist soldier as an old school friend and manages to secure his release on the condition that he deliver a message to his army superiors offering an exchange of prisoners. Later, when news from the front line is brought back to the camp, Roedel learns that one of the soldiers he spared rode into Lawrence and killed his father. Zygmunt Bauman usefully defines ambivalence as 'the possibility of assigning an object or an event to more than one category'.[22] Such a condition surely describes Roedel's predicament: that of simultaneously belonging to the categories of both North and South and being unable to give himself wholly and unconditionally to either cause.

The film traces Roedel's transformation from youthful idealism into bitter disillusionment and his subsequent efforts to distance himself from the Southern cause. The genesis of this latter transformation is the sacking of Lawrence and the death of his old friend, Jack Bull. Only Roedel and Daniel Holt, an African-American freed slave fighting for the Confederacy out of loyalty to his ex-master,

George Clyde, stand apart from their Southern brethren. Tolerated for different reasons, Holt and Roedel strive but ultimately fail to reconcile their contradictory identifications. For Roedel, having a Unionist father is sufficient to drive a wedge between himself and his fellow bushwackers. For Holt, riding with men who talk openly about scalping 'niggers' pushes him to breaking point. The unravelling of their loyalties first of all to nation and then to the South elicits both disillusionment and hope. As they contemplate their respective futures in the aftermath of the Lawrence massacre, Roedel asks Holt whether he intends to join up with the 'regulars'. Their subsequent exchange, filmed as they lie next to each other preparing to sleep, is instructive in so far as it reveals the similarities and differences between their positions and perspectives.

> Holt: You really askin' me? What cause you think I got, Roedel? When them Yankees come and kill George Daddy, his brothers and all his people, I stood with George Clyde.
> Roedel: Yeah, he was as good a friend to you as Jack Bull was to me.
> Holt: Yeah. And now he's both good and dead, as good and dead as he can be. Where that leave you and me, huh? Where that leave me?
> Roedel: Right here.
> Holt: That ain't nowhere for me. Reckon I just don't understand it. That day George Clyde died, it changed me. I felt something that day I ain't ever felt.
> Roedel: You felt that loss, that hollow feeling.
> Holt: No, what I felt was free.
> Roedel: I thought that's what George gave you when he bought you out.
> Holt: (*almost tearful*) Now that wasn't really his to give now, was it? With George Clyde, I believe I loved him, but being that man's friend wasn't no different to being his nigger and, Roedel, I ain't ever again gonna be anyone else's nigger.

As both men inch towards some kind of personal redemption that is neither easily realised nor excessively symbolic, one senses that what are seeing is history from the bottom up rather than the top down; that is, history that challenges attempts to impose a false coherence and order on events; history as process rather than product; history that is confusing, ideologically muted and ambiguous; history that is not intended to be an exact mirror of what it purports to be an account of; and history that acknowledges its own subjectivity and contingency. As Roedel says about the achievements and failures of the bushwackers' actions: 'It ain't right and it ain't wrong, it just is.'

Cold Mountain strives for a similarly complex engagement with history but falls well short of *Ride with the Devil*'s achievements for a number of reasons. First, it cannot decide whether it wants to be a film about the Civil War in particular or about warfare in general: the damage that violent conflict can exact on those caught up in the conflict, both on the front line and at 'home'. The trajectory of the film seems to favour the latter argument. Whereas the film opens with a spectacular re-staging of the Petersburg siege and represents the ultimately unsuccessful attempts by Unionist soldiers to break the siege in July 1864, it soon abandons any efforts to contextualise the war, or to explore the complex allegiances that led individuals to fight for one side or the other, or indeed to encourage audiences to reflect upon the specific effects of particular events. The film instead juxtaposes the epic journey of a deserting Confederate soldier, Inman (Jude Law), who must find his way home across stunningly beautiful but politically treacherous terrain, with the story of Ada (Nicole Kidman), his girlfriend, who must struggle against 'home-front' despotism and harsh personal circumstances in order to remain alive. By doing so, it quickly becomes a well-meaning, though not particularly specific, meditation on universal themes of war-weariness, disillusionment and survival. As the director Anthony Minghella acknowledges: 'It appears to be a story about the American Civil War, and I don't necessarily have an interest in war stories. But then I realised that was not the issue. It's more about a man's return from war, the after-effects of war, and the effects of war on the world away from the battlefield.'[23] Second, *Cold Mountain* falls short of *Ride with the Devil* because, despite its attempts to emphasise the appallingly random impact of the conflict on individual life (as Ada states, 'War messes up just about everything'), its structuring narrative, that of a soldier going home to be reunited with his lover, all but guarantees that both Inman and Ada will survive whatever happens to them, at least until their eventual reunion. For an episodic film centrally concerned with unpredictability and chance – what happens to ordinary lives in the chaos of war – there is a tedious predictability about *Cold Mountain*. Moreover, despite its polite anti-war sentiments and its admittedly unusual focus on the effects of the conflict on domestic life, even more unusually characterised by the relationship between Ada and a female drifter (Renée Zellweger) who helps her farm the land, Minghella's film is ultimately no more challenging as history than a well-produced 'coffee table' book that makes up for its lack of analysis with a plethora of beautifully photographed images.

As noted before, historical films can make the past meaningful in three different ways: by visioning, contesting or revisioning history.[24] Whereas *Cold Mountain* may just about 'vision' history – that is, put 'flesh and blood on the past' and give us some sense of what it may have been like for individuals caught up in the conflict and struggling to survive at home – *Ride with the Devil* does all three. It gives us some sense of how the Southern bushwackers were affected by the emotional and political 'realities' of the situations they found themselves in; how people's loyalties and identifications crossed and blurred boundaries of region, race, ethnicity and class; and how idealism mutated into disillusionment and ultimately in disengagement from the struggle. Perhaps not an entirely accurate view of the past, but certainly one that 'imparts an overall meaning of the past'[25] and gives us an experience of what an event like the sacking of Lawrence may have been like. Ang Lee's film also 'provides [an] interpretation that runs against traditional wisdoms'.[26] That is, the film contests the assumption that the Civil War was fought only by professional and well-disciplined armies clashing on the field of honour and that lines of allegiances and divisions were clear-cut and ineradicable. It is the figure of Holt, an African-American confederate, who most upsets traditional assumptions about the Civil War but as Daniel Woodrell, author of the source novel *Woe to Live On*, argues, 'I did enough research to make sure I was on solid ground with black Confederates. I found a photo of a 1906 reunion of Quantrill's guerillas, with this black man standing in the front row. Apparently, when he died, his pall-bearers were white men who'd fought for slavery.'[27] Holt may be a fictional character, then, but as the production notes explain, free and enslaved African-Americans did fight on the side of the Confederacy for any number of reasons: 'Some wanted to prove to white Southerners that blacks could be as loyal and trustworthy as whites . . . some were fiercely loyal to their white friends and masters . . . others saw service in the war as a welcome relief from the drudgery of plantation life', while most used the opportunity to edge closer to the front line and the freedom of the North.[28]

Lee's film also 'shows us the past in new and unexpected ways, [utilizes] an aesthetic that violates the traditional, realistic ways of telling the past, . . . [challenges] a normal dramatic structure [and] mixes genres and modes'.[29] Here the case *for* the film is less clear-cut, since one could argue that, in so far as both Holt and Roedel head westwards at the end of the film or, to quote *Adventures of Huckleberry Finn*, 'light out for the territories', it fulfils, par excellence, the expectations of the western. One could also argue that because Roedel ultimately renounces his violent ways and settles down with a new wife, Sue Lee (Jewel), and a baby sired by his dead friend Jack Bull, he has been saved, in quite conventional terms, by the redemptive power of family. But this is not national redemption coded as personal redemption. Roedel's trek westwards is motivated not by an expansive, confident desire to settle the frontier but, as with Huck Finn or the protagonist in Clint Eastwood's 1976 film *The Outlaw Josey Wales*, simply because there is nowhere left for him to go, and heading either North or South is no longer a viable option. Additionally, the pace of the narrative, unlike the wound-up, pump-action tendencies of many contemporary films, is deliberately uneven: stasis followed by motion, short bursts of high-octane action and blood-letting followed by extended periods of quiet contemplation when characters and audience alike can reflect on what has happened, reflect on the formal and thematic ambivalence that lies at the core of the film.

But the film's ambivalence and that of Jake and Holt, who find themselves 'assigned', in Bauman's terms, to more than one category, has a political significance that relates both to the historical moment of the 1860s and to the moment of its own production. *Ride with the Devil* uses its history to engage with and 'interrogate' the present and in the process manages to unsettle a contemporary tendency towards cultural and political stability and a preference for maintaining order.[30] In this sense, ambivalence is a disruptive force because, as Bauman puts it: 'the typically modern practice, the substance of modern politics, of modern intellect, of modern life, is the effort to exterminate ambivalence: an effort to define precisely and to suppress or eliminate everything that could not and would not be precisely defined'.[31] In the logic of the film, the Missouri bushwackers are dangerous because their refusal to be categorised casts them as outlaws as much as disciplined soldiers or bloodthirsty vigilantes. 'The battles and armies are back east,' one of them says. 'Here you just have people fighting.' And when asked why they haven't joined the Confederate army, another of them remarks, 'We'll fight in our own country, not where some general tells us to fight.'

Their fight, in the final analysis, is against uniformity, regulation and the relentless march of orderly progress, embodied by the homogeneous ideals and ambitions of their Yankee enemies. Their *bête noire* is 'the typically modern practice' of seeking 'to exterminate ambivalence'.[32] For one of the film's disillusioned Southern farmers, the seeds of their own destruction as a distinctive culture lies not in the superior weaponry or armies of their Northern counterparts but in their evangelical enthusiasm for education. 'Before they built a church even, they built a schoolhouse and they let in every tailor's son and farmer's daughter in the country,' he tells Jack Bull. 'They rounded up every pup because they fancied that everyone should think and talk the same free-thinking way they do, no regard to station, custom, propriety . . . And that is why they will win because they believe that everyone should live and think just like them. And we shall lose because we don't care one way or another how they live.' Ang Lee outlines nicely the link between such thoughts and the emergence of a new, American or Yankee-led, modernity:

> It seems so much of the world is becoming Americanized. When I read . . . *Woe to Live On* . . . I realised that the American Civil War was, in a way, where it all started. It was where the Yankees won not only territory but, in a sense, a victory for a whole way of life and thinking . . . It changed everyone. Everyone is equal, everyone has the right to fulfill himself: this is the Yankee principle . . . This is all very modern, and so is the new social order based on that. We learn to respect other people's freedom, too, even as we lose a certain connection to tradition . . . The Civil War was not only a physical war – blood and guts – but also a personal war, one which led to the new world that we are living in today: the world of democracy and capitalism.[33]

In this respect, *Ride with the Devil* is an important addition to the library of Hollywood's historical films not just because its protagonists stand in opposition to established historical orthodoxy. Rather, it is such a distinctive and welcome historical film because unlike, say, *The Patriot* or *Glory*, it embraces ambivalence and counters what we might call a contemporary trend towards the fixing of order and the allocation of ideas and people to particular narrowly defined roles. As such, it is also a film whose cultural and political significance resonates with our own contemporary moment. For Slavoj Zizek, 'postmodern forms of ethnic violence'[34] (or the kind of excessive outbursts of violence that we witnessed in Chechnya and the former Yugoslavia) are the product of the same 'enlightened' attempts to exercise control through the peaceful spread of a regulatory logic that inform the Northern 'takeover' in *Ride with the Devil*. This is not to suggest that excessive outbursts of violence are justified or justifiable, far from it; rather, that in a world of 'suffocating closure' they may have become for some people 'the only way to give expression to the dimension beyond particularity'.[35] This, then, is the 'Balkanisation' of America – and the world – prefigured by a hundred or so years in the feverish slaughter enacted by both sides in Lee's film. To this end, the film is 'something of a commentary on the internecine conflicts in today's world'[36] as much as it is an attempt to engage with a set of historical concerns related to the Civil War. Because if *Glory* and *Amistad* set themselves the task of expelling ambivalence, *Ride with the Devil*'s desire to take the opposite route means that it speaks, in critical rather than affirmative ways, about a particularly deadening modern preference for politeness, tolerance and order and an equally deadening and alarming need to disrupt, question and challenge this preference by using nihilistic violence.

NOTES

1 David Thelen, 'Making History and Making the United States', *The Journal of American Studies*, Vol. 32 No. 3, December 1998, p. 387.

2 Stephen Bates, 'Old wounds, new pains', *The Guardian*, G2, 24 August 1994, pp. 2–3.

3 Robert F. Maxwell in Maxwell Simpson, 'Something Old, Something New', *What's On In London*, 21 September 1994, p. 33.

4 Richard Schickel, 'Glory', *Time*, 18 December 1989, p. 70.

5 Mark Cooper, 'Ghosts of the Civil War', *The Face*, March 1990, p. 13.

6 Kurt Jacobsen, 'At war with the white view', *The Guardian*, 7 March 1990, p. 24.

7 See Derek Malcolm's short review, *The Guardian*, 1 March 1990, p. 24.

8 Nelson George, 'Old Glory', *The Village Voice*, 30 January 1990, p. 22.

9 Robert Burgoyne, *Film Nation: Hollywood Looks at US History* (Minneapolis: University of Minneapolis Press, 1997), p. 16.

10 Ibid., p. 26.

11 Jude Davies and Carol R. Smith, *Gender, Ethnicity and Sexuality in*

Contemporary American Film (Edinburgh: Edinburgh University Press, 2001), p. 73.

12 Brief summary of Davies' and Smith's analysis of *Glory* in *Gender, Ethnicity and Sexuality*, pp. 71–82.

13 See, for example, Todd Gitlin, *The Twilight of Common Dreams* (New York: Henry Holt, 1995); Naomi Klein, *No Logo* (London: Flamingo, 2001); Slavoj Zizek, *The Ticklish Subject* (London and New York: Verso, 1999); Michael Hardt and Antonio Negri, *Empire* (Cambridge, MA and London: Harvard University Press, 2000).

14 Hardt and Negri, *Empire*, pp. 200–1.

15 See Bill Nichols, *Representing Reality: Issues and Concepts in Documentary Films* (Bloomington, IN: Indiana University Press, 1992), p. 116.

16 As Hardt and Negri argue: 'This emerging social order does not create divisions but . . . recognises existing or potential differences, celebrates them, and manages them within a general economy of command. The triple imperative . . . is incorporate, differentiate, manage.' (*Empire*, pp. 200–1)

17 For a fuller account of this process or logic, see Zizek's account of 'Post-Politics' in *The Ticklish Subject*, pp. 198–9.

18 See Davies and Smith, *Gender, Ethnicity and Sexuality*, pp. 79–80.

19 Edward Countryman, *Americans: A Collision of Histories* (London and New York: I. B. Tauris, 1996), p. 373.

20 Shelby Foote, *The Civil War: A Narrative* (London: Pimlico, 1992), pp. 704–5.

21 Robert Rosenstone, 'Oliver Stone as Historian', in Robert Brent Toplin, ed., *Oliver Stone's USA: Film, History and Controversy* (Lawrence, KS: University Press of Kansas, 2000), p. 34.

22 Zygmunt Bauman, *Modernity and Ambivalence* (Cambridge: Polity, 1991), p. 1.

23 Anthony Minghella quoted in David Walsh, 'Not quite a serious work', *World Socialist Web Site*, http://www.wsws.org/articles/2004/jan2004/cold-j07.shtml (12/3/04).

24 Rosenstone, 'Oliver Stone as Historian', p. 35.

25 Ibid., p. 34.

26 Ibid., p. 35.

27 Daniel Woodrell in Michael Carlson, 'A writer at war and peace', *Daily Telegraph*, 19 October 1999, p. 24.

28 See Q&A with producer/screenwriter James Schamus in *Ride with the Devil*, Production Notes, p. 15. For a fuller account, see Ervin L. Jordan Jr's *Black Confederates and Afro-Yankees in Civil War Virginia* (Charlottesville, VA and London: University Press of Virginia, 1995).

29 Rostenstone, 'Oliver Stone as Historian', p. 36.

30 See Robert Rosenstone, *Visions of the Past: The Challenge of Film to Our Idea of History* (Cambridge, MA: Harvard University Press, 1995), p. 239.

31 Bauman, *Modernity and Ambivalence*, pp. 7–8.
32 Ibid., p. 7.
33 Ang Lee in *Ride with the Devil*, Production Notes, p. 3.
34 Zizek, *Ticklish Subject*, p. 198.
35 Ibid., p. 204.
36 Phillip French, 'Devils on horseback', *The Observer*, Review, 7 November 1999, p. 7.

Chapter 4

SAVING THE GOOD WAR: HOLLYWOOD AND WORLD WAR II IN THE POST-COLD WAR WORLD

World War II holds a celebrated position in the benign meta-narrative of American foreign relations. This narrative holds that the United States is a benevolent nation whose foreign policy is based not on pure self-interest but rather on the greater good of all humankind. As H. W. Brands suggests: 'If a single theme pervades the history of American thinking about the world, it is that the United States has a peculiar obligation to better the lot of humanity. . . Americans have commonly spoken and acted as though the salvation of the world depended on them.'[1] According to this meta-narrative, the US has only ever engaged in foreign policy that, while it may have advanced the national interest, also served some higher purpose in the history of human progress: the Spanish–American War was fought to free the Cuban people and others from domination by imperial Spain; World War I was fought to 'make the world safe for democracy'; World War II was designed to defeat the evils of Nazism and Japanese expansionism whilst establishing the 'Four Freedoms' for all peoples; the Cold War was pursued in order to defend the rights of free peoples everywhere against totalitarian aggression and subversion; and the New World Order and more recently the 'War on Terror' were established to defend civilised peoples the world over against the uncertainties and dangers of the post-Cold War era.

Clearly this meta-narrative ignores, discounts or minimises the importance of a host of brutal episodes and self-interested policies that riddle American history. The continent's indigenous population was displaced or destroyed as the United States expanded westward; Washington has waged war and imposed its will on peoples as near as Latin America and as distant as South East Asia; covert operations have been ordered to overthrow democratically elected governments;

economic and strategic imperatives have frequently taken precedence over moral considerations in the construction of policy; and Americans have proved themselves as capable as any other peoples of committing wartime atrocities. Yet despite the abundance of evidence to the contrary, the benign meta-narrative has remained a salient element of American national identity. As David Ryan points out, many of those historical experiences that were 'incompatible with the righteous image of the nation were basically written out of the sites of collective memory'.[2]

Such a process has occurred with the cultural memory of World War II, which has been 'converted over time from a complex, problematic event, full of nuance and debatable meaning, to a simple shining legend of the Good War'.[3] More than any other event in American history, including the revolution,[4] World War II has been mythologised and held up as an example of a 'golden age' that showcased America's 'national strength, collective courage, idealism, and other desirable traits'. The American experience of World War II has become regarded as 'a peak in the life of society when everything worked out and the good guys definitely got a happy ending'.[5] As Philip Beidler suggests: 'the glow of 1945 persists as a kind of beacon, a moment in which Americans' attitudes toward themselves and their relation to the world at least once seem to have been filled with a clarity and purpose – and perhaps even more importantly, a generosity of purpose'. The war maintains a positive grip on the American imagination and plays a central role in the nation's benign meta-narrative precisely because, since its passing, the clarity of purpose it provided has been 'no longer available' and has been 'so worthy therefore of attempting to locate and possibly recapture'.[6]

THE GOOD WAR

The US did emerge from the war more powerful economically, politically and militarily than it had ever been before. It was now officially a world power, a superpower in fact, that had largely escaped from the massive devastation that had been suffered by all the other major combatants in the global conflagration. It could more or less dictate the terms of the peace and the nature of the global system that would now emerge. American industry and the economy were booming, US fighting forces were the largest and best equipped in the world, and Washington held a monopoly over the ultimate power of atomic weaponry. In terms of elevating the US to the role of global super-power and consolidating the recovery from the years of economic depression, World War II had been a 'Good War' for the United States. There was also little question that the defeat of aggressive and expansionist Germany and Japan had been a worthy cause that served not only American national interest but also that of most other nations. Like any 'enduring myth', as Michael Adams observes, that of the Good War 'rests on a solid core of credible evidence'.[7] Yet it also ignores or downplays an array of less appealing aspects of America's war against Nazi Germany and Imperial Japan. Serious questions exist about the morality and necessity of firebombing Dresden and Tokyo, and of dropping atomic bombs on Hiroshima and Nagasaki. There was widespread disregard for the dignity and rights of the enemy, particularly in America's war in the Pacific, which John Dower has characterised as a 'war without mercy', where racism determined the way the Japanese were both depicted and treated.[8] This racially driven behaviour extended back to the homefront, with Japanese-Americans being sent to internment camps. Racism also remained rife within the American social structure, with segregation being maintained not only in public places in the South but also in the armed forces. American culpability in the Holocaust is also a matter of continuing debate and guilt concerning how much Washington knew about the genocide and why it did not act earlier to bring it to an end.[9] These areas of ambiguity, even shame, have been increasingly addressed by historians of World War II, as many have striven to consider the international perspectives of the war and the role of culture, gender, race, and other factors.

These and other troubling aspects of the Good War have largely failed to permeate the enduring myth, however. The critical interpretations of historians, writers and even filmmakers have 'done little to change general American attitudes'. As Beidler argues: 'Whatever the logic of history or memory, somehow World War II has shaken off all the challenges along the way.'[10] Michael Adams contends that it was 'Hollywood, more than any other agency' that made World War II into what he sardonically calls 'the best war ever' for the United States.[11] According to Beidler, post-war Hollywood films, combined with novels and other popular-cultural representations of the war, set in place reified and commodified images of World War II that would 'become enshrined themselves as forms of history and memory'.[12] John Whiteclay Chambers II and David Culbert agree that 'film and television depictions of war have evolved into the perceived "reality" of war' such that the 'public memory of war in the twentieth century has been created less from a remembered past than from a manufactured past, one substantially shaped by images in documentaries, feature films, and television programs'. Indeed, so large are contemporary television and film audiences that 'more people are experiencing the war through feature films and docudramas than actually participated in it'.[13] Adams concurs that Americans 'went to the cinema to see what the war had been like'. As a result, the war became 'a part of American folklore, captured forever in a manageable format and with a message acceptable to the public'. That message was essentially that World War II was a time of great American 'heroism and patriotism', in which the US defeated enemies that were unambiguously 'cruel, devious, and unprincipled'.[14]

It is a testament to the potency of World War II films as vehicles of propaganda and ideology that they were generally very effective at producing social and political consensus. As with other films we have analysed in this book, this potency can be explained both in terms of these films' claims to 'common sense' (who would argue against American heroism?) and by their invisible style and consequent pretensions towards verisimilitude – that is, if we cannot immediately identify a film's style as artifice, then its claims to 'realism' are enhanced. Classic World War II films were not, however, entirely gung-ho, pro-war affairs. In fact, an essential role in the archetypal film was a questioning soldier who doubted the necessity of American involvement in the war and challenged those in authority. Such figures were included even during wartime itself, since they asked the questions the public needed answering in order to grant their support to the US war objectives.[15] The heroic protagonists of the archetypal World War II Hollywood movie were also not flawless, uncomplicated characters. They often had a 'darkness within', a degree of cynicism and a chequered past. This was even the case for the greatest all-American celluloid hero, John Wayne, in the most celebrated of all American World War II films, *The Sands of Iwo Jima* (1949). Wayne's character, Marine Sergeant John Stryker, is a divorced, alcoholic, insubordinate loner. *The Sands of Iwo Jima* itself is not a 'dewey-eyed paean to combat glory' but rather a film that 'portrays war as unforgiving and cruel'. As if to prove this point, Stryker is killed in a random, almost meaningless way at the film's 'radically disruptive climax'.[16] Yet almost without fail, at least until the late 1960s, Hollywood's World War II films served the purpose of affirming the national perception that World War II was the Good War. Despite complexities of character and sometimes plot, the clear message was that during those extraordinary wartime years, Americans rose above their personal flaws, overcame their doubts and Great Depression-era cynicism, to fight the good fight, suffer the necessary sacrifices, and defeat the threat of evil from the Axis powers. It was, as Thomas Doherty suggests, 'the recollection of a securely victorious past' that served as an encouraging stalwart image during a Cold War that promised global annihilation should it lead once more to world war.[17]

THE BAD WAR

The experience of the Vietnam War, however, changed the way many Americans felt about war-making, the sacrifices that were worth making in the 'national interest', and the purpose and objectives of US foreign policy. The moral certitude of the World War II era, and indeed the early Cold War, was thrown into disarray by America's first defeat in war. The network of corruption, lies and abuse of power in Washington coupled with revelations of massacres and other heinous acts committed by US forces in Indochina served to undermine the way Americans thought of war as a unifying force that, when undertaken by the US, served some higher purpose. Vietnam provided the greatest challenge yet to the credibility of the benign meta-narrative of American foreign relations. Its effects could be felt in Hollywood's output, even if for many years studios were almost wholly unwilling to produce films that directly addressed the war in Vietnam. Instead, other genres such as westerns (*Little Big Man*), gangster films (*Bonnie and Clyde*), film noir (*Chinatown*) and indeed war films (*M*A*S*H*, *Patton*) were used as allegories for Vietnam and its impact on the homefront. As Jeanine Basinger argues, Vietnam brought about a 'period of disillusionment with combat' which led to the World War II combat film's format being 'inverted, perverted, destroyed, mocked, or satirized'.[18] Doherty agrees that while 'World War II films painted a portrait of victory and competence, of American true grit overpowering stormtrooper discipline and samurai fanaticism, Vietnam erased that image'.[19] Throughout much of the 1970s, the all-American soldier-hero was replaced as a Hollywood archetype by the unstable, if not downright psychotic, Vietnam veteran. Something of a revolution had taken place in American filmmaking, inspired by the cultural convulsions of the 1960s, that produced a new breed of films, dubbed the New Hollywood, that challenged old values, traditions and styles while reflecting the self-doubt, alienation, dissolution and confusion that seemed to grip the American psyche in the wake of Vietnam and Watergate.[20]

American attitudes toward the direction of US foreign policy and, in particular, the use of force remained ambiguous throughout the post-Vietnam period. Each US administration attempted to deal with or overcome the legacy of Vietnam and the apparent limits it placed on American power.[21] By the late 1970s, Hollywood finally began to use the Vietnam War as subject matter. Vietnam War films became a sub-genre of combat movies and played a significant role in the cultural coming to terms with the Vietnam experience that took place in American society. Some films attempted to reinterpret the American defeat as what President Reagan called 'a noble cause', even going so far as reinventing the war as an American victory (*Rambo: First Blood Part II*). Others were more critical of American involvement in Vietnam and endeavoured to portray an uncompromising view of combat that emphasised the insanity and horror of war while demonstrating the moral ambiguity or depravity of American actions, both at the institutional and individual level (*Apocalypse Now, Full Metal Jacket, Casualties of War*). The portrayal of war in Hollywood films changed significantly during this period, with conflict being more readily depicted as bloody, unpredictable and harrowing. The objectives of American foreign policy were often brought into question and authority figures were often treated with cynicism or even derision. Moreover, by taking their lead from the cycle of revisionist genre films that reached its apex during the 1970s, Vietnam War films like *Apocalypse Now* and *Full Metal Jacket* handcuffed their anti-authoritarian sentiments to a form which implicitly or explicitly challenged the 'classical' style of filmmaking by emphasising rather than concealing their own internal mechanics; revealing their own 'artifice' through jarring camera movements, discontinuous editing and over-determined mis-en-scene.

THE RETURN OF THE GOOD WAR?

By the end of the Cold War, the administration of George Herbert Walker Bush argued that the lessons of Vietnam had been learned and that it was time to move on. First in Panama and then in the Gulf War, Bush committed the largest number of US forces to combat since the Vietnam War. Particularly in the Gulf, Bush claimed the US had kicked the Vietnam syndrome once and for all. He delved back beyond Vietnam into the benign meta-narrative of American foreign relations to invoke the memory of the Good War to justify using force against Iraq. The invasion of Kuwait must be reversed, he argued, because history showed that aggressors must be punished rather than appeased, as Hitler was at Munich in 1938. Indeed, Bush made frequent comparisons between the Iraqi leader, Saddam Hussein, and Adolf Hitler. Bush's use of World War II analogies came as people were beginning to commemorate the 50th anniversaries of various World War II battles and other landmark events. From September 1989 to August 1995, the American public's attention became increasingly refocused on what was supposedly the United States' finest hour, when it had at first reluctantly and then whole-heartedly joined and ultimately won the fight against Nazism and Japanese imperialism. It was inevitable, perhaps, given the extensive media coverage on the various acts of commemoration being made fifty years on and the President's evocation of the era, that Hollywood would once again return to the subject of World War II. But what kind of World War II films would now be produced? Would they be more knowing than their predecessors, incorporating much of the new history on the war that considered alternative, critical viewpoints on aspects such as the motivations for war, the role of racism in the war's pursuit, the impact of combat on those who fought, and the reasons for targeting civilian populations in bombing raids?

The first batch of post-Cold War World War II films to emerge from Hollywood were anything but a raging success. In fact, they were regarded as 'box office poison' by most Hollywood executives, with one vice president claiming 'World War II is ancient history to the majority of the TV and movie audience – there's nothing real about it.'[22] *Fat Man and Little Boy* (1989) was a 'melodrama' about the Manhattan Project; *Memphis Belle* (1990) was an 'amnesiac' depiction of American bombing runs over Germany; *For the Boys* (1991) was a

Big Band musical vehicle for Bette Midler; and, worst of all, *Shining Through* (1992) was a 'wildly anachronistic espionage thriller'.[23] It was *Schindler's List* (1993) that finally broke the mould of World War II films failing to inspire both audiences and critics in the post-Cold War era. Steven Spielberg's film retells the story of Oskar Schindler, a Sudeten-German businessman who made his fortune operating a factory in Nazi-occupied Poland during World War II and went on to save over a thousand Jews destined for concentration camps by placing them on a list of 'essential' workers. The film won widespread critical acclaim, seven Academy Awards including Best Picture, and took millions at box offices worldwide. The success of *Schindler's List* opened the door for Hollywood to return wholeheartedly to World War II.

Between 1998 and 2001, four major-release films addressed various aspects of the American role in World War II. Spielberg's own *Saving Private Ryan* (1998) focused on the D-Day landings and their aftermath; *The Thin Red Line* (1998) addressed the American battle against the Japanese on Guadalcanal; *U-571* (2000) revolved around the seizure of a German Enigma code-breaking machine; and *Pearl Harbor* (2001) recreated not only the Japanese attack of 7 December 1941 but also the Doolittle air raid on Tokyo in April 1942. Each film wove fictional stories around these historical events and thereby brought to the foreground once more debates about the role of Hollywood both as historian and carrier of ideology. In the remainder of this chapter, we will first address the extent to which these films place their stories within an insightful historical context and thus provide an appropriately complex, multi-faceted perspective on historical events and their possible meanings; second, what their engagement with World War II reveals not only about the contested status of historical truth but also about our own contemporary moment; and third, how these films reconstitute American national identity in the post-Cold War world, particularly the ways in which they engage with questions of race and gender.

Saving Private Ryan depicts the D-Day landings at Omaha Beach on 6 June 1944, then focuses on the fictional story of a US Army squad's mission to retrieve from the fighting Private James Ryan whose three brothers have already been killed in the war. The film was a great international success. It grossed more money at box offices worldwide than it did in the United States.[24] In addition to its five Oscars, the film received other major national film awards in countries across the globe including Canada, Britain, France, Germany and Japan. Yet despite the film finding mass and critical appeal outside the United States, *Saving Private Ryan* is an almost entirely Americentric depiction of the Normandy invasion. Of the 150,000 Allied troops who landed in France on D-Day, there were 57,000 Americans. The rest were drawn from Britain, Canada, the Free French and other Commonwealth and European forces. By late July, the number of American troops in Normandy had risen to 770,000 but British and Canadian troops also totalled 591,000.[25] Yet in *Saving Private Ryan* there is almost no mention of the multinational nature of the invasion force. The film focuses solely on the efforts of the United States. In fact, America's allies are mentioned only once, and then in a derogatory manner, in a short discussion between Captain Frank Miller (Tom Hanks) and Captain Fred Hamill (Ted Danson) about the progress of the invasion. Miller observes dryly that 'We have the beach-head secured. Problem is Monty's taking his time moving on Caen. We can't pull out 'til he's ready, so . . .'. Hamill replies: 'That guy's overrated' to which Miller responds: 'No argument here.' The problem with this criticism of British Field Marshall Bernard Montgomery in the film is not that it is disingenuous. Montgomery had indeed promised to take the strategically important Caen on D-Day but failed to move on the city for several days and then weeks, much to the frustration and anger of the Americans, not least Allied Supreme Commander Dwight Eisenhower.[26] British and Canadian forces had met fierce resistance around Caen, however, where German defences were stronger than anywhere else in Normandy.[27] Military experts and historians remain in dispute over whether Montgomery's efforts at Caen should be praised or damned.[28] The main point here, though, is that aside from this brief, critical exchange about 'Monty' there is otherwise no mention in the film of America's allies and their actions on and following D-Day. *Saving Private Ryan*, therefore, privileges American actions above those of others involved in D-Day and sends the distinct message to its audience that it was the United States that almost single-handedly won the war against Nazi Germany. Indeed, since America's allies are only mentioned critically, the implication is that the US won World War II in spite of the lesser efforts of its fighting partners. How and why a film that essentially privileges an American perspective performed so well at the international box office is a question that we will return to later in the chapter.

It can be argued in Spielberg's defence that since the film focuses on soldiers who landed at Dog Green Sector on Omaha Beach, where only US forces invaded, it is not a problem that other Allied forces play no role in the film. From a historian's point of view, however, this fact highlights the lack of context in what has been praised in many quarters as the most 'realistic' cinematic representation to date of the events of D-Day. Indeed, the larger historical and political context of the Normandy invasion and World War II is almost entirely absent from the film. After the brief opening scene at what we are left to assume is an Allied graveyard in northern France, we are thrust immediately into the action without any contextual scene-setting. The sea laps around the beach defences on what the on-screen caption tells us simply is 'June 6, 1944. Dog Green Sector. Omaha Beach.' The slaughter that follows is not given any historical or political context by Spielberg. The depiction of the Americans landing at Omaha Beach may well be the 'most realistic presentation of combat' so far produced on film, as various World War II veterans have argued.[29] Or, as Jim Neilson remarks, the film's opening scenes are 'truly harrowing and equal, in graphic realism, any previous war movie'.[30] However, it is a highly dubious practice to uncritically laud the film's graphic realism without also interrogating the ways in which it colludes with recuperative attempts to code the conflict as righteous and also disengages with the wider significance of D-Day's events. As Howard Zinn argues, *Saving Private Ryan*, 'aided by superb cinematographic technology, draws on our deep feelings for the GIs in order to rescue not just Private Ryan but also the good name of war'.[31] Whatever the visceral, emotional impact of the film's opening action sequences, they also do little to satisfy many of the demands that we have placed on historical films. The audience is not given the opportunity to engage with the meaning and significance of the events being portrayed since there is little or nothing in the film to suggest what the larger context might be. Why are these men attacking this beach, at this time and with what purpose? What has occurred to bring them to this point? What is the significance of the operation they are undertaking?

John Whiteclay Chambers II and David Culbert argue that the greatest weakness of historical feature films is 'their apparent inability to examine complex causation'. They criticise Daryl F. Zanuck's earlier treatment of the Normandy invasion, *The Longest Day* (1962), for not containing 'one word about causation'. Their criticism can be levelled equally at *Saving Private Ryan*: 'The day of the invasion, June 6, 1944, comes from nowhere, and the film ends with no information about the probable result of the Allied landings.'[32] In *The Longest Day* there are rather laboured attempts to give some context to the day's events through the dialogue between characters. In *Saving Private Ryan*, any such attempts at explanation are kept to a bare minimum. There is the previously mentioned brief exchange between Captains Miller and Hamill, which amounts to little more than a laundry list of towns and cities that should be taken in order to facilitate the liberation of Paris. When it is determined that Private Ryan is helping defend a bridge over the Merderet River, we also get a brief explanation of the importance of this river and of Cherbourg as a deep water port for the push on Paris. Elsewhere, we are simply given short platitudes such as: 'Our objective is to win the war.'

There are also one or two brief exchanges of dialogue in Terence Malick's *The Thin Red Line* that attempt to set the film's depiction of C for Charlie Company's experiences on Guadalcanal into a wider perspective. Near the film's beginning, Brigadier General Quintard (John Travolta) leans over a map onboard a US Navy ship and gives some explanation to Lieutenant Colonel Gordon Tall (Nick Nolte) of the island's strategic significance: 'As you can see, this is their [the Japanese] road to Australia. This is their way of controlling the sea links to America. Now if we're going to stop the Japs' advance into the South Pacific, we're going to have to do it right there.' Quintard adds that no one wants the island itself but the Japanese have built an airfield there so it has become a significant threat. Tall was obviously listening, since later in the film, after his troops have made significant gains from the Japanese, he notes the importance of Guadalcanal. If the US can move bombers onto the island, he says, it 'means air power all around for a thousand miles in every direction'. He adds that 'Guadalcanal may be the turning point in the war.' Guadalcanal is at the eastern end of the Solomon Islands, just north-east of Australia, ten degrees below the equator. It was the furthest Japanese forces advanced in the war and a place of great strategic importance to both sides. For the Japanese it could provide a base for further advances toward Australia, the Fiji Islands or New Caledonia, while an American victory would not only protect those territories but also signal to the Japanese that the Allies were gaining an upper hand. The exchanges in the film do give some sense of this strategic importance, and Tall's suggestion that Guadalcanal would be the Pacific War's turning point is shared by historians. While Japanese forces had already been checked and repelled in earlier battles at Coral Sea and Midway, it was their 'failure on Guadalcanal' that forced them to 'go into reverse'. Following Guadalcanal, it was the US and its allies 'who were strategically on the offensive'.[33]

Despite these attempts to place the film's events within their strategic context, *The Thin Red Line* offers only a limited view of how the battle for Guadalcanal was fought. Historian Kenneth Jackson observes that the battle for the island 'was mostly over before this movie begins'. The film does not explain that the Japanese airfield was seized by US Marines before the end of the second day of fighting, on 8 August 1942, and then used to great effect by US forces. The 25th Infantry Division, featured in the film, did not arrive until several months later. Jackson also criticises the film for not explaining that:

> . . . neither the Japanese nor the Americans were initially able to get adequate reinforcements or supplies to their troops ashore, and that desperate naval battles by day and night continued throughout the fall. Both sides lost so many ships that nearby waters came to be known as 'Iron Bottom Sound'.[34]

Not only does the film give no indication that a major naval battle took place at Guadalcanal, it also ignores the significance of air power on the island even though it has been argued that the 'most decisive victories' were in the air.[35] We are also given no sense that the battle for Guadalcanal was over by February 1943. The film ends with the Japanese continuing to counterattack American advances and a voiceover tells us simply 'This war's not going to be over for a long time.'

The film has also been criticised for not rendering the island as American soldiers would have experienced it. In Malick's film, Guadalcanal is depicted as 'a paradise, replete with lush green mountains, tropical waterfalls, and glorious beaches' when it was actually 'mostly dense jungle, infested with ferocious ants, poisonous snakes, and malarial mosquitoes, not to mention lizards, crocodiles, spiders, leeches, and scorpions'. It was widely regarded by American servicemen as 'a tropical hell'.[36] Most of the many animals and birds shown in the film are beautiful, exotic creatures. Juxtaposed with the slaughter on the battlefield, these images serve well to demonstrate the surreal nature of war but they fail to convey how threatening the natural environment was to the GIs on Guadalcanal. One soldier does get sick, but aside from their fear of being killed by bullets or bombs, the Americans seem largely comfortable in what was actually oppressive heat, even though it is admitted in the film that water supplies are low.

Jackson concludes that 'the viewer learns too little about Guadalcanal' and that the film 'does not tell the viewer enough about history'.[37] Such criticisms are fair enough, but only to a point. Implicit in Jackson's demands of the film is the assumption that 'history' is ultimately recoverable. *The Thin Red Line* does not purport to be a definitive or even comprehensive history of the American battle for Guadalcanal. The war in the Pacific may provide the backdrop, but this is a film that, as Jackson himself admits, 'concerns itself with timeless issues of life, death, love, morality, evil, destiny, and fear'.[38] *The Thin Red Line*'s effectiveness as a pedagogical tool is less reliant on its 'accuracy' and more on its ability to encourage audiences to think critically about not only the particularities of the conflict but war generally and also the larger relationship between film and history. The film poses significant challenges to the quite rigid set of narrative conventions that war films usually follow and audiences expect. Malick's film not only eschews history, at least in any straightforward way; it barely has a narrative at all. As one reviewer puts it, the film is 'a near free-form essay in texture, shape and ideas' such that the 'historical base of the story hardly gets any screen time'.[39] *The Thin Red Line*, though, should not be judged solely on its status as a work of World War II history but on its effectiveness at evoking a more general sense of the chaos and contingency of war. As Geoffrey Mcnab concludes: 'Whatever its ideological bias or historical oversights, *The Thin Red Line* is hugely effective as a film about the absurdity of war.' War is shown as something 'messy and inchoate', with death and dying everywhere, especially as waves of GIs attempt to seize hilltop machine-gun bunkers.[40] Bullets rip through flesh, men die slowly and painfully, soldiers on both sides lose their minds, and no one seems immune from the random, unforgiving nature of war. The use of largely anonymous voiceovers to obliquely convey the thoughts of the various soldiers involved only adds to the confusion and sense of randomness. By asking the unanswerable question of why some men survive while other equally worthy men die in war, *The Thin Red Line* succeeds in its attempts to engage in a complex, philosophical discourse on the nature of combat. As such, it is a highly effective piece of cinema. Even if it only conveys a rather limited sense of the wider history of World War II and the specifics of Guadalcanal, the film gives a thought-provoking indication of what the experience of individual soldiers might have been like in the Pacific War. By framing the action in a distancing, almost alienating manner, the film opens up sufficient space for audiences to 'think' about what they are watching rather than merely to 'feel' and 'experience' the action; to think about the absurdities and consequences of war from a range of competing American perspectives, ranging from the grunt's eye to the military elite.

Like many of the Vietnam War films that preceded them, *The Thin Red Line* and, for that matter, *Saving Private Ryan* give relatively uncompromising views of what war does to individuals. This is particularly so in the way both films portray soldiers being wounded or killed. Stephen Ambrose observes that in earlier World War II films 'lots of men are killed . . ., but always in a clean shot that brings instant death. There are no wounds to speak of, no blood, no scenes depicting the true price of war, the damage that bullets and high explosives can do to the human body.'[41] This cannot be said of either *The Thin Red Line* or *Saving Private Ryan*. In the former, the killing of both Americans and Japanese is shown as bloody, indiscriminate, and often painful and slow. The strategies of defamiliarisation and disorientation adopted by *The Thin Red Line* are also highly effective in eliciting a critical, questioning response from audiences. The absence of obvious signposts instructing us how to 'read' or come to terms with images of battlefield slaughter point towards a radical ambivalence that structures Malick's film as a whole. While it never questions the fundamental reasons for fighting the war, the film's messy narrative and multiplicity of perspectives, its hallucinogenic mood and its visceral attempts to represent something of the violence and absurdity of war without striving to make any clear-cut political statement, makes it a 'difficult' film to watch.

Saving Private Ryan, meanwhile, has become widely hailed as the most 'realistic' combat film ever made. As Jeanine Basinger argues:

> The violence of *Saving Private Ryan*'s opening sequence (the D-Day landing on Omaha Beach) is overwhelming. . . the audience sees blood, vomit, dead fish, dismembered arms and legs, wounds spurting fountains of blood, torsos disintegrating while

being dragged to safety. Men drown, are wounded, and are shot and killed in a chaotic atmosphere of fear and bewilderment. Medics are forced to make ruthless decisions about the wounded ('Routine!' 'Routine!' 'Priority!') as they advance among what appears to be *every* soldier on the beach, all apparently dying.[42]

Basinger concludes that this opening sequence 'is a nightmare. Today's audiences are shocked into silence while watching. No one talks, and no one munches popcorn or rattles candy wrappers.'[43] While both *Saving Private Ryan* and *The Thin Red Line* tell us little about the wider history of World War II, the geopolitical objectives of the United States, or even the military history of how the invasions of Normandy and Guadalcanal led to the final defeat of Germany and Japan, do they fair any better at this more micro level? Both films certainly create what Robert Rosenstone would call a 'spectacle' but in doing so, do they convey 'a particular feeling' of what the 'past means' and challenge 'the images of the historical realities we think we know most clearly', as he suggests the best historical films can do?[44] In other words, do Spielberg's and Malick's films do a better job than earlier World War II films in conveying some sense of the myriad ways in which people experienced combat and its consequences during the war?

Basinger claims that 'Spielberg's mastery of sound, editing, camera movement, visual storytelling, narrative flow, performance and color combine to assault a viewer, to place each and every member of the audience directly into the combat experience'.[45] She concludes, however, that while earlier World War II films such as *Bataan* (1943) or, indeed, *The Longest Day*, were more physically 'unrealistic' than contemporary films such as *Saving Private Ryan*, the psychological and emotional impact of these earlier productions was just as effective. Indeed, *Bataan* was praised at the time of release for its 'gritty realism' and its violence was considered 'extreme'. Films of all genres that incorporate violence have increased in their bloodiness over the years, but this alone 'does not necessarily make them more realistic'.[46] In fact, as director Samuel Fuller concluded, the only way to present the experience of war on film would be to 'fire live ammo over the heads of the people in the movie theatre'.[47] Yet in *Saving Private* Ryan, Spielberg's technical skills as a filmmaker conspire not so much to assault viewers by placing them directly into 'the combat experience' – as Basinger argues – but rather to let audiences off the hook by permitting them to 'experience' combat without subjecting to proper critical scrutiny what Zinn calls the 'glory of military heroism'.[48] The role or function of spectacle here is crucial. Robert Kolker criticises Spielberg's 'theme-park style' ride through the combat on Omaha Beach in order to create for the viewer 'a deep unease and trepidation that, the film believes, parallels the battlefield experience'. He argues that Spielberg cannot allow himself to occupy an 'unremittingly bleak position' and must find a way either to mitigate or divert attention from the 'moral uncertainty' that such an image creates. For Kolker, then, Spielberg achieves this via recourse to spectacle:

> Through the manipulation of film stock and sound, through the creation of animated digital bullets, flying into the screen space, towards the soldiers from an unseen enemy, the viewer is given the opportunity to share the anxiety (if not the danger) of battle. Finally not so different from *Jurassic Park* . . . the audience is absorbed into the film's narrative space, and awe competes with despair.[49]

For all that Spielberg's images unsettle and disrupt our viewing experiences, they ultimately elicit no more than, as Kolker puts it, 'passivity: the longing gaze at the spectacle on the screen'. Far from challenging the viewer to reconsider their views on World War II, *Saving Private Ryan*, like other Spielberg films and much of American cinema, offers a spectacle that is closed to interpretation and therefore 'totally evades politics and history'. In Kolker's words, the films images are 'used to purchase emotion at the expense of analyzing alternatives or examining the details of history' and history itself is transformed into 'a spectacle that confirms power and hierarchy'.[50]

If the spectacle of war in Spielberg's film creates passivity in the audience and re-affirms existing power structures, it does so to an even greater degree in *Pearl Harbor* and *U-571*. These films attempt to convince us about the 'rightness' of their representations of history by taking Spielberg's 'theme park' style to its logical conclusions. They both caused controversy upon their release due to their apparently scant regard for the accepted historical record. *U-571* is a comic-book style action movie that depicts a US submarine crew seizing a German Enigma cipher machine and code booklets from a U-Boat in 1942, thus changing the course of the war in favour of the Allied cause. Yet, as many of the film's critics observed, this story is total fiction. The Enigma machine was actually retrieved from a disabled U-Boat, *U-110*, by the crew of the British destroyer HMS *Bulldog* on 9 May 1941, seven months before the US even joined the war. King George VI sent congratulations to the crew for what he considered to be 'perhaps the most important single event in the whole war at sea'. Moreover, as Hugh Sebag-Montefiore reveals in his history of the Enigma code-breaking saga, contrary to conventional wisdom it was not even this seizing of an Enigma machine that enabled the British to crack the code for the first time. That had been achieved through the deciphering of code-books captured from German trawlers. Indeed, the British had already seized other Enigma machines and apparatus. The main significance of the haul from *U-110* was not, therefore, that it single-handedly changed the course of the conflict but rather that the capture of the settings and procedures to be used for 'Offizier' Enigma messages enabled the British to decode doubly-enciphered messages being sent to U-Boat officers at sea.[51]

Whatever the circumstances that led to the breaking of the Enigma code, they were certainly not those portrayed in *U-571*. Although the film does acknowledge the actions of the Royal Navy at the head of its closing credits, it nonetheless raised the rancour of British reviewers who accused Hollywood of making a 'bogus and redundant' film that 'blithely ignores historical fact'.[52] One tabloid reviewer claimed that the 'manipulation of history that film-makers in general, and American ones in particular, are prone to threatens our whole view of history' and condemned the film as 'an insult to those who fought and died' in World War II.[53] This complaint even found its way into the hallowed halls of the British Parliament. MPs tabled a motion in the House of Commons which expressed regret for how the film 'detracted from the valour of the British sailors concerned.'[54] The issue even made it into Prime Minister's questions, where Tony Blair said he 'agreed entirely' with MP for Tamworth Brian Jenkins' assertion that *U-571* 'is an affront to the memory of the British sailors who lost their lives' in the operation to retrieve the Enigma machine and codes.[55]

Similar concerns were aired about the way *Pearl Harbor* ignores or diminishes the role of America's allies in World War II. The film's makers do indicate that the US should have given greater aid to Britain earlier and mocked-up newsreels praise the bravery of the RAF in repelling German attacks. Yet when the film's hero, Rafe

McCawley (Ben Affleck), volunteers to fight with Eagle Squadron in England, the clear implication is that Britain's hopes are lost without American assistance and leadership. As a battle-weary RAF officer tells Rafe, 'A lot of people frown on the Yanks for not being in this war yet. But if there are many more back home like you, God help anyone who goes to war with America.' The fact that it is Rafe who leads his British cousins when they fly out to meet the incoming Luftwaffe led film critic Peter Bradshaw to state: 'If you thought that the war in the Pacific would be one Second World War story which didn't need time out to patronise the Brits, you were wrong.' Rafe appears to be 'winning the Battle of Britain single-handed'.[56] Indeed, there is no mention in the film of the role played by Britain, Australia, New Zealand, or other participants in the war against Japan. Following the 'date which will live in infamy', this is very much America's war – and in *Pearl Harbor*, it is unquestionably the Good War.

Pearl Harbor is a film riddled with historical inaccuracies, fabrications and implausibility and, although they are not the sole basis of our critique, some of the film's more ludicrous 'inventions' are worth noting. Lawrence Suid, for example, makes the point that, 'so little of what appears on the screen bears even a remote resemblance to actual events leading up to the attack on Pearl Harbor, the actual attack, or the aftermath, including the Doolittle raid' that the film is rendered 'useless as a tool to teach students about the Japanese attack'.[57] Perhaps most tellingly, the film shows the architect of the Japanese attack, Admiral Isoroku Yamamoto, uttering the line: 'I fear all we have done is to awaken a sleeping giant.' Yet these words are not those of Yamamoto himself, but of the writers of the earlier film about Pearl Harbor, *Tora! Tora! Tora!* (1970). *Tora*, a joint American–Japanese production, had painstakingly attempted to piece together a faithful account of the calculations and miscalculations that led up to the attack before recreating the attack itself.[58] However, the director of *Pearl Harbor*, Michael Bay, is rather dismissive of *Tora*'s 'docudrama' approach and, making bold assertions for his own film, he insists that it manages to dramatise events and use them as a setting for a fictional love story while also upholding claims of historical realism: 'You will see what happened at *Pearl Harbor* like you have never seen it in any other movie. Our goal is to stage the event with utmost realism.'[59] Todd Garner, a senior Buena Vista production executive responsible for the film, makes a very similar point, although perhaps disingenuously he claims the producers are concerned that: 'Anything done less than perfectly would be disrespectful to the Americans who lost their lives there.'[60]

Pearl Harbor's faltering attempts at establishing the historical context are simplistic at best. Short newsreel excerpts (dubbed with a 'DJ' style voiceover) are used to inform the audience that, for example, in 1940 'even while France falls to Hitler, America still refuses to join the fighting', or later, that the Germans are bombing 'downtown London' – a description which underlines the film's unashamedly American perspective since, as Roger Ebert observes, 'at no time in 2,000 years has London ever had anything described by anybody as a "downtown"'.[61] As the film progresses, we are given snippets of information and fleeting efforts are made to explain what is happening and how it fits into the wider historical narrative of America's entry into World War II, but on the whole the film makes no real effort to interrogate the events leading up to the attack, nor does it place the attack itself in an appropriately full interpretative context.

As Anthony Lane puts it in *The New Yorker*, director Michael Bay's 'passion for geopolitical history tends to be exceeded by his interest in fireballs'.[62] When the love story is suspended and Pearl Harbor finally attacked, we are subjected to some forty minutes of unrelenting explosions, Americans being strafed with machine-gun fire, and warships sinking. One reviewer described the film rather aptly as '*Titanic* with bombs'.[63] Yet the action 'never rises above the level of a computer graphics video game'.[64] We're soon 'gorged on shots of bombs falling and ships toppling' since the violence in the film has 'no emotional resonance' and the 'horror of death in wartime registers only intermittently'.[65] Unlike in *Saving Private Ryan* and *The Thin Red Line*, death and dying are largely sanitised apart from when casualties arrive at the hospital. Although bodies are thrown into the air by explosions, most have their limbs intact; countless servicemen and civilians are fired upon and killed yet their bodies are not peppered with bullets and blood. As Peter Bradshaw wrote caustically in *The Guardian*, at times the film had 'about as much relationship to the reality of wartime combat as a Gap ad for khakis'.[66] If *Saving Private Ryan* and *The Thin Red Line* were attempts to engage in a more realistic, ambiguous rendering of World War II, all *Pearl Harbor* and *U-571* give us is a 'comic-book embodiment of American heroic ideals'.[67] The reliance on spectacular action sequences, even more so than in

Saving Private Ryan, evacuates both films of all moral complexities and asks nothing of the viewer except to marvel, goggle-eyed, at the computer-generated special effects and applaud when things are blown up, even if quite absurdly this means that American viewers of *Pearl Harbor* end up gorging themselves on the sight of Japanese bombs raining down on US Navy warships and personnel.

Films like *Pearl Harbor* constitute a worrying departure in Hollywood's engagement with American history and end up speaking as much to our own globalising moment as to the historical period that is supposedly being evoked. Kolker's analysis is useful, to a point, because it identifies the way in which a Spielberg-derived preference for spectacular images and 'closed' or apparently seamless narrative forms make it hard for audiences to identify the (invisible) ways in which they are being marshalled into positions of acceptance and consent. As Dana Polan suggests: 'spectacle offers an imagistic surface of the world as a strategy of containment against any depth of involvement with that world'.[68] Kolker is all too aware of the dangers that such practices pose to the demands of historical scholarship, which calls for complex, critical engagement with its subject.[69] Yet a film like *Pearl Harbor* does not have any of the pretensions to coherence seamlessly exhibited by Spielberg's films. Rather, as an example of recent blockbuster cinema, it is 'less interested in verisimilitude and spatiotemporal integrity than in pure sensation'.[70] In broader terms, as we have argued elsewhere in the book, this shift to a 'relentless privileging of aesthetics over politics' is linked to changes in the ways that films are financed, made and distributed in an increasingly global Hollywood film industry.[71] After all, watching someone getting blown up in slow-motion on a giant screen with sounds effects reproduced in Dolby stereo is arguably just as apprehensible to audiences in Taiwan as Tennessee, particularly if they are not required to dwell on the political implications of such scenes. For if it is entirely predictable that films like *Pearl Harbor* and *U-571* provide a skewed version of the past, then the more pressing question – and one that we'll be further developing in the next section – is how and why these films are depoliticising as historical texts.

THE GENDER WAR

The role of women has become an increasingly central concern in recent World War II historiography. The image of Rosie the Riveter as a symbol of the importance of women in the home-front war effort has long been part of the collective memory of America's war. Some 350,000 women also served in various non-combat capacities in the US Armed Forces during the conflict. In Hollywood's depictions of World War II, however, women 'for the most part figure in inter-woven romantic relationships or play other supporting roles'.[72] Rather than being central characters shown undertaking significant wartime duties and activities, the women in pre-1990s World War II films 'generally come to image the retrograde state of affairs described by Betty Friedan in *The Feminine Mystique*, as women returned to more traditional roles as wives, mothers, and homemak-ers. Especially in the "love and war" genre, sexual typecasting of female characters became a given.'[73] With greater emphasis now being placed on the importance of women in the war's historiogra-phy and American women in the 1990s having made significant soci-etal, political and economic advances, did Hollywood's new batch of World War II films offer more central, stronger roles to women? The answer is an almost unqualified no. In all four of the films we are addressing, women play only supporting or minor roles that on the whole reinforce traditional cultural (and Hollywood) assumptions about the role of women during wartime.

In *Saving Private Ryan*, it has been argued that women play pivotal roles: concern for the feelings and welfare of Ryan's mother provides the linchpin for the story at the heart of the movie; it is a woman who discovers Ryan's three brothers have been killed and brings this fact to the attention of her superiors; several of the characters talk about drawing strength from the women in their lives, particularly by dis-cussing their mothers and how they could have been better sons; Captain Miller claims to be fighting for the right to go back home to his wife; and at the film's end the aged Ryan seeks validation for the goodness of his life from his wife. Yet until these final moments, none of the women in the film are given a voice. They are mute characters. The first women we see in the film are a large pool of typists (a com-fortably traditional female role) who are typing condolence telegrams to the next of kin of dead American soldiers. As they type we hear a montage of voiceovers reading extracts from the telegrams. The voice-overs disempower the women, however, since they are all male voices. We do not even hear Mrs Ryan's cries when she crumples in anguish on her front stoop as an Army officer and her priest approach with the news of her sons' deaths. She is given no opportunity to voice her opinion on whether she wants her surviving son withdrawn from the war. Judging from the photos and the military colours displayed in her house, this home-on-the-range mother is likely to be fiercely proud of her sons and their willingness to fight for their country. She may, in fact, share her surviving son's wish to see his duty through and fight on. Yet she is given no opportunity to decide for herself. It is the men in authority who determine that she needs her son to be 'saved'.

Though war in *Saving Private Ryan* is shown to be a wholly male domain, there has been some debate as to whether the film subjects a fixed and heroic masculinity to critical examination. The men in the film are not portrayed as all-powerful hero warriors but rather as ordinary American men with inherent weaknesses they must overcome or at least confront in order to prevail in extraordinary circumstances. As Robert Kolker observes: 'The heroic male is under interrogation throughout *Saving Private Ryan*'. From the beginning of the film, the experienced Captain Miller suffers from traumatic stress as symbolised by his shaking hand and loss of hearing, the squad's rookie translator Upham (Jeremy Davies) struggles with cowardice, dying men scream for their mothers, and finally the elderly Ryan pleads with his wife for affirmation that he led a life worthy of the sacrifices made by others to save him. As Kolker concludes: 'In a film without women, this sudden need for a woman's validation expresses a basic male insecurity that runs through much of nineties cinema.'[74] Yet, in other ways, Spielberg's film merely continues a process of what Susan Jeffords calls the 'remasculinization' of American society; using cultural representations of war to ensure the 'renegotiation and regeneration of the interests, values and projects of patriarchy . . . in US social relations'.[75] As Jim Neilson observes, war in *Saving Private Ryan* is 'a masculinizing ritual'. The only survivors of Miller's squad – the cowardly and inexperienced Upham and the disrespectful, self-centred, mutinous Private Reiben (Edward Burns) – are redeemed only through their ability to act violently in the film's conclusion. As Neilson contends: 'It took this mission – this teaching (Miller is, after all, a teacher) by the surrogate father and the military – to change them, to make them men.'[76] Carol Cohn and Cynthia Weber, meanwhile, make the point that 'anything that is feminine [in the film] is extremely dangerous'. The death of several characters is attributed to an excess of sentiment or emotion, both coded in the film as 'feminine': Miller and most of his squad die to protect the feelings of Mrs Ryan; one squad member is shot dead by a sniper when he feels compassion for a female child; and Upham, the cowardly translator who is portrayed as a 'soft feminine kind of guy', convinces Miller not to kill a captured German who later returns in the deadly climactic battle. As Cohn and Weber conclude, when Upham shoots this German soldier upon his second capture, it is 'a recognition that his feminine sentiment of not wanting to kill someone was a mistake'.[77]

Although many of the men in *Saving Private Ryan* need 'feminine reassurance' that they are of 'heroic stature',[78] the film neither gives any real power or strength to those women nor attempts to challenge or even unsettle the dominant structures of patriarchy. The case against *The Thin Red Line* is less clear-cut. There were no American women on Guadalcanal until 1943, when Navy flight nurses began daily trips to evacuate the wounded. When the first US forces hospital was established on the island the situation was officially assessed as 'too rough' for female nurses to be stationed there.[79] Malick's film is set in 1942 and, as a result, the American women are shown only in flashbacks. The film begins with Private Witt (James Caviezel) absent without leave on an island paradise where he lives, works and plays among the indigenous peoples. The women here are shown as caring, happy mothers, who seem fully integrated into their idyllic society. It is here that Witt ruminates about death, hoping that he can face it with the same calm as his mother, who is shown briefly on her deathbed during a flashback. This theme of women as 'enablers' runs through the film, most vividly in the various flashbacks and musings of Private Bell (Ben Chaplin) about his wife. He describes her as his 'source of strength, love, purity' and 'my light, my guide'. Although these female characters are described and portrayed in the highest esteem, we know nothing of who they are, what they do, or how they perceive the war. They are little more than an imagined ideal. For Bell, this ideal is shattered toward the end of the film when he learns that his wife is leaving him for an Air Force captain and wants a divorce. The realities of the emotional and personal costs of war for domestic relationships are laid bare by Bell's sense of being betrayed. Witt's idyll is also shattered when he returns to the indigenous village. Instead of finding friendship, community, peace and love, he is ignored by the villagers; the men argue, the children suffer from disease, there are human skulls and bones stored in the huts, implying cannibalism, and the women are now all but absent.

Furthermore, in comparison to *Saving Private Ryan*, war is not seen in *The Thin Red Line* as a painful but seemingly necessary way to establish manhood. Rather, it is represented as corrupting, corrosive and destructive and as such the film seems to embrace a poetic nihilism. In one of the film's countless, anonymous voiceovers, one GI concludes: 'War don't ennoble men. Turns them into dogs. Poisons the soul.' As one reviewer observed, the battle sequences 'merely provide the backdrop to Malick's rambling, quizzical inquiries into military behaviour and the nature of evil; he's more interested in metaphysics than machismo'.[80] There are acts of heroism, most notably when Sergeant Keck (Woody Harrelson) throws his body upon a malfunctioning grenade to protect his nearby comrades, but these only reinforce the random insanity of conflict rather than glorifying it. Ultimately the discourse of masculine, individualist heroism has no place or meaning in the film and, by implication, in war itself. One of the main characters, First Sergeant Edward Welsh (Sean Penn), sums it up well: 'What difference do you think you can make? One single man in all this madness. You die, it's going to be for nothing.'

This kind of critical, nihilistic rhetoric is entirely and predictably absent from *Pearl Harbor*. In its place, we are presented with a sanitised view of gender relations in which men are recognisably heroic, lean and 'macho', and women, though sexualised, play an important role in the war effort. In other words, though ultimately quite reactionary, the ways in which *Pearl Harbor* attempts to both uncritically resuscitate a straightforward, secure masculinity and simultaneously acknowledge the contributions made by women draws attention to a depoliticising tendency both in the film itself and 'blockbuster' cinema in general. On the one hand, the film openly embraces a particular set of male expectations about the 'appropriate' way to represent the female body. Evelyn Johnson (Kate Beckinsale), the character at the centre of the love triangle that drives the main story, leads a group of nurses who are easily recognisable war-movie types: 'the fat one, the boy-crazy blonde, the shy girl with glasses and so on'.[81] Evelyn herself is the erotic object of the male gaze; the camera lingers on her svelte body, clad in tight dresses or blouses, lying on the rocks by the Pacific in her bikini, or pouting in her nurse's uniform. But although the film foregrounds her sexualised nature, it also wants to attribute to her some sense of agency and invest her role with some significance in terms of the overall war effort. As such, amid its crass romancing, patriotic bombast and spectacular pyrotechnics, the film does include some powerful images that show dramatically, and with closely observed detail, the contributions made by US Army nurses in World War II by focusing on the immediate aftermath of the Pearl Harbor attacks. Prior to the Japanese attack, the hospital in *Pearl Harbor* appears celestial, with pure white light streaming through gracefully flapping curtains on wards with spotless floors and bed-clothes folded neatly back on unused beds. The nurses themselves appear angelic in their bright innocence. Yet once the attack is under way, the hospital scenes are underscored by a greater degree of realism than any of the multimillion-dollar battle scenes around them. For a few minutes, at least, we are given a studied impression of how young women, empowered in their role as nurses, coped with their first harrowing experiences of war.

Many of the details portrayed appear to be taken directly from Barbara Brooks Tomblin's history of the Army Nurse Corps in World War II, *G.I. Nightingales*. The film shows much of what Tomblin describes as happening at Hawaiian hospitals on the day of the attack. It depicts the 'inevitable confusion caused by the large number of casualties' and recreates or draws upon many of the specific details of the nurses' accounts. These include Nurse Myrtle Watson's recollection of 'cutting patients out of traction and piling mattresses around their beds to protect them from stray bullets and flying glass'. Just as equipment shortages compelled nurses to improvise – 'fashioning tourniquets, for example, from belts, gas mask cords, and pistol shoulder straps' – Evelyn does likewise, using one of her stockings. Evelyn is also given the task of separating those 'who can be saved' from those who cannot. Nurses on Hawaii were given this power to make life-and-death decisions as they joined other medical staff in 'triaging patients, separating them into categories according to the kind and extent of their wounds'. Nurse Watson also remembers that sentimentality had no place in the hospital: 'bodies were piling up like cordwood wherever there was space'. This detail is also faithfully recreated in *Pearl Harbor* when the dead body of one of the off-duty nurses is unceremoniously placed on a pile of corpses. The film's depiction of the horror in the hospital ends with blood being mopped from the drenched floor of the formerly pristine ward. Watson again recalls that 'Red became the prevailing color, as blood seemed to work its way into every nook and cranny of the hospital.'[82] Alone among the four World War II films we address, therefore, *Pearl Harbor* shows women actively participating in the war effort and depicts them as strong, focused individuals capable of rising above their fears to perform meaningful, significant tasks. Indeed, in these scenes at least, they are even portrayed as stronger than some of their male counterparts.

What the film gives with one hand, however, it takes away with the other. Outside of these quite brief scenes, the gender politics of the film are typically reactionary and the serious points made are countervailed by the comic-book love story and the sexual stereotyping that dominate the rest of the film. Evelyn herself seems to dismiss the importance of her own actions. Indeed, for her, the whole Japanese attack constitutes something of an annoying distraction; an event that first of all interrupts her blossoming relationship with Rafe, and second, sets in motion events that results in her abandoning Rafe for his best friend Danny Walker (Josh Hartnett). The film offers no sustained analysis of the role played by women in the Pacific War and, as such, replicates the gender logic of most films in the combat genre, whereby men fight and women offer their love and support. In so far as it makes tentative efforts, in the post-attack hospital scenes, to acknowledge and include the contributions made by women, and incorporate these scenes into a film that ultimately codes women as subordinate, *Pearl Harbor* is symptomatic of the way in which many contemporary Hollywood films deal with the question of difference. In *Pearl Harbor*, and for that matter any number of blockbuster films, gender differences are initially discounted (women like Evelyn can do anything that the men can do), then re-affirmed (women like Evelyn are sexualised) and then managed within a diffuse order or system that pretends to acknowledge everyone's point of view as equal but that actually privileges the perspective of the white male protagonists. As with most films in the combat genre, in *Pearl Harbor* and the other World War II films analysed here, the 'absence of women is maintained' with female characters playing effectively or literally peripheral roles.[83]

THE RACE WAR

As we discussed in earlier chapters, the fact Hollywood has, in recent years, been more willing to address the issue of race and racism in its films has not meant that cinematic representations of racial differences are entirely free of the kind of racism and prejudice that affected earlier films. Rather, as with gender, domination has assumed newer, friendlier forms. As such, although we should not automatically ridicule efforts made by films like *Pearl Harbor* to appear to be inclusive and tolerant of racial differences, we should remain wary of any such attempts. The *New York Times* observed that the film, despite its uncomplicated, often cartoonish depiction of life during wartime, is 'strenuously respectful of contemporary sensitivities'.[84] One of the heroic supporting characters is based on Doris 'Dorie' Miller, the first African-American to be awarded the navy Cross. This inclusionary gesture is one that should be applauded not least because in earlier World War II films there were 'virtually no black Americans represented, save accidentally, and then only in the menial roles to which they were actually confined for the most part in wartime'.[85] As Thomas Doherty points out: 'The main barrier to equal treatment of blacks in the combat film was the unequal treatment of blacks in the military services.'[86] The US Armed Services remained segregated until July 1948. In the navy, black Americans were restricted to roles in the Steward's Branch. Miller was Ship's Cook, Third Class, on the battleship *West Virginia*, although he also had a combat assignment to one of the ship's anti-aircraft guns. When the call to battle stations came on 7 December 1941, he found his assigned gun was damaged so he helped move the wounded to safety, carrying his captain below decks to the first aid station. He then went back above decks and manned another anti-aircraft gun for which he was not trained. Miller recalled afterwards that 'it wasn't hard. I just pulled the trigger and she worked fine. I had watched the others with these guns. I guess I fired her for about 15 minutes. I think I got one of those Jap planes. They were diving pretty close to us.'[87] Initially both the navy and the American press were 'less than forthcoming with news of his action' but in May 1942 Miller's decoration for courage under fire was well publicised.[88] Miller was killed in action in the South Pacific the following year but he was not forgotten: in 1973 the US Navy named a frigate after him, the USS *Miller*.[89]

Just because *Pearl Harbor*'s makers decided to include a figure based on Miller as one of its supporting characters, however, does not immunise the film against accusations of racism or at least a problematic tokenism when dealing with questions of race. As Geoffrey Mcnab notes: 'we learn little about this character; he feels like a token presence, as marginalized in the movie as the real-life Miller was in the racist, pre-Pearl Harbor navy'.[90] A. O. Scott agrees that the 'Dorie Miller subplot smacks of demographic base covering and self-congratulatory bad faith.'[91] Like most of the actors in the film, Cuba Gooding Jr, who plays Miller, is given little of substance to say in his half-dozen or so short scenes. He complains to Nurse Johnson that although he joined the navy 'to become a man, he is instead a cook who has never been allowed to fire a weapon (though this was not true of the non-fictional Miller) but instead must 'clean up after other sailors eat'; the subtext being that these are feminine, servile duties. Otherwise, he is shown physically asserting his manhood by winning a boxing match, and he is complimented by his captain, who then dies in his arms during the attack, causing him to rise above decks to shoot down a Japanese fighter (although it looks as though he also sends a hail of bullets flying towards a neighbouring American warship). What agency Miller is given in the film is very limited, and nowhere are the larger issues of racism and segregation explored or even witnessed. Aside from his relatively lowly assignment, Miller is treated fairly, even equally, by everyone he encounters. Even during his boxing match against a brawny white sailor, it is his rank rather than his race that draws contempt from his opponent and the assembled crowd.

That racism is entirely elided in *Pearl Harbor* does not reflect the historical 'reality' of World War II, but rather reflects the contemporary ideological concerns and preoccupations of the film's makers. Racism, of course, was not only rife in American society in 1941, but was also a major influence on the way the US perceived and treated the enemy, particularly the Japanese. Much of the wartime racial stereotyping of the enemy was perpetuated in post-war Hollywood films. Representations of Japanese and German barbarism did abate somewhat as time passed and the defeated powers became important allies in the Cold War and also increasingly important markets for Hollywood's output. Indeed, Japan is now the second-largest national cinema market after the United States and plays a significant role in the ownership of American-based film studios. This reality of the increasingly globalised film industry was clearly not lost on the makers of *Pearl Harbor*, who made deliberate efforts to 'humanise' the Japanese pilots and their commanders. A 'culturally sensitive version' of the film was even re-edited for Japanese audiences.[92] Michael Bay insisted effusively before the film's release that 'We totally depict the Japanese as very heroic, very dignified. . . In no way do we treat them as demons.' After all, he claimed, they were 'just doing a job' when they attacked Pearl Harbor.[93]

The Japanese in the film are shown as well-trained, patriotic, thoughtful and honourable, and their officers appear reticent, even regretful about launching the attack. In a particularly effective scene we see one of the Japanese pilots preparing for the attack and hear his prayer: 'Revered father, I go now to fulfil my mission and my destiny. I hope it is a destiny that will bring honour to our family. And if it requires my life, I will sacrifice it gladly to be a servant of our nation.' Yet the film's apparent respect for cultural differences barely conceals a cynical tokenism in which marketplace tolerance is preached but only in so far as it serves the interests of the film's global marketers without upsetting an uncomplicated vision of white American righteousness. Despite pretensions towards inclusionism, *Pearl Harbor*, as Anthony Lane argues, 'gives the enemy a dramatic shrift so short that even the most red-blooded American viewers may feel a trifle embarrassed'.[94] Roger Ebert observes that most of the Japanese dialogue is 'strictly expository; they state facts but do not emerge with personalities or passions'. He concludes that the film's portrayal of the Japanese is 'so oblique that Japanese audiences will find little to complain about apart from the fact that they play such a small role in their own raid'. Also, aside from one dentist and a doctor (who is actually accused of being a 'filthy Jap'), 'the almost total absence of Asians in 1941 Hawaii is inexplicable'.[95] After the raid on Pearl Harbor, the Japanese themselves more or less disappear from the film. The recreation of the April 1942 'vengeance' attack on Tokyo that gives the film a victorious flag-waving finale for the US military is viewed almost entirely from the perspective of the Doolittle raiders (named after their commander Lieutenant Colonel James H. Doolittle). We are given no view from the ground and know nothing of the damage caused either physically or psychologically. By the time of our final view of the Japanese, as they bear down on our stranded heroes somewhere in occupied China, they have been reduced to nothing more than faceless comic-book villains.

The Thin Red Line offers a more complex and sympathetic portrayal of the Japanese. The fact that we are left with no doubt that they are capable of great brutality – the first evidence of the Japanese on Guadalcanal are the mutilated bodies of dead American soldiers – is not the sum total of the film's interest in the 'enemy'. Initially they remain faceless, unknown and menacing to both the film's protagonists and the viewer, but only until the hill-top machine-gun bunkers are finally breached. After this, the stereotype of the Japanese as super-warriors who are invincible, merciless and willing to fight to the death is challenged by images of terrified, emaciated young men who appear as much, if not more adversely affected by the horrific trauma of close combat than their American counterparts. When the Americans overrun a Japanese camp we see chaotic scenes of petrified men uncertain whether to fight, surrender or kill themselves. It seems almost all are suffering from starvation, and many are clearly out of their minds with madness. Many of the images are deeply compassionate: one Japanese soldier, for example, is seen crying over the body of a dead colleague. The Americans appear bemused by what they find, and this bemusement serves to further unsettle uncomplicated assertions about the morality of the American mission in the Pacific. In one particularly affecting sequence, a voiceover spoken by a dead Japanese soldier challenges his American killers to consider: 'Are you righteous, kind? Does your confidence lie in this? Are you loved by all? Know that I was too. Do you imagine your suffering will be less because you loved goodness, truth?' Although it is the only time we hear a Japanese viewpoint, it is a powerful moment because it compels the viewer to think about how combat affects all sides in war and implicitly acknowledge that concepts such as 'right' and 'wrong' are contingent and wholly dependent on perspective.

Not only are the Japanese portrayed with compassion in *The Thin Red Line*, but the Americans themselves are shown to be capable of brutal, immoral acts. For example, two surrendering Japanese soldiers are killed, one of them being beaten to death, and at the Japanese camp some GIs are shown picking over the bodies of their dead and dying enemies. The notion that the Pacific War was racially motivated, however, is never explored and in fact the American treatment of the Japanese is relatively sanitised. Some American servicemen on Guadalcanal and elsewhere in the Pacific campaign developed a fetish for collecting 'grisly battlefield trophies' such as Japanese 'gold teeth, ears, bones, scalps, and skulls'. Such practices were well-publicised in the American press during the war but find no place in Hollywood's latter-day renderings of the conflict. *Life* magazine, for example, ran a 'human-interest story' complete with full-page photograph of an attractive blonde whose fiancé had sent her a Japanese skull as a souvenir. The same magazine also ran a well-known photograph showing Japanese skulls being used as ornaments on US military vehicles. As John Dower concludes, it is 'virtually inconceivable' that the same practices could have been carried out on German or Italian war dead and promoted back home without causing an 'uproar'.[96]

Even though some of the more extreme American behaviour during the war is not depicted, we are given a more 'warts-and-all' perspective in *The Thin Red Line* and *Saving Private Ryan* than we are in *Pearl Harbor*, *U-571*, and most of Hollywood's earlier World War II films. Audiences brought up on a diet of Vietnam War films have become used to images of American soldiers committing heinous acts in pursuit of a lost cause. In both *Saving Private Ryan* and *The Thin Red Line*, then, we are given a more morally ambiguous portrayal of American soldiers than in earlier World War II films. In *Saving Private Ryan*, for example, a GI calls out to his colleagues 'Don't shoot! Let 'em burn!', as flame-engulfed Germans fall screaming from a machine-gun turret, surrendering troops are shot in cold blood, and a group of retreating Germans are shown being trapped in a trench and slaughtered from above by surrounding American soldiers. In one of *Saving Private Ryan*'s most effective scenes, the only surviving German from an assault on a machine-gun position that resulted in the death of the American squad's medic is forced to dig graves for his fallen colleagues and, he presumes, himself. A debate ensues over what should be done with him during which he pleads desperately for his life by praising all things American, singing the 'Star Spangled Banner' and rejecting Nazism by crying out 'Fuck Hitler'. In this pivotal scene, then, unusually we see a German soldier who is allowed to exhibit humanity rather than remaining a faceless nemesis, while the morality of his American captors is called into question. The 'natural order' of things is re-established, however, when his life is eventually spared because, as Captain Miller says, it would be 'against the goddamned rules' to shoot him. One palpable aspect of historical realism in *Saving Private Ryan* is the way it portrays Americans dealing brutally with surrendering soldiers and prisoners of war.[97] Indeed, the German released after the battle at the machine-gun position returns to his ranks and is among the Germans who attack and kill most of Miller's squad during the film's climax. He surrenders again but is recognised and, as discussed earlier, this time shot by Upham, the American who had pleaded for leniency for him when he was first captured. The moral ambiguity of American actions in the war is also shown earlier in the film, when Captain

Miller refuses to help a stranded French family get their children to safety. Miller makes the squad's purpose quite clear: 'We're not here to do the decent thing. We're here to follow fucking orders.' Although *Saving Private Ryan* raises some potentially intriguing questions about the conduct and morality of American soldiers caught up in the intensity and violence of war, it ultimately retreats into more conventional cinematic territory with the Americans emerging victorious and heroic. As Kolker concludes, the viewer is offered the 'dangers of subversion rendered harmless by the affirmation of secure convention'. Although almost all of Miller's squad are killed during their mission, the film concludes with the 'hope that a larger morality of commitment and growth' will emerge from the destructive forces of the war.[98]

CONCLUSIONS: THE ALL-AMERICAN WAR

Since Hollywood has become an increasingly globalised industry in recent years, it might be expected that its output would reflect a more inclusive view of historical events. Yet with recent World War II films this is anything but the case. While there may have been some efforts made not to offend audiences in certain cinema markets, most notably Japanese viewers of *Pearl Harbor*, on the whole each of the films analysed here pays scant attention not only to historical context but also global sensibilities. These are Americentric films where allies and enemies alike are given short shrift in stories that focus on 'a group of exclusively American heroes, operating in an historical . . . vacuum'.[99] All the films under discussion in this chapter re-affirm, albeit to varying degrees, a vision of the United States as the world's leading power and ultimately a force for good in the world. They operate within an ideological framework of what historian John Fousek identifies as 'American nationalist globalism'. This framework emerged as a result of American success in World War II itself, which enabled the US to take on the mantle of a 'fully matured great power' that was ready to 'usher in a new golden age in its own image'. Within this framework of American nationalist globalism, Fousek argues, Americans viewed 'national self-interest and global altruism' as 'identical', such that 'what was good for America was good for the world'. The basic assumptions of US policy makers across party lines during the early Cold War were that 'US power was global in scope. The interests of the US and the rest of humanity were convergent. And the US was the natural, destined leader of the world – possessing values, institutions, and "a way of life" to which all other peoples aspired.'[100] Essentially these are also the assumptions that lie at the very centre of the benign meta-narrative of American foreign relations. Clearly the Cold War era shook these assumptions to their very core, not least as a result of the debacle in Vietnam, but like the myth of the Good War itself they have remained remarkably endurable. Since Vietnam, and particularly in the post-Cold War period, foreign-policy makers and advocates on both sides of the American political spectrum have made attempts to revive and consolidate these notions of benign American power. Their actual policies might have revealed their self-interested hegemonic designs but rhetorically at least both liberal and conservative (in the American senses of the words) visions of the United States and its role in world affairs have been informed by an underlying assumption of American benevolence. These liberal and conservative visions, and the extent to which they can be thematically reconciled, can be seen operating in Hollywood's recent renderings of World War II. The form and scale of these films, however, and the extent to which they are made, marketed and distributed with an increasingly global film-going audience in mind, suggests that the rendering of history in contemporary Hollywood films is not simply a matter of 'business as usual'.

The main question that *Saving Private Ryan* poses is 'Was the war worth it?' Before Captain Miller dies he tells Private Ryan to 'Earn it', to live a life that is worthy of the sacrifices that have been made to save him. We then see the old Ryan ask his wife whether he has indeed led 'a good life'. By extension, the audience is being asked to consider whether it has earned the life that those who fought and died in World War II made possible through their sacrifice. The answer Ryan receives is that of course he has. The implication is clear: the war itself may have been terrible but it was both necessary and righteous and, in the end, it enabled Ryan – and others like him – to lead a 'good life'. The images of the Stars and Stripes that bookend the film underline the pivotal role played by the US in securing freedom not just for Ryan and other Americans but also for the world. Although Spielberg's vision in this and his other films has been characterised as essentially conservative, on the American political spectrum he is firmly within the liberal camp, donating substantial sums to the Democratic Party's coffers each year. He appears cognisant of American society's imperfections – its inequalities, its discrimination against minorities, its abuses of power at the highest levels and its failures in foreign policy – yet he still believes fundamentally in the ideal of America and its achievability, indeed its perfectibility. None of the characters in *Saving Private Ryan* are flawless, many of them do awful things, but from the film's perspective, they do so almost unquestioningly in the name of good. For all its combat 'realism' and its portrayal of morally condemnable acts of violence by Americans, *Saving Private Ryan* is a film that conforms to the popular, benign view of World War II. As Howard Zinn observes, there is 'never any doubt that the cause is just. This is the good war.'[101] It is almost as though Vietnam never happened, even though so much of that conflict's impact on the way combat is now presented in Hollywood movies is present in the film. Certainly we are shown the pain, suffering and 'realism' of the effects of war on individual soldiers but the politics of the Vietnam War seem to have all but disappeared. As Jim Neilson puts it: 'A filmmaker raised on the criminal duplicity of American armed forces in Vietnam, Spielberg blithely accepts the notion that in World War II the military's motives were noble and selfless. This, after all, was the good war, a war far different from Vietnam.'[102] Moreover, as Zinn notes, if the defeat in Vietnam 'caused large numbers of Americans to question the enterprise of war', then *Saving Private Ryan* seeks to recapture a pre-Vietnam innocence. As such, for all of its spectacular violence and feigned verisimilitude, Spielberg's film is not anti-war. Rather, *Saving Private Ryan* 'rescues the good name of war' and the 'glory of military heroism' while 'implicitly rebuking his generation for its protest and lack of patriotism'.[103] World War II is once again heralded as a model for American wars whereby sacrifices are made in the name of a just cause. War can be good, was good in World War II, and redemption can come through violence. It is an American liberal view of war as something that is sometimes necessary in order to achieve some higher purpose.

The Thin Red Line offers a rather different perspective. It is a more intellectually challenging, thought-provoking and questioning film than *Saving Private Ryan*, or for that matter *U-571* or *Pearl Harbor*. Limited as it may be as a historical account of the battle for Guadalcanal, the film nevertheless raises considerable doubts about the undertaking of war in general and more specifically the motivations behind World War II. It challenges both militarism and the point of war, and suggests that World War II was neither the beginning nor the end. As the film admits in conclusion: 'This war's not going to be over for a long time.' The implication here is not simply that World War II would not reach a rapid close but that war itself will be perpetual and indeed that a propensity for war is central to American foreign policy. Earlier in the film, in typically wistful manner, it is suggested that this propensity may well be down to 'property, property', but Malick's film never develops a coherent critique of the economic imperative underscoring American dominance in the global realm. For all its ruminations on the meaning and effects of war, *The Thin Red Line* actually does little to directly challenge or undermine the myth of the Good War or the benign meta-narrative of American foreign relations. The enemy is given a human face but there is little engagement with how they may view the course of the war differently than the Americans. Like the other World War II films considered here, *The Thin Red Line* still focuses almost exclusively on American soldiers and privileges the role of the United States above those of its allies in the Pacific War, who warrant no mention in the film. Guadalcanal was 'an overwhelmingly American affair'[104] but viewers looking to this film for clues about the wider conflict against the Japanese will get no indication that Australian, British and other troops played a vital role. As with *Saving Private Ryan*, World War II, as seen through the lens of *The Thin Red Line*, is an American war in which American soldiers prevail.

Many Cold War era World War II films such as *The Longest Day* and *Tora! Tora! Tora!* made efforts at 'impartiality' largely in order to demonstrate that Americans, Germans, Japanese, British and French were 'now acting together against a Communist threat from the east'.[105] Where these earlier films were somewhat concerned with forging Cold War unity, the more recent batch are instead (in spite of worldwide box office considerations) seemingly dedicated to promoting American global dominance in terms of values, courage, hardiness, and the willingness to do whatever is necessary to establish and maintain international order and stability. While *Saving Private Ryan* and *The Thin Red Line* may do so in more subtle ways, *Pearl Harbor* and *U-571* have fewer qualms about actively promoting American ideals and exceptionalist notions of American greatness. *Pearl Harbor* is essentially about one of the worst days in American military, diplomatic and political history, yet the film manages to effectively snatch victory from the jaws of defeat. First, it sends its two central heroes up in fighter planes to take out a few Japanese aircraft at the end of the attack on Pearl Harbor and then in its finale recreates the Doolittle raid on Tokyo, both with much patriotic breast-beating. These triumphant scenes have been criticised for being 'excessively jingoistic' and liable to trivialise 'the suffering of the victims' at Pearl Harbor.[106] What they do, however, is reflect the film's conservative agenda and underscore a belief in the might and righteousness of American military interventions. The Doolittle raids, we are told in the film's closing monologue, helped change the course of the war and of world affairs for the better: 'America realised that she would win and surged forward. It was a war that changed America and the world.' The war is depicted in the film as a rite of passage that brought the US to its apparently rightful place as benign global leader: 'America suffered but America grew stronger. . . The times tried our souls and through the trial we overcame.'

The US is further privileged above its allies in *U-571*, where an act of British 'wartime heroism' is 'casually recast as American'. Will Hutton blames 'the increasing nationalism in the US' which is 'reflected by Hollywood's careless disregard for historical truth'. Far from being a film driven by the imperatives of a globally-minded Hollywood, *U-571* changed its story specifically to meet the perceived wishes of an American audience. As Hutton puts it, quite simply 'US audiences do not want to watch British success.' He argues that a few American companies control so tightly global film distribution that 'the cultural impact of film is founded almost entirely on the priorities of another civilisation'.[107] The case should not be understated since American films made up between 75 and 90 per cent of the biggest-grossing films during the 1990s in some twenty-four foreign territories with reliable box office data, and 90 to 100 per cent in a further eighteen. World War II films fit in the most popular category, action and adventure films, which make up 'Hollywood's greatest export staple', particularly to South and East Asia, as well as being 'by far' the most successful form of films inside the United States itself.[108] Their popularity, however, seems not to be based on the values they seek to promote or their vision of the meaning of American history. In fact, these films appear successful in spite of their ideological biases, which are unlikely to be well-received in many parts of the world where resentment at perceived US cultural, political, economic and military imperialism runs high. They are popular, however, precisely because for many audiences they operate at a level at which one reviewer suggests *Pearl Harbor* works best: 'as a bang-and-boom action picture, a loud symphony of bombardment and explosion juiced up with frantic editing and shiny computer-generated imagery'.[109] It is form and style as much, if not more than content that accounts for the burgeoning popularity of this new type of 'blockbuster' film that speaks to the cultural and political logic of our globalised moment. As Franco Moretti argues, it is the 'abrogation of language' in favour of 'explosions, crashes, gunshots, [and] screams' in action films that 'facilitates their international diffusion'[110] – that is, a preference for undemanding spectacle over challenging content.

Perhaps because filmmakers have their eyes on as large a share as possible of the global cinema market, there is not a great deal of effective history in any of the recent World War II films to emerge from Hollywood. They do give visions of particular aspects of the combat experience in World War II, engage to a certain degree with questions concerning the morality of war, and make some effort to show the racial and gender aspects of the conflict. On the whole, though, they do not offer alternative viewpoints on the history of the war or challenge much of the conventional wisdom about its causes, course or outcomes. In fact, they are most useful as reflections of certain contemporary concerns about the role of the US in the world and the use of American military force. As a whole, although they contain some challenging images, they tend to reinforce the perception of World War II as the Good War, or indeed as the Best War Ever in American history.

NOTES

1 H. W. Brands, 'Preface', *What America Owes the World: The Struggle for the Soul of Foreign Policy* (Cambridge: Cambridge University Press, 1998).

2 David Ryan, *US Foreign Policy in World History* (London and New York: Routledge, 2000), pp. 10–11.

3 Michael C. C. Adams, *The Best War Ever: America and World War II* (Baltimore, MD: Johns Hopkins University, 1994), p. 2.

4 For example, Americans have consistently regarded World War II as the most just war the United States has ever fought, placing it above the Revolutionary War that sealed US independence from Britain. See, for example, *Gallup Poll: Public Opinion 1991* (Wilmington, DE: Scholarly Resources Inc., 1992), p. 57.

5 Adams, *The Best War Ever*, pp. 1–2.
6 Philip D. Beidler, *The Good War's Greatest Hits: World War II and American Remembering* (Athens, GA and London: University of Georgia Press, 1998) p. 3.
7 Adams, *The Best War Ever*, p. 5.
8 John W. Dower, *War Without Mercy: Race and Power in the Pacific War* (New York: Pantheon, 1986).
9 See David S. Wyman, *The Abandonment of the Jews: America and the Holocaust 1941–1945*, 2nd ed. (New York: The New Press, 1998); Robert H. Abzug, *America and the Holocaust: A Brief Documentary History* (Basingstoke: Macmillan, 1999).
10 Beidler, *The Good War's Greatest Hits*, pp. 2–3.
11 Adams, *The Best War Ever*, p. 11.
12 Beidler, *The Good War's Greatest Hits*, pp. 3–4.
13 John Whiteclay Chambers II and David Culbert, eds, *World War II, Film and History* (New York and Oxford: Oxford University Press, 1996), pp. viii, 3–6.
14 Adams, *The Best War Ever*, pp. 11, 14.
15 Jeanine Basinger, *The World War II Combat Film: Anatomy of a Genre* (Middletown, CT: Wesleyan University Press, 2003).
16 Thomas Doherty, *Projections of War: Hollywood, American Culture, and World War II* (New York: Columbia University Press, 1993), p. 273.
17 Ibid., p. 280.
18 Jeanine Basinger, 'Translating War: The Combat Film Genre and *Saving Private Ryan*', *Perspectives: American Historical Association Newsletter*, Vol. 36 No. 7, October 1998, p. 47.
19 Doherty, *Projections of War*, p. 282.
20 See Peter Biskind, *Easy Riders, Raging Bulls: How the Sex-Drugs-and-Rock'n'Roll Generation Saved Hollywood* (New York: Simon & Schuster, 1998); Leonard Quart and Albert Auster, *American Film and Society Since 1945*, 2nd ed. (Westport, CT: Praeger, 1991), pp. 108–34.
21 See Trevor B. McCrisken, *American Exceptionalism and the Legacy of Vietnam: US Foreign Policy Since 1974* (Basingstoke: Palgrave, 2003).
22 Quoted in Doherty, *Projections of War*, p. 297.
23 Doherty, *Projections of War*, p. 297.
24 *Saving Private Ryan* grossed $216,335,085 in the US while taking a total of $480,000,000 worldwide. See http://www.the-numbers.com/movies/1998/SVPRI.html (9/7/03).
25 Stephen E. Ambrose, *The Victors: Eisenhower and His Boys – The Men of World War II* (New York: Simon & Schuster, 1998), p. 210; Martin Folly, *The United States and World War II: The Awakening Giant* (Edinburgh: Edinburgh University Press, 2002), p. 99.
26 Ambrose, *Victors*, pp. 206–10.

27 Folly, *US and World War II*, p. 100; Edwin P. Hoyt, *The GI's War: American Soldiers in Europe During World War II* (New York: Cooper Square Press, 2000), pp. 375, 387.

28 Ambrose, *Victors*, p. 207.

29 Jeanine Basinger, 'Translating War: The Combat Film Genre and *Saving Private Ryan*', *Perspectives: American Historical Association Newsletter*, Vol. 36 No. 7, October 1998, p. 1.

30 Jim Neilson, 'Review: Stephen [sic] Spielberg and the Lost Crusade', *Cultural Logic: An Electronic Journal of Marxist Theory and Practice*, Vol. 2 No. 1, http://eserver.org/clogic/2-1/neilson.html (20/2/02).

31 Howard Zinn, 'Private Ryan Saves War,' *The Progressive* (October 1988) http://www.progressive.org/zinn1098.htm (1/7/03).

32 Chambers and Culbert, *World War II, Film and History*, pp. 150–1.

33 Dan Van Der Vat, *The Pacific Campaign* (Edinburgh: Birlinn, 1992), p. 298.

34 Kenneth Jackson, '*The Thin Red Line*: Not Enough History', *Perspectives Online*, April 1999, http://www.theaha.org/Perspectives/issues/1999/9904/9904FIL6.CFM (1/7/03).

35 See Van Der Vat, *The Pacific Campaign*, p. 297.

36 Jackson, '*The Thin Red Line*'; see also Ronald H. Spector, *Eagle Against the Sun: The American War with Japan* (New York: Viking, 1984).

37 Jackson, '*The Thin Red Line*'.

38 Ibid.

39 Cam Winstanley, 'Film of the Month: *The Thin Red Line*', *Total Film*, April 1999, p. 85.

40 Geoffrey Mcnab, 'The Thin Red Line', *Sight and Sound*, March 1999, p. 54.

41 Stephen E. Ambrose, '*The Longest Day* (U.S., 1962): 'Blockbuster History', in Chambers and Culbert, *World War II, Film, and History*, p. 102.

42 Basinger, 'Translating War', pp. 1, 43.

43 Ibid., p. 43.

44 Robert A. Rosenstone, *Visions of the Past: The Challenge of Film to Our Idea of History* (Cambridge, MA: Harvard University Press, 1995), pp. 238–9.

45 Basinger, 'Translating War,' p. 43.

46 Ibid., pp. 43–4.

47 Quoted in Basinger, 'Translating War,' pp. 44.

48 Zinn, 'Private Ryan Saves War'.

49 Robert Kolker, *A Cinema of Loneliness*, 3rd ed., (Oxford: Oxford University Press, 2000), p. 307.

50 Ibid., pp. 323–4.

51 Hugh Sebag-Montefiore, *Enigma: The Battle for the Code* (London: Weidenfeld & Nicolson, 2000); Hugh Sebag-Montefiore, 'Enigma Variations', *The Guardian*, G2, 25 May 2000, p. 2.

52 Xan Brooks, 'U-571', *Guardian Unlimited*, 2 June 2000, http://film. guardian.co.uk/News_Story/Critic_Review/Guardian_review/0,4267, 327462,00.html (9/7/03); Tom Tunney, 'U-571', *Sight and Sound*, July 2000, http://www.bfi.org.uk/sightandsound/reviews/details.php?id= 572& body=review (9/7/03).

53 Thomas Quinn, 'Sunk by the Yanks Again: Hollywood is Twisting Historical Truth in the Name of Big Bucks', *The Mirror*, The A List supplement, 2–8 June 2000, p. 4.

54 Lucy Ward, 'Economics of Truth: MPs attack Rewriting of Wartime History for Box Office Gain', *The Guardian*, 7 June 2000, p. 11.

55 'Prime Minister's Questions, 7 June 2000', *House of Commons Hansard Debates*, http://www.parliament.the-stationery-office.co.uk/pa/cm 199900/cmhansrd/vo000607/debtext/00607-04.htm#00607-04_sbhd1 (1/7/03).

56 Peter Bradshaw, 'Torture! Torture! Torture!', *The Guardian*, Friday Review, p. 12.

57 Lawrence Suid, 'Movie Review: *U-571* and *Pearl Harbor*', *The Journal of American History*, Vol. 88 No. 3, December 2001, http://www.history cooperative.org/journals/jah//88.3/mr_20.html (1/7/03).

58 See Bernard F. Dick, *The Star-Spangled Screen: The American World War II Film* (Lexington, KY: University of Kentucky Press, 1996), pp. 243–9.

59 Interview with Michael Bay, *National Geographic Beyond the Movie: Pearl Harbor*, http://plasma.nationalgeographic.com/pearlharbor/ ngbeyond/movie/index.html (9/7/03); and quoted in Suid, 'Movie Review'.

60 Quoted in John Patterson, 'Bruckheimer Goes to War', *The Guardian*, Friday Review, 27 October 2000, p. 3.

61 Roger Ebert, 'Pearl Harbor', *Chicago Sun-Times*, 25 May 2001, http:/ /www.suntimes.com/ebert/ebert_reviews/2001/05/052501.html (10/7/03).

62 Anthony Lane, 'Bombs Away: Love and Rivalry in 'Pearl Harbor',' *The New Yorker*, 4 June 2001, p. 82.

63 Peter Preston, 'Titanic with Bombs', *The Observer*, Review, 3 June 2001, p. 7.

64 Lawrence Suid, '*Pearl Harbor*: Bombed Again', *Naval History*, August 2001, http://www.usni.org/NavalHistory/articles)1/Nhsuid8.html (30/7/03).

65 Geoffrey Mcnab, 'Pearl Harbor', *Sight and Sound*, July 2001, http://www.bfi.org.uk/sightandsound/2001_07/pearl_harbour.html (9/7/03); A. O. Scott, 'Pearl Harbor: War is Hell, but Very Pretty', *New York Times*, 25 May 2001.

66 Bradshaw, 'Torture! Torture! Torture!', p. 12.

67 Tunney, 'U-571'.

68 Quoted in Kolker, *A Cinema of Loneliness*, p. 324.

69 Kolker, *A Cinema of Loneliness*, p. 324.

70 Robert Stam and Toby Miller, eds., *Film and Theory: An Anthology* (Oxford: Blackwell, 2000), p. 228.

71 Debbie Lisle and Andrew Pepper, 'The New Face of Global Hollywood: *Black Hawk Down* and the Politics of Intervention', *Cultural Politics*, forthcoming.

72 Beidler, *The Good War's Greatest Hits*, p. 7.

73 Ibid.

74 Kolker, *A Cinema of Loneliness*, pp. 306–7.

75 Susan Jeffords, *The Remasculinization of America: Gender and the Vietnam War* (Bloomington, IN: Indiana University Press, 1989), pp. xi–xiv.

76 Jim Neilson, 'Stephen [sic] Spielberg and the Lost Crusade'.

77 Carol Cohn and Cynthia Weber, 'Missions, Men and Masculinities: Carol Cohn discusses *Saving Private Ryan* with Cynthia Weber', *International Feminist Journal of Politics*, Vol. 1 No. 3, Autumn 1999, pp. 464–75.

78 Kolker, *Cinema of Loneliness*, pp. 306–7.

79 Barbara Brooks Tomblin, *G.I. Nightingales: The Army Nurse Corps in World War II* (Lexington, KY: University Press of Kentucky, 1996), pp. 43–5.

80 Mcnab, 'The Thin Red Line', p. 54.

81 Scott, 'Pearl Harbor'.

82 Tomblin, *G.I. Nightingales*, pp. 14–17.

83 Basinger, *The World War II Combat Film*, p. 260.

84 Scott, 'Pearl Harbor'.

85 Beidler, *The Good War's Greatest Hits*, p. 6.

86 Doherty, *Projections of War*, p. 211.

87 'Ship's Cook Third Class Doris "Dorie" Miller,' *National Geographic Beyond the Movie: Pearl Harbor*, http://plasma.nationalgeographic.com/pearlharbor/ngbeyond/people/index.html (9/7/03).

88 Doherty, *Projections of War*, p. 212.

89 'Ship's Cook Third Class Doris "Dorie" Miller'.

90 Mcnab, 'Pearl Harbor'.

91 Scott, 'Pearl Harbor'.

92 Mark Simkin, 'Pearl Harbour Film Launch in Japan', transcript, *AM* programme, ABC Radio, Australia, 22 June 2001, http://www.abc.net.au/am/s317121.htm (9/7/03).

93 Interview with Michael Bay, *National Geographic Beyond the Movie*.

94 Lane, 'Bombs Away', p. 82.

95 Ebert, 'Pearl Harbor'.

96 Dower, *War Without Mercy*, pp. 64–6.

97 For an account of American attitudes toward surrendering Germans

and prisoners of war, see Gerald F. Linderman, *The World Within War: America's Combat Experience in World War II* (New York: The Free Press, 1997), pp. 108–14.

98 Kolker, *A Cinema of Loneliness*, pp. 323–4.

99 Tunney, 'U-571'.

100 John Fousek, *To Lead the Free World: American Nationalism and the Cultural Roots of the Cold War* (Chapel Hill, NC: University of North Carolina Press, 2000), pp. 1–8.

101 Zinn, 'Private Ryan Saves War'.

102 Neilson, 'Stephen [sic] Spielberg and the Lost Crusade'.

103 Zinn, 'Private Ryan Saves War'; Neilson, 'Stephen [sic] Spielberg and the Lost Crusade'.

104 Van Der Vat, *The Pacific Campaign*, p. 250.

105 Ambrose, *'The Longest Day'*, p. 105.

106 Mcnab, 'Pearl Harbor'.

107 Will Hutton, *The World We're In* (London: Abacus, 2003), p. 51.

108 Franco Moretti, 'Planet Hollywood', *New Left Review*, Vol. 9, May/June 2001, pp. 90–3.

109 Scott, 'Pearl Harbor'.

110 Moretti, 'Planet Hollywood', p. 94.

Chapter 5

OLIVER STONE AND THE DECADE OF TRAUMA

More than any other American film director in recent years, Oliver Stone has looked to American history for his inspiration and subject matter. In doing so, he has also attracted greater controversy and passionate criticism than any of his contemporaries. The plaudits and condemnations come almost in equal measure. Stone is praised by some historians for advocating 'a strong thesis about the meaning of the past' and presenting a 'powerful interpretation of contemporary American history'.[1] Some have even claimed that he is 'the most influential historian of America's role in Vietnam'.[2] Yet other historians deem Stone's renderings of historical subjects 'disgraceful' or a 'disaster'.[3] As such, he has been accused of an 'arrogant distortion of the historical record' that amounts to the 'rape of US history'.[4]

Stone has gone to great lengths to try to answer his critics by writing articles, op-ed pieces and letters, conducting interviews with historians, appearing at academic conferences, publishing referenced film scripts and contributing to an academic book assessing his work. In recent years he has insisted that he is not a historian. Nor, despite the beliefs of some critics, has he ever claimed to be one. Instead, Stone sees himself as a 'historical dramatist' in the tradition of the Greeks and William Shakespeare. He argues that he mixes fact and fiction in his work in attempts to reveal larger 'truths' about recent American history and to challenge the often comfortable narratives and conclusions of traditional American historians.[5] With his trilogy of Vietnam War films (*Platoon, Born on the Fourth of July* and *Heaven and Earth*) and his two political dramas (*JFK* and *Nixon*), Oliver Stone has produced a body of work that reconfigures the history of what might be called the traumatic decade from the assassination of John F. Kennedy in 1963 to the resignation of Richard Milhous Nixon in 1974. The events of this decade – multiple political assassinations; widespread civil upheaval and unrest; an increasingly bloody and unpopular foreign war that ended in the defeat of American objectives; and the revelations of corruption and abuse of power at the highest levels – shook the very fabric of American society and threatened to finally destroy the belief in American exceptionalism.[6] As Robert Kolker observes, these events were 'processes of unravelling, unfinished and unfinishable narratives':

> At their most abstract, they are stories of collapse, deflation, loss, and free-floating anxiety. They tell of the coming apart of ideologies of triumph, presence, security, and agency, substituting in their place vague, incomplete murmurings of bewilderment, abandonment, misapprehension, and aggression.[7]

It is this absence or collapse of certainty surrounding traditional understandings of 'America' and American history that fascinates, preoccupies and drives Stone's historical films. As a scriptwriter and director, Stone is not afraid to focus the audience's gaze upon the darker, questionable aspects of the United States' recent political and social past. In order to assess Oliver Stone's contribution to the study of American history it is necessary to first consider how the perspective on history he offers may differ from that of both other filmmakers and many traditional historians; second, what purpose Stone's films serve in terms of the promotion of historical inquiry; and third, how radical an agenda Stone is advocating though his historical dramatisations. In other words, whether his films affirm or critique the dominant cultural and political ideologies of their own moment of production.

CONTESTING HISTORY

It has been argued that Stone 'bucks a current trend in movie production' by making films that 'examine the dark side of American life and leave audiences uncomfortable'.[8] Stone's films certainly 'contest' history and 'provide interpretations that run against traditional wisdom or generally accepted views.'[9] For this very reason, the criticisms and condemnations of his work have been particularly impassioned and often quite vicious. Stone has gone to great lengths to try to justify the historical perspectives he has placed on film and to answer the condemnations he has received. Such efforts seem to reflect a desire or need to be accepted by the mainstream as a legitimate voice. Yet Stone has consistently and deliberately focused his camera on subject matter and major themes that are inherently controversial, challenging, and often at odds with commonly accepted historical narratives. Stone has striven through his films to contest or undermine the benign meta-narrative of US history or what he calls 'America's official story'. As Stone said of *JFK*, his intention was to make his audience 'leave the theater ready to think about things and, I hope, rethink them, and begin to wonder about some of the givens, some of the sacred cows, some of the official story'.[10]

Stone's Vietnam trilogy, for example, offers a view of American interactions with the outside world and its consequences for American society that constantly assaults the viewer and brings into question the familiar myths about the benign nature of the American mission in the world. *Platoon* (1986) was the first mainstream, popular Hollywood production to focus purely on the American combat experience in Vietnam. Earlier films had contained combat scenes from Vietnam but they did so either obliquely (*The Deer Hunter*, *Apocalypse Now*) or they were films that largely failed at the box office and therefore had little impact on the public's perception of the war and its meanings (*Go Tell the Spartans*, *The Boys in Company 'C'*).[11] *Platoon* opened the way for mainstream Hollywood to confront combat in Vietnam and had a major impact on the processes of coming to terms with the experience of Vietnam that occupied American culture from the mid-1980s into the early 1990s. It did so with what was widely hailed as unprecedented realism. John Wheeler, chair of the Vietnam Veterans' Memorial Fund, argued that: '*Platoon* makes us real. The Vietnam Memorial [on the Mall in Washington, DC] was one gate our country had to pass through; *Platoon* is another. It is part of the healing process. It speaks to our generation. Those guys are us.'[12] Vincent Canby, reviewing the film for the *New York Times*, marvelled that 'Never before . . . have I seen in a war movie such a harrowing evocation of fear, which functions like adrenaline but feels like a headache, the kind that rises and falls but never quite disappears.'[13] For his part, Stone was the first writer and director of a major American film about the Vietnam War who was a veteran of the conflict. He had volunteered to fight in Vietnam and had been decorated with the Bronze Star for Valor and a Purple Heart. Though overburdened by ideological leanings and melodramatic flourishes, Stone's interpretation nonetheless had the legitimacy of survivor testimony and thus, in eyes of some critics, carried greater 'moral authority' and 'cultural value' than treatments by non-veterans.[14] Stone was roundly praised for conveying the 'feel' of combat in Vietnam. As Susan Mackey-Kallis suggests: 'our awareness of the grime, sweat, and pain of the young recruits as they hump through the jungles of Southeast Asia is almost visceral. We smell their fear, taste their dry-mouthed exhaustion, and sense their confusion and despair.'[15]

Despite the plaudits, however, *Platoon*'s realism is tempered by significant melodramatic tendencies and the film also follows many of the conventions of the combat genre. The story centres on the journey of a young soldier, Chris Taylor (Charlie Sheen), from his arrival in country as a naive, innocent rookie through to his departure as a battle-hardened, mature if wounded warrior. During the film he must undergo many tests of his courage and manhood, and is subjected to the conflicting influence of two father figures – the 'good' Sergeant Elias (Willem Dafoe) and the 'bad' Sergeant Barnes (Tom Berenger). The film follows an episodic structure from the nerve-ridden first patrol, through a terrifying night-time ambush, the horror of a village massacre, and ultimately the brutal climactic battle with its apocalyptic aftermath. There are also recognisable character types: the inexperienced youth, the father figure who dies, the absence of women except as victims, the largely faceless and numerically overwhelming enemy. These and other conventions, together with Stone's tendency towards melodrama, are rife throughout the film.

Yet, in social and political terms, *Platoon* does to an extent step beyond the bounds of mainstream Hollywood and 'attempts an examination of the breakdown in rational order and the inherent racism and brutality of many Americans in Vietnam'.[16] Most significantly, the film is more than willing to explore the less palatable aspects of American activities in Vietnam. The scant regard for the humanity of the Vietnamese is made abundantly clear. In a pivotal scene, after finding the mutilated bodies of their colleagues, the platoon descends upon the nearest Vietnamese village to seek out those responsible. What follows graphically evokes memories of the My Lai massacre: a disabled teenager is made to dance with machine-gun fire before his skull is smashed to pieces with the butt of a gun; a woman is shot in the head by Sergeant Barnes (Tom Berenger) because she will not be quiet, causing another soldier to cry 'Let's go for it. Let's do the whole fucking village'; Barnes then threatens to execute the dead woman's young daughter unless her father confesses to Viet Cong allegiance. After Sergeant Elias (Willem Dafoe) intervenes, the whole village is nonetheless torched, the men and some of the women are taken away in shackles, and a teenage girl is gang raped. This hugely effective scene received much critical and public attention, and was the precursor to other such examinations of American brutality toward the Vietnamese in films such as *Casualties of War*. Elsewhere in the film, American soldiers are shown quite deliberately killing each other, a GI is shown cutting the ear from a dead Vietnamese soldier as a trophy, and after the climactic battle an uninjured soldier is shown stabbing himself in the leg so that his tour of duty can reach an early end. All these images unnerve the viewer and upset many of the more conventional devices deployed elsewhere in the film. Stone also makes some attempts to engage with the class and racial aspects of America's war in Vietnam. The protagonist, Chris, is a white middle-class volunteer to Vietnam but shows some awareness that the drafted members of his platoon are disproportionately from the lower classes: 'Well, here I am . . . with guys nobody really cares about . . . they're poor, they're the unwanted, yet they're fighting for our society and our freedom.' Cultural divisions within US society are also reflected in the two opposing groups at the platoon's base camp, where Barnes leads the reactionary, alcohol-swilling group telling bigoted jokes to the sounds of 'Okie from Muskogee', while Elias is in the more communal, dope-taking crew, kicking back to Smokey Robinson's 'Tracks of My Tears'. Stone also gives some attention to the disproportionate burden placed on black Americans to do the fighting in Vietnam and explores, to some extent, the continued racism they faced within the armed forces. As Clyde Taylor argues, however, despite some advances, *Platoon* still bows to 'familiar limits of discourse in its deployment of black troops'. Although they may be more than the token presence afforded them in earlier films, they nonetheless 'occupy a second tier where they are deployed as shadows deepening the moral conflict between Elias and Barnes'.[17] Although it may be a departure from earlier films on Vietnam, the ambiguity of Stone's politics in *Platoon*, as we will discuss later in the chapter, nonetheless renders the film less radical than might be assumed.

In what has been described as 'a bitter, seething postscript' to *Platoon*,[18] Stone took his critique of the Vietnam War much further in *Born on the Fourth of July* (1989). This film is based on the story of an all-American boy who volunteers for Vietnam with bravado and an over-riding sense of patriotism only to return an ostracised, disillusioned paraplegic who turns against everything he once loved. The transformation is all the more shocking since the protagonist, Ron Kovic, is played by Tom Cruise, an actor renowned for his chiselled good looks and most famous for being the 1980s equivalent of John Wayne in the Reaganesque, anti-Soviet action movie *Top Gun* (1986). Although Cruise begins the movie as the quintessential, blue-eyed, all-American boy, he is transformed not only into a paraplegic but also the antithesis of the American hero, even managing to 'look physically unattractive with lank, unwashed long hair, a drooping moustache, and a sagging beer belly'.[19] The film again shows American soldiers firing upon Vietnamese civilians and killing their own in the confusion of battle. Kovic returns home, not to a hero's welcome, but to a squalid veterans' hospital, a society that shuns him, and friends and family who no longer understand him or seem to know him. The clear message is that Vietnam has corrupted the very soul of America and caused the US to lose its way. Stuart Klawans argued in *The Nation* that the film 'probably tells you more about American society and politics than all previous Vietnam movies combined' while offering 'more political honesty than anyone could expect from Hollywood'.[20] Historian Jack E. Davis goes even further, arguing that '*Born* is more honest and forthcoming than the typical institutional history, and it rejects the ancestor worship pouring forth from public history.' Stone's film is 'an actual inquiry rather than a presentation'. It is framed around 'a historical problem, addresses critical questions about the American experience, and offers an interpretation of the recent past that approaches that found in scholarship'.[21] In other words, Stone has engaged with the existing historical discourse on the Vietnam War in order to address through his film the reasons for US involvement, how the war affected individuals and communities in the US, and what the conflict reveals about the wider project and meaning of 'America'. In so doing, it can be argued that he succeeds in adding something to that discourse.

Stone offers a critique of the political and social conditions that led the US into Vietnam and encouraged many of the nation's best and brightest to support and fight the Cold War. His contention is that the kind of unbridled patriotism celebrated in World War II movies and Fourth of July parades, played out in childhood war games and imprinted on the American psyche by Cold War political rhetoric, drew the United States inexorably away from its finest values and traditions into the abyss of Vietnam. Even John F. Kennedy, who elsewhere Stone celebrates as a hero, is made culpable for America's fall from grace. Kennedy's Inaugural Address assertion that Americans will 'bear every burden' in defeating communism is portrayed as a call to arms to Kovic, contributing directly to his naive 'America – love it or leave it' attitude. Stone examines the impact the war had on the American home-front more effectively than in any previous Hollywood film, focusing not only on the tensions within a particular community over the treatment of one of its sons but also on the wider impact of the anti-war movement. Whereas later, in *JFK* and *Nixon*, Stone asserts that self-interested political forces betrayed the true course of the United States, throughout much of *Born on the Fourth of July* he challenges the audience to think about whether there are traits inherent in American society and its founding myths that led to militarisation and blind patriotic fervour in the early Cold War years. The very notion of an exceptional America seems to be under investigation, though, as we shall see later, the film's apparent radicalism is undermined by its willingness to strike a compromise and welcome Kovic back into the fold at the end. Indeed, it is worth noting that such a strategy indicates how subversive and recuperative agendas are working in tension with one another throughout the film and indeed in Stone's oeuvre as a whole.

Critics of the film complained that Stone, apparently with Kovic's cooperation, manipulated and changed facts from the veteran's autobiography. Specifically, the film portrays a visit by Kovic to the family of a Marine colleague he believes he killed in a 'friendly fire' incident in Vietnam, and also the brutal policing of both a 1970 Syracuse University anti-war rally and a riot at the 1972 Republican National Convention. None of these events actually occurred, causing some critics to accuse Stone of distorting history and even lying.[22] The director freely admits that 'several incidents and facts were changed, and some mistakes were made', including the portrayal of police brutality at Syracuse. However, he insists that the embellishments in the film serve a higher purpose, making larger points about the impact of the war on American society, and that they are 'a valid and powerful form of artistic license'.[23] Although at times he does resort to 'sensationalism, composite images and even fiction', Stone nonetheless makes 'an important contribution to history' by offering 'a valid alternative viewpoint' on the nature of US foreign interventions and their effects on American society to that promulgated by the 'mythic legacy of World War II'.[24] The film effectively articulates the tensions and schisms produced by the Vietnam war within American society and manages to convey something of the period's emotional and intellectual confusion by giving us some sense of what it might have been like both for those who went to Vietnam and those who stayed at home.

In the conclusion to Stone's Vietnam trilogy, *Heaven and Earth* (1993), he again shifts attention, this time viewing the war largely from a Vietnamese perspective, and indeed from that of a woman. With very few exceptions, Hollywood's engagement with Vietnam, and indeed that of many historians, has been very much from the American point of view. There has been little focus on the Vietnamese, the complexities of their lives and culture, their reasons for fighting for independence, and the impact upon them as individuals and as a society. Indeed, many Vietnam films, from *The Green Berets* to *Rambo*, have been criticised for 'an impulse to villainize the enemy and an inability to overcome . . . inherent racist tendencies'.[25] In *The Deer Hunter*, for example, the Vietnamese are portrayed 'almost uniformly as a repellent, savage people' who are 'almost without exception either demonic or decadent variations of the "yellow peril"'.[26] To some extent, Stone's treatment of the Vietnamese in *Platoon* was applauded for replacing the stereotypical 'leering, yellow-eyed "gooks"' of earlier American films about the war with 'the beautiful, dark, leaf-draped ghosts of soldiers . . . flying through the bush, impossible, even often in death, to embrace'.[27] Such representational strategies, of course, flirt with an Orientalist tendency to associate the East with the exotic and sensual as well as the barbarous. Nonetheless, in so far as Stone depicts the Vietnamese 'not as madmen full of hate and a maniacal notion of torture, but as simple and dedicated men and women who fought and died to drive out the invader as their countrymen had done for ten thousand years before them',[28] his Vietnam films constitute a significant, if perhaps flawed, advance in Hollywood's treatment of America's wartime adversaries. It is difficult at times, however, to pin down Stone's racial and, for that matter, gender politics. Despite the laudatory remarks of some reviewers, in neither *Platoon* nor *Born on the Fourth of July* are the Vietnamese given any kind of a voice or 'meaningful characterization'.[29] Women also, if they are present at all, have tended to be marginalised or are 'typically passive' in Stone's films.[30] In *JFK*, for example, the scenes between Jim Garrison (Kevin Costner) and his wife (Sissy Spacek) have been characterised as 'traditional gender melodramatics', wherein a neglected wife berates her obsessive, work-focused husband for not

prioritising his family enough.[31] Indeed, David Breskin complained to
Stone in an interview that the 'women in your work tend to be prosti-
tutes, bimbos, housewives, stick figures. And if they're developed at
all, they tend to be either emotionally cold or sort of along for the ride,
as appendages to the male characters.' Stone's rather inadequate
response was to argue that his films are 'about ideas which primarily
concern men'. He did, however, also draw attention to those women
who play more central roles and are independent, strong figures, specifically Kyra Sedgewick's character Donna in *Born on the Fourth of
July*.[32] To this small list could be added Joan Allen's superb performance as Pat Nixon, the President's wife, in *Nixon*, although even her
role is somewhat perfunctory and serves merely to add to our perspective on Nixon himself. Moreover, in both films, the protagonists have
mothers whose overbearing presence and pious religiosity are shown
to be partly responsible for their weaknesses.

Stone claims he did not make *Heaven and Earth* 'in response to
critics' complaints that my films neglected or denigrated women'. He
did admit, however, that Hollywood's films about Vietnam, including his own, 'had always been about Americans and, as such, were
ethnocentric if not racist'.[33] By choosing to make a film about Vietnam
that privileged the perspective of a Vietnamese woman, therefore, he
was making a laudable political statement. The problem that many
critics had with the film, however, was not with its intentions but
rather its execution. Based on the autobiographies of Le Ly Hayslip,
the film follows her life from childhood in the Central Highlands,
through encounters with French, Vietnamese Communist, American
and South Vietnamese troops, to a life of work and pregnancy in
Saigon, and eventually marriage to an American and emigration to
the bewildering suburbia of California. The film was not well
received by critics or the movie-going public. It was criticised for
having an 'overloaded plot' that 'suffocates [its] simplistic thematic
framework'.[34] Although it is quite a conventional film that flirts with
sentimentality and attempts to compress too much into its two hours,
in many ways it is nonetheless a highly effective piece of work. As in
other films, Stone attempts to unsettle his audience and challenge
particular views that many might have held about Vietnam and
about the wishes, needs and objectives of the Vietnamese people.
While there may be little depth of argument, audiences are at least
confronted with the idea that the Vietnamese were not fighting the
French and then the Americans at the will of the Kremlin but for

reasons of nationalism and the desire for independence. Americans are again seen perpetrating or condoning heinous acts, most graphically when Le Ly (Hiep Thi Le) is tortured by a South Vietnamese officer under the compliant eye of a US military adviser. Villagers are torn from their ancestral lands and rounded up into strategic hamlets for their 'protection'. Possible informants are even forced to confess by watching their friends being thrown from helicopters. As Julia Foulkes observes, however, 'none of the many sides of this war comes off more virtuous than any other'.[35] The Vietnamese Communists summarily execute suspected traitors and Le Ly is raped rather than being shot by two of her comrades. Villagers are also not merely victims but actively engage in the war, being readily recruited by the National Liberation Front and perpetrating attacks against their foreign invaders. The film conveys most effectively how rural Vietnamese life was forever changed by years of war and shows how villagers struggled to cope with the ebb and flow of fighting with no clear front-lines that saw their land pass almost ceaselessly in and out of the control of the various protagonists in the conflict. Le Ly has argued that the film could have done more to portray the daily lives of the Vietnamese but she is largely happy with Stone's interpretation of her life.[36]

The film's greatest achievement is that it draws attention to some of the major effects war can have on women. Whereas most American war films concentrate on the impact of war on men, *Heaven and Earth* engages with the experiences of women in combat; the use of sexuality, sexual abuse and rape as tools of war; issues of prostitution and the role of women in black-market profiteering; the consequences of unwanted wartime pregnancies; and the fate and treatment of Amerasian children. Some of these issues may only be addressed at the surface level but it is significant that a film by a highly influential Hollywood director should include such issues at all. As Foulkes concludes: 'Through numerous tragedies, Le Ly and her mother depict the travails of survival for women in war. The agonizing compromises of morality and honor forced by life in a war and its aftermath achieve a resonant humility in the portraits of Le Ly and her mother.'[37]

By examining the war in Vietnam through the eyes of a Vietnamese woman, Stone addressed two major perspectives neglected in his earlier work and challenged his audience to consider the war and its human impact from a different perspective than most would have been comfortable with. Perhaps as a result, *Heaven and Earth* did not attract the same kind of critical and commercial success that Stone had enjoyed with *Platoon* and *Born on the Fourth of July*. On the evidence of the film's reception, there seemed to be little appetite for exploring the impact of the war on America's adversaries and victims rather than on the American psyche itself. And while Le Ly Hayslip's worthy sentiments about the importance of remembering what happened in Vietnam and her implicit acknowledgment of the function that films can play in this respect should be noted – 'Military action brought a holocaust to Vietnam,' she remarked, 'Americans have to face that disaster honestly so that it cannot happen again'[38] – it seems that few Americans at the time of *Heaven and Earth*'s release were ready or willing to do so.

If the Vietnam trilogy chips away at the benign meta-narrative of American history, then Stone's political couplet of *JFK* (1991) and *Nixon* (1995) seems to want to bring the whole façade crashing down. In these films, he suggests that hidden powers among the highest of American authorities colluded in the assassination of John F. Kennedy (and, indeed, Bobby Kennedy and Martin Luther King Jr) and that the military industrial complex effectively controls US foreign policy. Both films caused a furore in the American media and among academics, particularly historians. For example, Alexander Cockburn claimed that, in *JFK*, Stone's 'history is bogus and his aesthetics questionable'.[39] George Will was even more damning: '*JFK* is an act of execrable history. . . In this three-hour lie, Stone falsifies so much that he may be an intellectual sociopath, indifferent to truth.'[40] Beyond contesting the now commonly-refuted conclusion of the Warren Commission that Lee Harvey Oswald acted alone in the assassination of President Kennedy, *JFK* offers a number of competing perspectives on how and why Kennedy was killed. It pivots around the investigations of New Orleans District Attorney Jim Garrison and his attempts to bring a local businessman, Clay Shaw (Tommy Lee Jones), to trial in a failed bid to prove that a conspiracy lay behind the assassination.

Even those who find good things to say about the film agree it is 'replete with inaccuracies and distortions' and that it abounds with 'factual errors'.[41] It is unnecessary to repeat here the long list of composites, compressions and creations that Stone undertook in his film. It is the film's broader messages about the significance and reasons for the assassination that are worthy of some attention. One of the central claims is that Kennedy was assassinated to prevent him withdrawing the US from Vietnam. There is some debate among historians over what course Kennedy's policies would have taken, including that towards Vietnam, should his presidency not have ended prematurely. Stone's main inspiration for making such a claim, John Newman, argues that Kennedy's final policy document on Vietnam proves he was planning to withdraw 1,000 troops ahead of a complete withdrawal by 1965. A mere four days after Kennedy's death, this order was cancelled by Lyndon Johnson and the war soon escalated further.[42] Although Kennedy did send some mixed messages about his intentions toward South East Asia, most historians of the war strongly refute the contention that withdrawal was imminent. Robert Buzzanco argues: 'Far from being a dove, Kennedy was the driving force behind the American intervention in Vietnam' who had a record of 'constant reinforcement and escalation'.[43] He had raised the number of US military personnel in Vietnam from 700 to over 16,000, introduced the strategic hamlets programme, and initiated a number of counterinsurgency operations in the pursuit of a limited war against the Vietnamese Communists. On the day of his death he had planned to tell the Dallas audience: 'We in this country in this generation, are – by destiny rather than choice – the watchmen on the walls of freedom. . . Our assistance . . . to nations can be painful, risky and costly, as is true in Southeast Asia today. But we dare not weary of the task.'[44] There is little hard evidence to support the claim that Kennedy would have withdrawn from Vietnam and much to suggest that, with the same advisors and circumstances that Johnson inherited, JFK would have followed much the same course as his successor. Indeed, it has been argued that the assassination of the South Vietnamese President Diem, in a coup that was effectively sanctioned by the Kennedy White House, was a more pivotal event in the deepening of the American involvement in the war than was Kennedy's own death three weeks later.[45] However, precisely because Stone asserts with such force and confidence that Kennedy was on the brink of a withdrawal from Vietnam, and overlooks the less palatable aspects of Kennedy's own South East Asia policy, the film effectively closes down rather than opens up debates about culpability. In the logic of the film, the blame for Vietnam is passed neatly onto a motley crew of 'players' including Johnson, the military, the CIA, the Mafia and big business. At the same time, and despite Stone's earlier criticism of Kennedy in *Born on the Fourth of*

July, the assassinated president is entirely and problematically exonerated.

Nevertheless, in *JFK*, Stone does challenge head-on one of the central, comforting aspects of the benign meta-narrative of recent US history: that Lee Harvey Oswald murdered John F. Kennedy without any support or help from others, particularly not those in positions of power. The film's claims about the nature and character of political conspiracies, and its uncovering of a web of interlocking power relations underpinning these conspiracies, draw attention to the corrupting influence of big business and special interests in American political life. As Marcus Raskin contends, 'it is absurd to argue that conspiracies do not exist'. It is, he suggests, 'far better and more accurate to begin from the assumption that conspiracies are common, especially in politics'.[46] Similarly, Michael Rogin argues that, since the mid-1960s, 'reasonable people have had to doubt the Warren Commission, lone assassin . . . version of the killing of Kennedy' and have 'had to acknowledge . . . the power of secret government in the United States, hidden both in its unaccountable decision making at the top and its covert operations on the ground'.[47] The activities of the CIA in Cuba, Guatemala, Iran, Chile and elsewhere; the uses of the civilian and military intelligence agencies against domestic dissenters; and the abuse of power at the highest levels during the Watergate and Iran-Contra scandals all bear witness to the darker side of American history that Stone wants to confront and accuses many traditional historians of ignoring or downplaying. Moreover, as we will discuss further in the conclusion to this chapter: 'Evidence for the withholding within government of information that might shed light on Kennedy's death is overwhelming'.[48]

In *Nixon*, Oliver Stone continued to explore themes of conspiracy and corruption, again revealing his willingness to 'dwell in the darker shadows of history',[49] though given his subject – the US president most mired in scandal and disgrace – he might perhaps have expected to raise less ire than he garnered for *JFK*. On the contrary, however, several historians poured even more scorn on the film. As with *JFK*, Stone had gone to some lengths to legitimise his account of Nixon's life, including publishing an annotated screenplay complete with footnotes, facsimiles of Watergate documents and supporting essays from academics and former Nixon advisors. Such a strategy, however, worked to outrage certain historians to new levels of indignation. Stephen Ambrose, for example, accused Stone of a 'peacock like display' of 'fraudulent' scholarship that was in effect 'too thin to cover his basic contempt for real scholarship'.[50] Joan Hoff went further, accusing Stone of the 'rape of US history' and the 'representational, pornographic rape not only of Nixon but of the presidency itself'. Stone had, she argued, objectified and commodified Nixon and 'seduced and silenced' the film's audience by 'leaving no room for discussion of facts or debate'.[51] Certainly Stone had again conflated certain situations, invented scenes, wrongly attributed dialogue to certain characters, and had generally used much dramatic license. That said, he never claimed to have provided a 'literal' recreation of Nixon's private life or political career. In fact, the film begins with a disclaimer stating that what follows is 'a dramatic interpretation of events and characters based on public sources and an incomplete historical record. Some scenes and events are presented as composites or have been hypothesized or condensed.' What Stone had sought to do, in making *Nixon*, was render an exploration of the power and paranoia surrounding one of the twentieth century's most intriguing American political figures and raise questions about the nature of the American political system itself; whether this system, as a result of increased secrecy and the concentration of power in the hands of a few, had created a life of its own, no longer controllable by elected officials and the constitutional checks and balances. Such a task is an ambitious one, particularly for a filmmaker working within the confines of the Hollywood system, and it is not one at which Stone faultlessly succeeds. Yet, as Robert Brent Toplin suggests: 'Stone's characterizations of the seamy side of politics arouse our thinking about the way power may be wielded beneath the surface of politics. His allusions to conspiracy suggest a variety of troubling activities at high levels that deserve our attention.'[52] Although there is much that is symbolic, sensational and spectacular about Stone's film, it does not, as some critics claim, neatly close off further discussion. Rather, it compels the audience to ask questions about the nature and corruption of government in the United States and whether self-interest and the promotion of elite concerns dominate political affairs at the expense of the public good. The film, then, is essentially a 'clever integration of fact and personal theorizing' on the part of Oliver Stone and, as such, does not provide the viewer with clear-cut, pre-packaged answers. Rather, it constitutes 'just one of many possible explanations that we can consider in trying to understand Nixon's personality'[53] and the myriad of demons that may have driven him.

Stone's films do ask important questions about history. Little is straightforward, particularly in *JFK* and *Nixon*. His films amount to what Kolker calls 'cinematic interrogations of historical and cultural figures and movements'.[54] Particularly in *JFK*, 'viewers hardly have time to ponder what is true, what is speculation and what is fiction'.[55] Indeed, *JFK* quite deliberately avoids advocating a single, particular explanation for Kennedy's assassination. Instead, there are so many conflicting suggestions of complicity that, as one reviewer quipped, 'it was hard to leave the theatre without momentarily double-checking your own whereabouts on 22 November 1963'.[56] In raising these questions, the film, as Toplin notes, 'asks the audience to think for itself and begin the process of deconstructing the meaning of its own history.'[57] It calls upon audiences to take to task official versions of history and ask whether alternative versions might exist and, in fact, be more convincing. As the mysterious X (Donald Sutherland) says to Garrison: 'Don't take my word for it. Don't believe me. Do your own work, your own thinking.' This is the central message of the film: no one should take for granted what we are told about history; everything is open to debate, interpretation, revision and further exploration. In this sense, *JFK* encourages historical inquiry rather than perverting, distorting or destroying it, as some have charged. Indeed, by suggesting 'competing possibilities for what happened', Stone's film, as Rosenstone argues, emphasises 'the artificial and provisional reconstruction of any historical reality'.[58] Or, as Garrison puts it at the end of his courtroom summation, looking directly into the camera: 'It's up to you.'

A DIFFERENT FORM OF STORYTELLING

When considering whether or to what extent Oliver Stone, as a filmmaker, challenges the narrative conventions of the Hollywood movie, it is important to make a distinction between the form and style of his Vietnam films and later examples like *JFK* and *Nixon*. Each of the episodes in Stone's Vietnam trilogy follows a relatively conventional narrative. As noted earlier, *Platoon* views war as a 'rite of passage for young men' and offers a 'generic "war is hell" critique' rather than addressing Vietnam itself more specifically.[59] *Born on the Fourth of July* follows Kovic's story chronologically, whereas the book it is based upon has a non-linear narrative, jumping back and forth through time and actually ending with Kovic's wounding in a way that allows the reader more distance to reflect on the deeper meanings of the story.[60]

Instead, the film encourages audiences to focus on Kovic's re-assimilation into the social and political mainstream following the Democratic National Convention in 1976 rather than asking potentially difficult questions about institutional shortcomings and the bankruptcy of political rhetoric. In formal terms, as Kolker observes, 'Stone leaves little room for inquiry. . . Every cut and movement of the camera is assertive.'[61] *Heaven and Earth*, too, tells a relatively straightforward chronological story that follows the life-changing dramas of the film's protagonist from the innocence of childhood to adult self-discovery. The way in which history is told in *JFK* and *Nixon*, however, challenges the formal logic of much mainstream American filmmaking and, for that matter, most written histories. As Robert Burgoyne observes: 'the temporal structure of *JFK* departs radically from the sense of continuity that traditionally defines the national past'. *JFK* begins with a largely chronological, context-setting montage of newsreel reports and other contemporary clips that establish a society seemingly 'moving along parallel pathways in a homogenous time, punctuated by clear-cut historical events'.[62] But as soon as the President is shot, the linear narrative begins to unravel and Stone uses a wide variety of formal techniques to disrupt the passage of time as we would expect to see it unfold in a conventional film. As one critic put it, Stone's use of rapid editing and flashback, and his splicing together of original and recreated footage, constitutes 'a pummelling style, a left to the jaw, a right to the solar plexus, flashing forward, flashing backward, crosscutting relentlessly, shooting in tight, blurring, obfuscating, bludgeoning the viewer'.[63] In formal terms, then, the intent and effect of such a practice is, as Burgoyne suggests, to show time 'as a dimension that can be manipulated, a dimension that is open to doubt, ambiguity and suspicion'. History, therefore, is best understood as 'a site of contradictory, mundane, and abstracted details'[64] and Stone's film draws our attention to the fact that any understanding of the past must be conditional on the information available, the way it is presented, and the perspective from which it is both projected and received. Robert Kolker puts it well:

> *JFK* insists that we pay attention not merely to stories, but to the images through which they are told, and to those doing the telling. It is a film about discourse, process, power, and ideology, about speaking things into existence by investigating and demonstrating how events are represented, so that learning is accom-

plished by understanding process and coming to terms with power.

JFK, therefore, is an effective and significant piece of historical film-making because it 'requests the viewer's active engagement in its methodology'.[65]

In *Nixon*, too, chronology is discarded as Stone deploys an array of flashbacks, non-sequential scenes and the rapid intercutting of images, both archival and re-enacted. This approach, as Ian Scott argues, allows for 'the distortion of logic, and the breakdown and pressure of concealment thus acts as a physical presence destroying the administration in its last two years'.[66] Watching *Nixon* is an unsettling, sometimes confusing and often disturbing experience. The film has great emotional impact but it is also challenges the viewer to give intellectual consideration to what appears on the screen. As Kolker contends:

> *Nixon* is open, large, and broad, sometimes nearly hysterical in its drive to generate images of explanation, narratives of historical clarification, and psychologies of character. Stone keeps countering his subject's desire to scuttle behind the history he helped deform by shoving him and that history out into the open, forcing him to confront it along with the viewer.[67]

Like *JFK*, Stone's examination of Richard Nixon offers no single, clear interpretation. Rather, history in *Nixon* 'is synthesis, facts retold, explained, represented, seen, and reseen through a variety of points of view'.[68]

In films such as *JFK* and *Nixon*, Stone is effectively challenging the logic of much traditional historical scholarship. Rather than suggesting that disciplined research can lead us towards some kind of transcendent historical truth, history in these films is conceived of as a clash between competing versions of the truth. As Kolker puts it: 'History is the result of many conflicting narrative layers, a dialectic of stories, each feeding on the other, each claiming the truthfulness of its representation, each a version formed by ideology, point of view, moral and political perspective, cultural context and desire.'[69] Stone's rendering of history is deliberately confrontational, deliberately unsettling and thus necessarily problematic, contestable and incomplete. As Stone himself argues: 'we dramatists are undertaking a deconstruction of history, questioning some of the given realities. . . we call into question the very idea of reality. We play with your mind.' Our point is that what some historians see as dishonest and misleading can also be regarded as challenging and thought-provoking. Stone acknowledges that his films are 'a way of attacking the current consensus' among the historical community but in so doing he does not expect, nor would he want, viewers to uncritically and wholeheartedly accept his perspective.[70] Though Stone makes some very forceful assertions in *JFK* and *Nixon*, the overall tone of these works is not to make problematic claims to the 'truth' but rather to challenge audiences to think for themselves and arrive at their own conclusions.

One of the greatest concerns of Stone's critics is that the conflation of fiction and non-fiction in his films is 'historically contaminating and exploitative of unsuspecting viewers', particularly 'the young'.[71] Arthur Schlesinger Jr, for example, worries about the 'impact of *JFK* on the unwary young'.[72] Though we have expressed concern elsewhere in this book about the tendencies of some films and filmmakers to privilege style and aesthetics at the expense of developing coherent political positions, the assumption that modern audiences simply accept everything they see on the cinema screen as literal truth is condescension of the highest order. As Marita Sturken argues, younger viewers 'raised on MTV' and the fast-cutting, non-linear techniques used in *JFK* and *Nixon* are actually 'more likely to have the image skills to read Stone's montage sequences than older viewers'.[73] Stone himself is convinced that viewers know that they are watching an interpretation of history rather than a literal recreation. In fact, he argues that his 'ambivalent and shifting style . . . makes people aware they are watching a movie and that reality itself is in question'.[74] Sturken contends that the 'infantilizing' of the audience on the part of critics is 'merely a foil' for the belief that Stone's techniques of storytelling have the effect of 'contaminating' history. Such a viewpoint not only regards audiences as 'susceptible and manipulable' but also 'understands memory and images as pure and unchanging texts'.[75] As we have argued throughout this book, history is not settled and stable but open to constant interpretation and reinterpretation. Oliver Stone, perhaps more than any other contemporary American writer and director, is engaging with American history in ways that make manifest its ultimately unknowable nature.

STONE'S POLITICS

In his review for the *Journal of American History*, Thomas Reeves claims there is 'an intense hatred of the United States' underlying *JFK*'s story of conspiracy and corruption at the highest level.[76] Such a claim, however, entirely misses the root nature of Oliver Stone's historical inquiries. In all his historical films, Stone challenges the benign meta-narrative of American history but he does not, ultimately, dismantle the notion that the United States is an exceptional nation. His attempts at ideological critique are countered by a corresponding desire to re-affirm certain enlightened values and principles that the United States throughout its history has sought to claim as its own. Stone's critiques are rooted in a conviction that Kennedy's assassins, those controlling Nixon, and the architects and perpetrators of Vietnam, were all somehow responsible for soiling the image of America as an enlightened, progressive, beacon to the world. Like many American critics before him, Stone shares in the foundational myth of America as an 'exceptional' nation and mourns the denigration of this myth by the power-hungry, self-interested minions of what he calls the 'Beast'. In Stone's view, the system, corrupted as it may be, remains essentially good. Ultimately, Stone's films are infused with a recuperative politics that strives, to convince audiences that victory for the 'good' can be snatched from the jaws of nihilism and defeat, and though corrupted, apparatuses of power can still serve enlightened ends. For example, in so far as Jim Garrison uses the courts to try to expose the plot that killed Kennedy in *JFK*, Stone seems to be suggesting that the institutions he holds responsible for the social and political traumas of the 1960s and 1970s will eventually bear up the evidence of their own duplicity. As such, Stone does not advocate a revolutionary change in the structures of American society and politics but rather appeals to the myth of 'America'. Stone argues that the Kennedy assassination is not the product of deep-seated problems that have affected American social and political life from its inception but is rather the point where the 'betrayal' of America and 'American values' begins.[77] Problematically, as Sturken observes, 'the primary force of this narrative involves the establishment of a state of prior innocence'.[78] Stone regards the assassination as an event that 'changed the course of history. It was a crushing blow to our country and to millions of people around the world. It put an abrupt end to a period of innocence and great idealism.'[79] For Stone, the United States' 'fall from grace' began with Kennedy's murder and the subsequent 'descent into hell' was the Vietnam War. His films are a clarion call to all Americans to seek out the 'truth' about their history and, by doing so, to 'restore Camelot to its former glory'.[80] Herein lies the paradox at work in Stone's films. While he acknowledges that 'postmodern history may represent a dialogue among many truths', he nonetheless attempts to strive for '*the* truth' in his films or at least encourages his audience to seek it out.[81] As Kolker argues, Garrison's courtroom summation, 'with its plea to redeem the fallen king, threatens to negate the film's larger plea to question, probe and analyze images and discover how history is made by asking us to return to the safe fold of sentimental archetypes, where our rulers are royal and our obeisance therefore unquestioned'.[82]

John F. Kennedy is one of the most iconic figures in the benign meta-narrative of American history – the youthful, attractive, intelligent leader who best represented the ambitions of a new generation but who was tragically struck down before he could fulfil his potential. In both *JFK* and *Nixon*, Stone buys wholeheartedly into the myth. Although *JFK* says very little about the substance of Kennedy's presidency, it is nonetheless an exercise in the 'conscious aggrandisement of the public memory of John Kennedy'.[83] Stone's film is a 'hagiographic depiction of John F. Kennedy as a champion of truth, justice, and peace' and is, as Michael Kurtz puts it, 'highly biased and one-dimensional'.[84] Towards the end of *Nixon*, with resignation imminent, the president admits that Kennedy is what the American people want to be whereas he, Nixon, is what they are. Stone clearly regards Kennedy as 'the purest and most enlightened of heroes'.[85] He is the knight in shining armour who is struck down before he can slay 'the Beast'. Stone's central assumption, that all was well in America prior to Kennedy's assassination, ignores much evidence indicating that belligerence and secrecy were mainstays of US politics and foreign policy long before that fateful morning in Dallas. Kennedy's administration alone had orchestrated the failed Bay of Pigs invasion of Cuba, attempted at least half a dozen times to assassinate Fidel Castro, taken the world to the brink of nuclear war during the Cuban missile crisis, given its blessing to the removal from power and assassination of South Vietnamese President Diem, greatly increased the US military presence in Vietnam and overseen massive rises in defence spending.

Given Stone's reverential view of JFK, he might have been expected to adopt a 'scorched earth policy toward Nixon'.[86] Yet the disgraced president is given a rather sympathetic portrayal. As Ian Scott observes: '*Nixon* discovers ambiguity in the man and a twisted humanity and tortured history that professes personal tragedy.'[87] Stone has himself admitted that 'it's tough not to feel some compassion for a guy who just never thought he was good enough to join the establishment, even when he emblemised that very entity'.[88] Following the Kent State killings, for example, Nixon ends up privately expressing regret about this and other events in his life. Although he does so 'without the least comprehension of their meaning other than his feelings of loss and regret',[89] it is an image that seems contrary to the widespread view of Nixon as a crook who cared little about the consequences of his actions. The film ends with archive footage of Nixon's funeral, attended by all the surviving US presidents from Ford to Clinton, complete with a salutary voiceover from Stone himself. As Kolker suggests, the problem here 'lies with the potential damage done to the text itself, because the sympathy and the sentiment throw off the ironic, condemnatory exposure that has gone before'.[90]

This pattern of critique and rehabilitation or recuperation is characteristic of Stone's other films. Generally, the political messages of Stone's films are more ambiguous, or certainly less radical, than it might at first appear. *Platoon*, for example, is far from being an antiwar film. As Sydelle Kramer argued in *Cineaste* at the time of the film's release, the film's melodramatic structure requires us and its protagonist Chris to choose between war as an instrument of fairness and justice as represented by Sergeant Elias, or war as an instrument of evil as personified by Sergeant Barnes. There is no thought that the rejection of war would be a better answer. Rather, *Platoon* is a film about 'violence for the greater good – violence as redemption'. Chris does not learn to 'abandon violence' but rather how to properly use it.[91] Although critics have argued the film 'gives us a Vietnam without patriotic rhetoric or self-sacrificial heroics',[92] the death of Elias, arms raised Christ-like, is one of the most blatant glorifications of sacrifice and martyrdom in war ever committed to film. *Platoon* may not be as unsubtle as *Rambo: First Blood Part II* (1985), in which Sylvester Stallone attempts to single-handedly refight the Vietnam War and 'win this time'. But Stone's film gives little indication of the war's origins or its motives, and does not engage in the wider debates over the war's moral ambiguity or its impact on American society and politics. Although it emphasises the darker side of the American encounter with South East Asia, by suggesting that the war could have been won if only Americans had been 'true to ourselves' rather than fighting each other, the film does not depart too far from President Reagan's attempts to recast the war as a 'noble cause'. *Platoon* may give a 'realistic' representation of life as a grunt soldier and draw attention to class, racial and cultural cleavages within the US Army but, as Marita Sturken observes, 'it reveals little about other aspects of the war – its complexity as a technological and strategic war, its government and military policies, or its effects on the Vietnamese people'.[93] In fact, on this latter point, since one of the main arguments of the film is that in Vietnam the Americans 'did not fight the enemy, we fought ourselves, and the enemy was in us', Stone's film has 'the impact of erasing the war of and with the Vietnamese, not only the terrible numbers of their dead but the story of the skilled Vietnamese army and guerrillas that ultimately defeated the United States'.[94]

In a similar manner, *Born on the Fourth of July* seeks to reintegrate Kovic into the fold and thus blunt some of the criticisms directed by the film against institutional and governmental culpability in his degeneration. Kovic's personal journey takes him from an all-American childhood through several kinds of hell before he is ultimately redeemed at the 1976 Democratic National Convention. Reviewing the film for *Newsweek*, David Ansen argued that 'the movie is a tirade against the authoritarian macho mentality that led us into Vietnam'.[95] But although the film does critique the reasoning that took the US into Vietnam, it does not reject the mythic pre-Vietnam 'apple pie' and 'picket fence' idyll that the march to war was intended to preserve. Indeed, the 'Hometown, USA' of Kovic's childhood is 'a place, in Stone's eyes, without cynicism, despair, or doubt, [in] an era when being American was something to proclaim with assurance and optimism to the rest of the world'.[96] Here, and in his other films, Stone buys into the basic myth of American exceptionalism and the benign meta-narrative of American history, arguing not that it is a flawed belief in the first place but merely that its promise has been betrayed by corporate, governmental and criminal elites. Indeed, by arguing that the killing of Kennedy, the war in Vietnam, and the abuses of executive power under LBJ and Nixon betrayed the true course of American history, Stone is essentially affirming the idea of the US is a special nation but that it lost its way during the 1960s. This uncritical acceptance of the essential good of 'American' values and principles means that, far from deconstructing the myth of America, Stone advocates a return to basic principles and the right-eous path of American historical development as an antidote to the mess and confusion of his films' decade of trauma.

Indeed, while Kovic's own story sees him condemn what he calls the American Dream as a 'fucking lie', it ultimately sees him become an 'enlightened hero',[97] who embraces rather than rejects his national identity and its values and beliefs. Kovic's emotional and political growth throughout the film is 'deeply within the tradition of American ideology', especially because it occurs through 'hard phys-ical struggle and a painful growth of consciousness'.[98] Kovic's journey is synonymous with 'America's discovery of truth through the Vietnam experience'. The film's recuperative agenda, therefore, is all too clear. Stone has admitted that he wanted to get 'to the truth of Vietnam' in order to 'help advance the healing of those who had fought and to enlighten those who one day may be drafted to fight'.[99] In ideological terms, the film is best understood as an integral part of the post-Vietnam healing process and a sustained collective effort on the part of many Americans to confront and come to terms with the experience of Vietnam and its consequences during the 1980s and early 1990s. By the film's end, as Kovic prepares to take to the podium at the 1976 Democratic National Convention, he is able to declare to a journalist that although 'it's been a long way for us vets. Just lately, I've felt like I'm home. You know, like maybe we're home.' He then takes to the stage as 'It's a Grand Old Flag' plays, not with irony, but as an expression that Kovic, and by implication all Americans, has regained some belief in the values and principles for which America has stood traditionally. Susan Mackey-Kallis argues that this is not an uncomplicated redemption but a reminder that 'Americans should love their country, with judgment rather than innocence, not out of blind patriotism but with the knowledge that its actions are some-times wrong'.[100] Nonetheless, the implication, as in Stone's other films, is that if only Americans were true to their founding principles and values, then American domestic politics and foreign policy would be both exemplary and inspirational.

CONCLUSIONS

Oliver Stone is ultimately, as Robert Kolker has argued, 'a fascinating example of how much film still influences the culture and how much that influence will be attacked when it begins to impose on conventional wisdom'.[101] Stone's historical films have been so passionately attacked and defended in both popular and academic circles that, if nothing else, they have elevated to a higher level the profile of contemporary historical engagement and debate. In the case of *JFK*, Stone's interpretation of American history had the rare, if not unique, effect of a feature film mobilising public policy with the passing into law of the President John F. Kennedy Assassination Records Collection Act of 1992. This act established the Assassination Records Review Board (ARRB) to 'locate, identify, review, and release' several million pages of documents and other evidence that Stone asserted in his film had been withheld from the public record by various government agencies. In its final report, the ARRB acknowledged that it was *JFK* that had been directly responsible for the public outcry that pressured the US Congress into establishing the review board. As historian Michael Kurtz concludes:

> Oliver Stone performed a great service. He aroused so much interest in the assassination that a whole generation of scholars is currently conducting research into the newly released documents. He gave the establishment a much-deserved blow to the solar plexus. His allegations of a systematic suppression of millions of pages of documentary materials by various government agencies have been proved true by the release of those materials under the act that he played a critical role in having enacted. . . For all of *JFK*'s faults and shortcomings, few producers and directors can claim such an impact from their movies, and few historians can claim such an impact from their works.[102]

In addition to this specific, tangible consequence of Stone's work, his films also have the potential to greatly affect the way their viewers regard history and thus serve a useful pedagogical purpose. The result is not, as his severest critics fear, that his audience will unthinkingly accept Stone's interpretations as gospel. Rather, those who see Stone's films are more likely to ask questions about the history they think they know and to critically evaluate the basis upon which historians and filmmakers build their interpretations.

Stone is also more than willing to address elements of recent American history that other filmmakers and many historians find too contentious to approach. As film critic Roger Ebert observes: 'In a time when few American directors are drawn toward political controversy, Stone seeks it out. He loves big subjects and approaches them fearlessly.'[103] Stone's approach is also likely to ask serious questions about the power structures at play in American politics and society, and the forces that shape conventional views of the course of American history. Ian Scott regards this as another unique aspect of Stone's filmmaking: 'Who else is even considering attacking the social, economic and political foundations of American society in modern Hollywood without the façade of an alternate genre approach, whatever the flaws of his ideological approach?'[104] But radical as much of Stone's agenda may be, ultimately he is making historical and political assertions that are rooted in the founding myths of the United States. Stone may attack elements of the benign meta-narrative of American history but such a critique exists in tension with an antithetical and ultimately quite conservative desire to re-affirm some mythologised, foundational, Edenic notion of America as the answer to the perceived malaise of contemporary times. In other words, to do as Garrison implores the jury in *JFK*: 'Show the world that this is still a government of the people, for the people, and by the people.'

Roger Ebert admits that 'movies are not the best way to make a reasoned argument' because they 'traffic in emotions'.[105] But, as Jack Davis concludes, Stone manages to 'convert critical ideas into engaging visual moments'. In *Born on the Fourth of July*, as in other films, he asks his audience 'not to simply witness or contemplate his film's images' but to '*feel* the trauma of Ron Kovic and of Vietnam'. He encourages them to 'experience history not on an intellectual level but on an emotional one', believing that the 'emotional will have a more lasting effect than the intellectual'.[106] It is in Stone's passion for his subjects, his passion for challenging conventional views, that much of his power as a historical filmmaker or historical dramatist lies. He asks unsettling questions of his audience and implores them not to accept historical accounts at face value, presumably including his own. As we have argued elsewhere, there is a danger inherent in asking audiences to 'feel' rather than 'think' but, unlike Spielberg,

Stone manages to address this concern. While Stone's films rely on the emotional impact of spectacle and controversial assertion, they also at least strive to engender critical engagement among their audience. They provoke as much as they reassure, shock as much as they cajole, and outrage as much as they conserve. If nothing else, Stone makes an extremely strong argument in favour of the idea that filmmakers have a right to contribute to the discourse about the meaning of the past.

NOTES

1 Robert A. Rosenstone, 'Oliver Stone as Historian', in Robert Brent Toplin, ed., *Oliver Stone's USA: Film, History and Controversy* (Lawrence, KS: University of Kansas Press, 2000), pp. 27–8.

2 Randy Roberts and David Wilky, 'A Sacred Mission: Oliver Stone and Vietnam', in Toplin, *Oliver Stone's USA*, p. 67.

3 William W. Phillips, '*JFK* review', *Journal of American History*, Vol. 79 No. 3, December 1992, pp. 1264–5.

4 Joan Hoff, '*Nixon* film review', *American Historical Review*, Vol. 101 No. 4, October 1996, pp. 1173–4.

5 Oliver Stone, 'Stone on Stone's Image (As Presented by Some Historians)', in Toplin, *Oliver Stone's America*, pp. 40–65.

6 See, for example, Daniel Bell, 'The End of American Exceptionalism', *The Public Interest*, Fall 1975, reprinted in Daniel Bell, *The Winding Passage: Essays and Sociological Journeys 1960–1980* (New York: Basic Books, 1980).

7 Robert Kolker, *A Cinema of Loneliness*, 3rd ed., (Oxford and New York: Oxford University Press, 2000), pp. 69–70.

8 Robert Brent Toplin, 'Introduction', in Toplin, *Oliver Stone's USA*, p. 8.

9 Rosenstone, 'Oliver Stone as Historian', p. 35.

10 Quoted in Susan Mackey-Kallis, *Oliver Stone's America: 'Dreaming the Myth Outward'* (Boulder, CO: Westview Press, 1996), p. 42.

11 See Albert Auster and Leonard Quart, *How the War was Remembered: Hollywood and Vietnam* (New York: Praeger, 1988).

12 Quoted in Mackey-Kallis, *Oliver Stone's America*, p. 63.

13 Vincent Canby, '"Platoon" Finds New Life in the Old War Movie', *New York Times*, 11 January 1987, section II, p. 21.

14 Marita Sturken, 'Reenactment, Fantasy, and the Paranoia of History: Oliver Stone's Docudramas', *History and Theory*, Vol. 36 No. 4, Theme Issue 36: 'Producing the Past: Making Histories Inside and Outside the Academy', December 1997, pp. 67–8.

15 Mackey-Kallis, *Oliver Stone's America*, p. 63.

16 Kolker, *Cinema of Loneliness*, p. 72.

17 Clyde Taylor, 'The Colonialist Subtext in *Platoon*', *Cineaste*, Vol. XV No. 4, 1987, pp. 8–9.

18 Vincent Canby, 'How an All-American Boy Went to War and Lost His Faith', *New York Times*, 20 December 1989, p. C15.

19 Mackey-Kallis, *Oliver Stone's America*, p. 37.

20 Quoted in Mackey-Kallis, *Oliver Stone's America*, p. 75.

21 Jack E. Davis, 'New Left, Revisionist, In-Your-Face History: Oliver Stone's *Born on the Fourth of July* Experience', in Toplin, *Oliver Stone's USA*, p. 136.

22 Diana West, 'Does "Born on the Fourth of July" Lie?', *The Washington Times*, 23 February 1990, pp. E1, E8.

23 Oliver Stone, 'On Seven Films', in Toplin, *Oliver Stone's USA*, pp. 236–8.

24 Davis, 'New Left', pp. 136, 145–6.

25 Bruce Weigl, 'Stone Incountry: A Platoon of the Mind', *Cineaste*, Vol. XV No. 4, 1987, p. 11.

26 Auster and Quart, *How the War was Remembered*, p. 63.

27 Weigl, 'Stone Incountry', p. 11.

28 Ibid.

29 Sharrett, 'Born on the Fourth of July', *Cineaste*, Vol XVII No 4, 1990, p. 49.

30 Toplin, 'Introduction', p. 18.

31 Kolker, *Cinema of Loneliness*, pp. 79–80.

32 David Breskin, *Inner Views: Filmmakers in Conversation*, expanded ed. (New York: Da Capo, 1997), pp. 125–9.

33 Stone, 'On Seven Films', p. 241.

34 Julia L. Foulkes, 'Heaven and Earth: Film Review', *American Historical Review*, Vol. 99 No. 4, October 1994, p. 1272.

35 Ibid., p. 1273.

36 Le Ly Hayslip, *'Heaven and Earth'*, in Toplin, *Oliver Stone's USA*, pp. 184–5.

37 Foulkes, 'Heaven and Earth', p. 1273.

38 Le Ly Hayslip, *'Heaven and Earth'*, p. 185.

39 Quoted in Mackey-Kallis, *Oliver Stone's America*, p. 39.

40 Quoted ibid.

41 Michael L. Kurtz, 'Oliver Stone, *JFK*, and History', in Toplin, *Oliver Stone's USA*, p. 169.

42 John M. Newman, *JFK and Vietnam: Deception, Intrigue and the Struggle for Power* (New York: Warner Books, 1992).

43 Robert Buzzanco, *Vietnam and the Transformation of American Life* (Oxford: Blackwell, 1999), pp. 64–8.

44 Quoted in Gerard J. DeGroot, *A Noble Cause?: America and the Vietnam War* (Harlow: Longman, 2000), p. 79.

45 Ibid., pp. 78–82.

46 Marcus Raskin, '*JFK* and the Culture of Violence', *American Historical Review*, Vol. 97 No. 2, April 1992, p. 491.

47 Michael Rogin, 'JFK: The Movie', *American Historical Review*, Vol. 97 No. 2, April 1992, pp. 501–2.

48 Ibid.

49 Mark C. Carnes, 'Past Imperfect: History According to the Movies (Interview with Film Director Oliver Stone)', *Cineaste*, Vol. 22 No. 4, Fall 1996.

50 Stephen Ambrose, '*Nixon*: Is It History?', in Toplin, *Oliver Stone's USA*, p. 202.

51 Hoff, '*Nixon*: Film Review', p. 1173.

52 Toplin, 'Introduction', p. 17.

53 Ibid.

54 Kolker, *Cinema of Loneliness*, p. 71.

55 Toplin, 'Introduction', p. 10.

56 See Max Holland, 'After Thirty Years: Making Sense of the Assassination', *Reviews in American History*, Vol. 22 No. 2, June 1994, p. 192.

57 Toplin, 'Introduction', p. 15.

58 Rosenstone, 'Oliver Stone as Historian', p. 36.

59 Mackey-Kallis, *Oliver Stone's America*, p. 63.

60 Ron Kovic, *Born on the Fourth of July* (New York: Corgi, 1990); Christopher Sharrett, 'Born on the Fourth of July', p. 50.

61 Kolker, *Cinema of Loneliness*, p. 71.

62 Robert Burgoyne, *Film Nation: Hollywood Looks at US History* (Minneapolis: University of Minnesota Press, 1997), pp. 90–6.

63 Richard Grenier, 'Movie Madness', *Times Literary Supplement*, 24 January 1992, pp. 16–17, quoted in Sturken, 'Reenactment, Fantasy, and the Paranoia of History', p. 76.

64 Burgoyne, *Film Nation*, pp. 91–3.

65 Kolker, *Cinema of Loneliness*, p. 75.

66 Ian Scott, *American Politics in Hollywood Film*, (Edinburgh: Edinburgh University Press, 2000), p. 146.

67 Kolker, *Cinema of Loneliness*, p. 86.

68 Ibid., p. 83.

69 Ibid., p. 78.

70 Quoted in Carnes, 'Past Imperfect'.

71 Sturken, 'Reenactment, Fantasy, and the Paranoia of History', p. 75.

72 Arthur M. Schlesinger Jr, 'On *JFK* and *Nixon*', in Toplin, *Oliver Stone's America*, p. 214.

73 Sturken, 'Reenactment, Fantasy, and the Paranoia of History', p. 76.

74 Carnes, 'Past Imperfect'.

75 Sturken, 'Reenactment, Fantasy, and the Paranoia of History', p. 76.
76 Thomas C. Reeves, '*JFK*: Movie Review', *Journal of American History*, Vol. 79 No. 3, December 1992, pp. 1263.
77 Stone quoted in Mackey-Kallis, *Oliver Stone's America*, p. 27.
78 Sturken, 'Reeanctment, Fantasy and the Paranoia of History', p. 72.
79 Stone quoted in Mackey-Kallis, *Oliver Stone's America*, p. 33.
80 Mackey-Kallis, *Oliver Stone's America*, pp. 35–6.
81 Ibid., p. 24.
82 Kolker, *Cinema of Loneliness*, p. 80.
83 Scott, *American Politics in Hollywood Film*, p. 127.
84 Kurtz, 'Oliver Stone, *JFK*, and History', p. 172.
85 Reeves, '*JFK*', p. 1263.
86 Roger Ebert, '*Nixon*', *Chicago Sun Times*, 20 December 1995, http://www.suntimes.com/ebert/ebert_reviews/1995/12/1012232.html (4/11/03).
87 Scott, *American Politics in Hollywood Film*, p. 148.
88 Quoted in Scott, *American Politics in Hollywood Film*, p. 149.
89 Kolker, *Cinema of Loneliness*, p. 91.
90 Ibid., pp. 91–3.
91 Sydelle Kramer, '*Platoon*', *Cineaste*, Vol. XV No. 3, 1987, pp. 49–50.
92 Leonard Quart, 'A Step in the Right Direction for Hollywood', *Cineaste*, Vol. XV No. 4, 1987, p. 7.
93 Sturken, 'Reenactment, Fantasy, and the Paranoia of History', p. 68.
94 Ibid., p. 69.
95 Quoted in Mackey-Kallis, *Oliver Stone's America*, p. 75.
96 Mackey-Kallis, *Oliver Stone's America*, pp. 75–6.
97 Ibid., p. 81.
98 Kolker, *Cinema of Loneliness*, p. 74.
99 Davis, 'New Left', pp. 136, 144.
100 Mackey-Kallis, *Oliver Stone's America*, pp. 81–2.
101 Kolker, *Cinema of Loneliness*, p. 95.
102 Kurtz, 'Oliver Stone, *JFK*, and History', pp. 174–7.
103 Roger Ebert, 'Heaven and Earth', *Chicago Sun-Times*, 24 December 1993, http://www.suntimes.com/ebert/ebert_reviews/1993/12/895982.html (4/11/03).
104 Scott, *American Politics in Hollywood Film*, p. 106.
105 bert, 'Heaven and Earth'.
106 Davis, 'New Left', p. 141.

Chapter 6

FROM CIVIL RIGHTS TO BLACK NATIONALISM: HOLLYWOOD V. BLACK AMERICA?

If contemporary filmmakers have felt compelled to do away with the explicit racism of pre-Civil Rights Hollywood movie-making and make African-Americans the subjects rather than the objects of their gaze, then the vexed question of how successfully have their ambitions been realised needs to be addressed. For while there has long been a slow trickle of 'worthy' films made by white liberal directors whose integrationist politics usually requires initially hostile black and white protagonists to put aside their differences and prejudices and join forces to tackle some kind of 'outside' threat (that is, *In the Heat of the Night, Mississippi Burning* and *The Hurricane*), there has also been a small but growing number of films made by African-American directors (that is, Spike Lee, Mario Van Peebles) whose focus is predominantly African-American subjects and which tend to privilege conflict and confrontation rather than reconciliation and assimilation. *Do the Right Thing, Malcolm X, Panther* and *Dead Presidents* would be examples of this type of film.

Such a distinction has provoked scholars like Manthia Diawara and Ed Guerrero to differentiate between what they refer to as 'Black independent cinema'[1] or 'a new black film wave'[2] and mainstream Hollywood cinema, although Diawara in particular is careful to draw attention to the multiple ways in which 'mainstream cinema . . . feeds on independent cinema and appropriates its themes and narrative forms'.[3] Nonetheless, despite such cross-fertilisation, the appropriateness of such a distinction, for Guerrero at least, remains. The lines of demarcation are clear. On the one hand, Hollywood has 'tended to focus narrowly its increasingly shallow product on escapism, sentiment, glamour, romance and more recently spectacular orgies of violence and sexploitation' and has thus been responsible for subjecting African-Americans to a grim diet of marginalisation and stereotyping in order to hold 'in place the white-dominated symbolic order and racial hierarchy of American society'.[4] On the other hand, what Guerrero calls the looming possibility of a 'black film industry' – heralded by the emergence of movie stars like Denzel Washington and Halle Berry and by the growing influence of 'black cultural expressions, styles and ideas on consumer culture'[5] – in turn speaks about a seismic shift in the ways in which African-Americans make, finance, watch and feature and participate in films generally. As Guerrero argues: 'the new black filmmakers are subtly shifting the terrain of the contest for the popular representation of blackness by taking their depictions of black life to higher levels in terms of funding, production standards and perhaps most importantly the broad circulation of their films among popular audiences'.[6]

At stake is not only the question of how these black 'independent' films represent the struggle for racial equality and the emergence of Black Nationalism as a social, cultural and political force from the early 1960s onwards. Rather, it is also the viability of the distinction between Hollywood and this so-called black independent cinema in the first place. For Guerrero, this distinction would seem to be straightforward. Films like *Mississippi Burning* (1987) and *The Hurricane* (2000), made by white directors and financed exclusively by major film studios, are necessarily contaminated as historical texts by their collusion in systems of production and consumption which either consciously or unconsciously reflect white interests and concerns. Those films made by black filmmakers, meanwhile, have the ability and, crucially, the freedom to tell alternative histories, ones which privilege black perspectives and viewpoints. *Panther* (1995) – a film made by Mario Van Peebles about the rise of the Black Panther Party for Self-Defense in California in the late 1960s and told from a largely sympathetic perspective – would seem to belong to the latter group. The film certainly divided audiences on its release, typically along racial lines. So while David Horowitz of the Los Angeles Center for the Study of Popular Culture took the unprecedented step of buying advertisement space in *Variety* in order to denounce the film as a 'two-hour lie' and a 'blackwash' and the Panthers themselves as 'cocaine-addled gangsters',[7] a group of prominent African-American figures in the entertainment world, including Spike Lee, Jesse Jackson and Danny Glover, countered Horowitz's campaign with similarly placed adverts that lauded the film's success in bringing to the (main)screen a previously ignored moment of black cultural and political history. As director Mario Van Peebles put it, 'Rarely in the history of Hollywood have African-Americans themselves had the opportunity to present our history, our hopes, our dreams, the story of our lives in our own way.'[8]

The issue is not whether *Panther* manages to somehow accurately represent the history, hopes and dreams of African-Americans in general – surely an impossible task – but rather that a film about black revolutionaries was made at all and, more importantly, that it was made in such a way that did not wholly succumb to the demands and ambitions of nervous studio executives. Van Peebles has described the tortuous process of bringing his father Melvin's script to the screen: 'We went to the studios five years ago. One studio said they'd be happy to do the Panther story but it had to be from a "mainstream" perspective . . . We just put the script back on the shelf.'[9]

The same could not be said of Alan Parker's *Mississippi Burning* or Norman Jewison's *The Hurricane*, films which courted controversy for doing exactly what *Panther* refused to: privileging a 'mainstream' (that is, white) perspective and marginalising the role played by black characters in the struggle for social and political justice and equality. In the case of the former, the fact that Parker's film chose to focus on the role played by two fictional white FBI agents in hunting down the killer of three Civil Rights workers in Mississippi in 1964 and largely overlook the efforts of black people themselves in orchestrating protest and resistance was defended by the director on the grounds that a different film could not have been made within Hollywood during the 1980s.[10] *The Hurricane*, meanwhile, is a film about the struggle to overturn a problematic conviction imposed on boxer Rubin Carter (Denzel Washington) for a multiple homicide. The eventual success of the case is portrayed as being largely the product of hard work carried out by three well-meaning Canadians. The efforts of Carter himself and the black activists and lawyers who had represented him before their intervention are overlooked. The point here is not to dispute the veracity or importance of the Canadians' involvement in Carter's story, nor to claim that the FBI in *Mississippi Burning* did nothing to unearth the killer of the three Civil Rights workers. Rather, it is to suggest that a reductive focus on the issue of historical accuracy obscures the far more significant question of 'why?': why did *The Hurricane*'s makers choose to elect the Canadians as Carter's ultimate saviours? Or, for that matter, why did they decide to underplay Carter's propensity for aggression and violence and emphasise only his saintly resolve? Or, in the case of *Mississippi Burning*, why did its makers elect not to focus on the struggles of black characters themselves? Answers to such questions can, of course, only be speculative but we suspect that they can be found in the ascendancy of a particular type of liberal multicultural politics. The fact that *The Hurricane*'s ending looks forward to a harmonious, race-less utopia speaks implicitly about the yearnings of a particular strain of 1990s liberalism and entirely ignores the deep racial divisions and distrust which continue to characterise post-Civil Rights race relations.

What of the distinction, then, between Hollywood and black independent cinema and this rather problematic linkage between historical authenticity and artistic autonomy? It may well be fair to argue that black 'independent' filmmakers might have more freedom to decide what goes into and what is excluded from their films but to conclude that their films will necessarily tell a version of black history that is more 'authentic' or closer to the 'truth' overlooks two important factors; first of all, as Tommy L. Lott puts it, 'the fact that . . . there is less disparity between the film practices of black independents and black filmmaking in Hollywood',[11] and second, that history itself is not some kind of fixed reality waiting to be unearthed by an appropriately deferential scholar. What follows in this chapter emerges from these twin premises: that we need to find new ways of talking about film and history that acknowledge its contested, contingent status, and that we need to find new ways of talking about Hollywood and independent films that challenge the assumption that the former will always be contaminated by repressive ideologies and the latter will necessarily be wholly free of the corrupting influences of ideologies of nationalism, capitalism and patriarchy. The internal logic of *Panther* and *The Hurricane* might indicate the appropriateness of such a distinction but not, as we will see, *Malcolm X* (1992) and *Ali* (2001). What we need not do is congratulate films and filmmakers for occupying a place outside of ideology per se but rather to explore the complex ways in which *all* films simultaneously collude with and contest dominant ideologies and discursive formations. The question of how these overlapping and conflicting processes affect the construction of history in the retelling of the lives of Malcolm X and Muhammad Ali constitutes a key line of inquiry in this chapter.

LOOKING FOR MALCOLM: SPIKE LEE'S *MALCOLM X*

Almost forty years after his death and twelve years after the release of Spike Lee's landmark film, Malcolm X remains something of an enigma; a poor black street hustler turned devout Muslim who continued to speak on behalf of the impoverished community of his upbringing; a firebrand Black Nationalist who came to temper his racial separatist message in the wake of a second Islamic conversion; a once fervent supporter and then a fierce enemy of the Nation of Islam; an avowedly patriarchal figure who nonetheless was utterly dependent on the support and love of his wife, Betty Shabazz; a heterosexual icon who may or may not have shared homosexual experiences in his youth. Nomenclature alludes to this mutability: from Malcolm Little he became Detroit Red, Malcolm X and finally El-Hajj Malik El-Shabazz. It is hardly a surprise, then, that he should represent different things to different people: to Ossie Davis, 'our black shining prince . . . our living black manhood'; to Spike Lee, 'a role model . . . [and] strong black man who was telling white people point blank what the truth is'; to James Baldwin, 'My father, my brother'; to Guru, a proto-rapper who 'stood for righteousness and not compromising your beliefs . . . [and who] had a programme: let's get organised and fight back'; and to Angela Davis, a revolutionary figure whose premature death foreclosed on the possibility that he might have ended up identifying with 'the global feminist movement today'.[12] As Marlon Riggs famously put it: 'Malcolm constitutes the quintessential unfinished text. He is a text that, we as Black people, can finish, that we can write the ending for, that we can give closure to – or reopen – depending on our own psychic and social needs.'[13]

One of the pivotal moment's of Lee's *Malcolm X* comes an hour or so into the film during the incarceration sequence where Malcolm (Denzel Washington) is being exposed to the teachings of Elijah Muhammad and the Nation of Islam for the first time. Outside in the prison yard, Baines (Albert Hall) asks Malcolm to tell him who he is. The film cuts between close-ups of their expressions: Baines' insistent and unyielding, Malcolm's awkward and confused. 'Alright, I ain't Malcolm Little, I ain't Red and I damn sure ain't Satan,' he says, after a long pause. 'That's right,' Baines tells him, 'so who are you?' Malcolm frowns and says, 'I don't know.'

It is a powerful moment not simply because it prefigures Malcolm's initial conversion but rather because it draws attention to the problematic nature of subjectivity; that is to say, the uncertainty which ensues once assumptions about our own subjectivity have been exposed as a socially engineered lie. It is here, perhaps, that the film comes closest to realising what Terrence Rafferty describes as the radical potential of *The Autobiography of Malcolm X* (1965), the as-told-to book written by Alex Haley during and after Malcolm's split with the Nation of Islam. 'By all accounts,' he argues, 'it was a period of intense spiritual confusion for him, and that not fully acknowledged uncertainty may be the source of the book's most mysterious, paradoxical quality . . . The Malcolm of the autobiography is an extraordinary literary creation – a strong, boldly drawn character whose meaning is fluid, ungraspable, fathomless.'[14] In other words, it is here that the film comes closest to inscribing Malcolm X not as a strong, boldly drawn character, for he is drawn this way throughout, but rather as someone 'ungraspable and fathomless', a complex and multifaceted figure – 'the quintessential unfinished text' – able to simultaneously speak to and on behalf of diverse, even conflicting, constituencies. To put it another way, what this scene alludes to is the moment where 'difference', to use Stuart Hall's definition, is no longer 'radical and unbridgeable' but rather becomes 'provisional, conditional and conjectural'[15] and where all that once seemed solid, to paraphrase Marx, suddenly melts into air.

It is perhaps inevitable but also something of a disappointment, therefore, that much of the rest of the film draws back from such radical uncertainty and relentlessly sets out to fix Malcolm X within a linear narrative of conversion that nevertheless privileges one particular stage or moment of this process: what Joe Wood describes as the realisation of a coherent black ideology whereby Malcolm becomes 'a face for the Nation's "true" Black spirit and nationalist ideology'.[16] This fixing of Malcolm X, iconising him within a particular role and function, is inevitable because of the didactic nature of the project, a matter that will be addressed later in this section and that, in turn, informs the form and content of the film itself. But it is disappointing not simply because the film ends up serving the kind of rigid nationalism that, as Wood puts it, Malcolm had rejected before the autobiography was finished or even because in doing so it closes itself off to the more fluid and 'available' Malcolm: an identity or an ideology that 'is not particularly Islamic, not particularly nationalist, not particularly humanist'.[17] Rather, the disappointment arises from the fact that the film itself, as a result of this need to frame

Malcolm X's life as a linear, teleological progression towards an already demarcated and unambiguous end-point, seems quite conventional, or at least appears that way once the inflammatory nature of its subject has been duly noted. In the end, we're left to wonder how different Lee's *Malcolm X* is from other Hollywood biopics like *Cry Freedom* or *Gandhi* or, in structural terms, from the archetypal American rags-to-riches story whereby the protagonist's ultimate 'success' depends upon his or her ordered progression from one fixed point to another.

To dismiss Lee's film as standard Hollywood fare is of course unfair, given the struggle that he faced in bringing such uncompromising subject material to the big screen. Facing hostile Warner Brothers executives who wanted to cut the film's projected running time and budget on the one hand, and indignant black radicals like Amiri Baraka on the other (Baraka is alleged to have said, 'we will not allow Malcolm X's life be trashed to make middle class negroes sleep easier'[18]), the simple fact that Lee made what Ellis Cashmore described as 'the most ambitious movie by a black director about a black subject'[19] speaks for itself. As Rafferty argues, 'the most conspicuous achievement of [the film] is its very existence – or, rather, its existence in the form of a three-hour-and-twenty-minute epic biography distributed and (largely) financed by a major Hollywood studio'.[20] Still, the question of whether *Malcolm X* constitutes a Hollywood film or a 'black' film, and whether these two categories are mutually exclusive, *does* require our attention.

For Guerrero, the emergence of 'a liberated black cinema'[21] in the 1980s necessarily marked a decisive split with the Hollywood mainstream, so that while filmmakers like Spike Lee continued to receive financing from the major studios, their cultural and political engagement with radical, more complex ways of framing blackness (and whiteness) marked them as distinctive from the majority of Hollywood's filmmakers and the system's repressive racial ideologies. Guerrero's distinction is not merely a cultural and political one but rather an economic one, too, and he uses the controversy surrounding *Malcolm X's* budget and running time to draw attention to ultimately unsuccessful attempts on the part of Warner Brothers executives to censor the film through economic subterfuge: 'Obliquely, the enduring issues of industry control and co-option of black expression were subtly focused, via budget limitations, on the film's running time.'[22] For Guerrero, then, Lee's *Malcolm X* stands at the vanguard of a 'liberated black cinema' not merely because of its representational practices and attendant racial politics but also because, in order to make the film according to his own agenda and 'vision', Lee was compelled to elicit the financial support of a group of black investors including Bill Cosby, Magic Johnson, Tracy Chapman, Oprah Winfrey, Michael Jordan, Janet Jackson and Prince as a way of 'persuading' the studio to kick in the remainder of what was required to complete the film. At a press conference at the Schomburg Center for Research in Black History and Culture in Harlem, Lee pointed out that such irregular financing arrangements necessarily affected the question of ownership: 'These are black folks with some money who came to the rescue of the movie. As a result, the film will be my version. Not the bond company's version, not Warner Brothers'.'[23]

Still, the idea that Lee's 'vision' is somehow unmediated and therefore pure, or at least free of the corrupting influence of Hollywood, remains problematic, as is the assumption that *Malcolm X*, as part of a liberated black cinema, necessarily has a radical aesthetic and political orientation. Such assessments, as Lott points out, depend on 'too rigid a dichotomy between independent and studio films' since there is less of a difference than might be expected between the output of black filmmakers working within Hollywood and those who are independent. About *Malcolm X*, Lott argues, 'there can be no doubt that Lee's representation of Malcolm X was influenced by the box-office demand for his film to have 'cross-over' appeal'.[24] Lott's point is an instructive one but since he also fails to explain either how the film may have been influenced by 'box-office demands' or, for that matter, what precisely he means by the term 'cross-over' appeal, we will have to develop this line of inquiry ourselves. Here, once again, the question of intent and effect – for whom the film was made and for what purpose(s) – is central, and rather than arguing that Lee's representation of Malcolm X's life is either free from or indelibly tainted by studio interference, our point is that the form and content of the film is beholden, first and foremost, to its status as history lesson. That is to say, what is disappointing about the film – its linearity, its formal conventionality and its iconising of Malcolm X – is a result of its function as a particular *kind* of instructive, uplifting educational experience.

So what kind of experience is Lee offering and who are his intended audience? Lee himself seems clear: 'I want people, especially black people, to come out of the theatre motivated, spiritually uplifted, and have a deeper understanding of the man Malcolm X and try to apply what he was trying to do to their present life today.'[25] So while Lee's claim that 'we just told the truth'[26] urges us to read the film as authentic, the more pressing issue is how Lee's stated ambitions – to motivate, uplift and educate particularly black people – have influenced what kind of biopic he has made and how he has made it. It is here that Lee finds himself caught in an impossible double-bind. If, as Paul Gilroy argues, the majority of those younger black males wearing Malcolm X baseball hats and T-shirts (presumably one of Lee's key target audiences) 'look back at Malcolm X from a position of absolute stunning ignorance of the politics that spawned him',[27] then the film's message and the way in which this message is expressed need to be appropriately direct. Certainly, as Guerrero acknowledges, 'the black audience, at least as consumers, is just as enlightened and – problematically – colonised as the white'.[28] Which is perhaps why *Malcolm X*, a Spike Lee *and* a Warner Brothers film, contains none of the stylistic flourishes and formal inventiveness that characterised Lee's earlier *School Daze* (1988) and *Do the Right Thing* (1989). But in playing things straight and re-presenting Malcolm X's life using a conventional linear narrative structure and a formal style typical of mainstream American cinema, one is left to wonder whether, apart from its subject and its cast and crew, there is anything distinctive or rather distinctively African-American about Lee's film.

It would be churlish and quite wrong to suggest that *Malcolm X* fails to either motivate, uplift or educate its audiences, but not perhaps to question what kind of education audiences might expect to receive from the film: do its instructive or didactic qualities allow for sufficient space for us as an audience to *think* for ourselves? This last point is posed as a question rather than a statement because we are all too aware that audiences, black and white, read films, or scenes in films, often in very different ways. Such a claim requires closer consideration. The film has a fixed trajectory charting its subject's transformation from pusher, via a prison-based conversion, to prophet. Essentially, then, it is about his journey from a life of crime and degradation to spiritual and political enlightenment, and thus serves as exemplar and cautionary tale, the best and worst of what could happen to black males living in mid-twentieth-century America. The film's vibrant opening scenes, embodied by colourful zoot suits, jitterbug music, dance-hall vibes and restless, swirling camerawork, signify a dynamic black culture nonetheless built upon the shiftless, transient foundations of racial accommodation and subservience. Malcolm's subsequent descent into crime is nihilistic rather than political, an understandable if not inevitable consequence of poverty, alienation and the kind of self-loathing implied by the painful practice of 'conking' – applying a mixture of corrosive lye, Vaseline and eggs to one's hair as a way of straightening it and thus making it look 'white', as Malcolm says to Shorty (Spike Lee) early in the film. A drug-addled Malcolm's personal nadir is reached during a later 'conking' scene, where the pain of the process barely registers; that is, until a lack of water means he cannot rinse out the mixture in time and is forced to use toilet water. In the same moment, police officers storm the apartment and arrest him and Shorty for armed burglary, for which they receive a minimum sentence of ten years.

For Manthia Diawara, the spiritual conversion in the second part of the film and the autobiography is overshadowed by the story about Malcolm's criminal exploits in the first part, and one of the reasons that Malcolm X is so popular particularly with young black males is that they 'see a mirror image of their own lives in the experiences of Detroit Red'.[29] Perhaps so, but despite the riotous colour and energy of the film's early scenes, Lee's primary ambitions as a filmmaker and an educator are realised only during and after Malcolm's conversion in prison and by his subsequent political and spiritual awakening during his rise through the ranks of the Nation of Islam. It is only in the context of the second half of the film that Lee's stated insistence that school children, especially black ones, should skip classes to go and see the movie makes sense, because what Lee wants to show them is a particular Malcolm X; dedicated, fiery, politically astute, attuned to the concerns and difficulties associated with being a black man in a racist, white-controlled world. In other words, these scenes are instructive because what we see is Malcolm talking the talk and walking the walk; that is, we see him effectively confronting figures of white authority (for example, the priest in prison played by Christopher Plummer, or the police officers who assault and lock up Brother Johnson), gently chiding 'unenlightened' black 'brothers and sisters' (Archie, Laura, Shorty) whose actions end up reaffirming the supremacy of the 'white devils' and engaging constructively with like-minded Nation of Islam activists and with enthusiastic, receptive black audiences who want to hear his Black Nationalist rhetoric.

Buoyed by Denzel Washington's quietly mesmeric performance as Malcolm, the scenes where he addresses audiences in the temple or on the streets of Harlem are the most effective of the film, and it is difficult not to be energised by the political fervor and righteous anger of Denzel-as-Malcolm, but the didactic seriousness of the project could also be its shortcoming. Lee's often heavy-handed sign-posting ends up instructing us how to watch and interpret particular scenes, rather than allowing us to draw our own conclusions, and thus the history lesson that we receive is an old-fashioned one where historical 'truths' are presented in pre-packaged, bite-size chunks for audiences to consume without questioning their veracity or asking whether alternative readings might be possible. In one of the film's most intriguing scenes, when Malcolm is first introduced to Betty Shabazz (Angela Bassett), he warns her that he is 'a hard man when it comes to women', at which point the scene cuts to Elijah Muhammad telling Malcolm that 'too many of our women have the devil in them'. The scene continues in a similar fashion, cutting between Malcolm lecturing Betty about women's roles and Elijah Muhammad doing likewise with Malcolm, and one is left to wonder whether Lee is implying that Malcolm is speaking his own mind or being influenced, even indoctrinated, by his mentor's teachings, particularly given subsequent revelations about Elijah Muhammad's secret womanising. The idea that Lee might be poking fun at Malcolm's unswerving and ultimately misguided loyalty to his master is an intriguing one, particularly given the film's willingness to develop Betty as a more significant character than she appears in the autobiography. But such scenes are the exception; more common are those in which the sign-posting is clear. The authenticity of Malcolm's conversion to the Nation of Islam, for example, is underlined by the appearance in his cell of a glowing apparition of Elijah Muhammad; or the 'correct' way to behave during one of Malcolm's speeches is indicated by a close-up panning shot along a row of black Americans listening to him as if for the first time.

It is worth noting how similar these scenes are, in style if not content, to the one discussed Chapter 2 from Spielberg's *Amistad*, where Yamba, one of the African slaves, as Kolker explains, '"naturally" discovers the rightness of the Christ story by looking at pictures'.[30] In other words, while *Malcolm X* is a conversion narrative with a diametrically opposed trajectory – one in which a mediating white consciousness is usurped by a black one – methodologically it achieves this ambition, in a manner reminiscent of Spielberg, by convincing us, through the type of scene that we described above, of the inherent 'rightness' of its project. Just in case the message is unclear, additional emphasis is supplied by overdetermined moments in which the usually 'invisible' ideological thrust of the film is fleetingly made all too visible. Thus, the formal logic (if not the politics) of the opening scene in Spielberg's *Saving Private Ryan*, where the American flag is showcased and celebrated, is reproduced by the opening scene of Malcolm X, where shots of the flag are intercut with the grim videotaped footage of four LAPD officers beating Rodney King and then with images of the flag burning and eventually mutating into the shape of an 'X'. The political messages of both films are very different, of course, but the formal technique used to convey these messages is markedly similar. For Guerrero, *Malcolm* X is the antithesis of a Hollywood film precisely because, via this kind of juxtaposition, Lee is effectively refusing to 'let Hollywood off the political hook by preventing his depiction of the meaning of Malcolm's life from being safely regulated, a la mainstream cinema, to the ghetto of the historical past.'[31] But one could just as well argue that Lee's heavy-handed way of doing so is eerily reminiscent of Spielberg, as is Lee's flair for marketing his film and merchandising its products. Swap a *Jurassic Park* mug for an 'X' embossed cap. Certainly in so far as the opening scene, as Terrence Rafferty says of the film as a whole, gives you the answer right away, it also 'deprives you of the deepest meaning of Malcolm's adventure: the pleasure and satisfaction of thinking the problem through in your own way, in your own time'.[32]

A brief look back at the film's production history sheds further light on the ways in which Lee took control of the material in order to develop it in a particular direction and for a particular end. The 'official' story goes something like this. The autobiography was originally optioned by producer Martin Worth in 1968. Worth then commissioned James Baldwin to write a screenplay. 'Baldwin wrote the first script [but] . . . was really drinking heavily and eventually another writer named Arnold Perl helped him finish it.'[33] The problems were numerous but among the more pressing ones was the question of 'how to juggle [and blend] the many personas of [Malcolm X] . . . into a coherent story.'[34] Interest waned and was revived, eventually in the 1980s, by Norman Jewison, who was then usurped by Lee as project coordinator on the grounds that 'he . . . or any white man wasn't qualified to do this film'.[35] Lee, then, revived the Baldwin–Perl script and took to rewriting it himself, mostly focusing on the final third. '[It] had to be changed,' Worth argued, 'because we now know more about his death than when Jimmy was writing. It wasn't the best part.'[36] Then Baldwin's sister, Gloria, demanded that Baldwin's name be removed from the credits. 'Don't ask me why,' Lee is said to have remarked.[37]

So much for the 'official' story. Critics of the film tell a different story. Terrence Rafferty and Jonathan Rosenbaum, for example, have gone back to Baldwin's original screenplay, One Day, When I Was Lost, and have noted the numerous, significant ways in which it was altered by Lee, in part, to 'soft-pedal' Malcolm X's criminal activities:

> Lee's Malcolm does a little numbers running, snorts cocaine once, and participates in an antically staged burglary. The auto-biography and Baldwin's script show him selling dope, steering rich men to whip-wielding black whores, and becoming crazed and violent from constant coke use.[38]

Rosenbaum, meanwhile, draws upon Baldwin's The Devil Finds Work and describes Baldwin's frustrations over the ways in which Perl, in the late 1960s, was simultaneously 'translating' his script and 'siphoning' all the meaning out of it. In Baldwin's version, for example, the short scene where Malcolm first meets West Indian Archie plays out in a subtle, understated manner; as Rosenbaum explains, 'Malcolm orders a drink from the bar, Archie and his friends, sitting at a nearby table, make jokes about his naivete while obliquely acknowledging that they used to be like him themselves; then after Malcolm stumbles over Archie's shoes, Archie invites him to sit down at his table.'[39] This scene was altered by Perl so that Malcolm's stumble prefigured a tense showdown; 'a shoot-out from High Noon with everybody in the bar taking bets as to who will draw first'.[40] In Lee's revised version of the script, this scene is 'refined' once again. Rosenbaum explains:

> A big bully collides with Malcolm at the bar, derides him for not saying "Excuse me," calls him an "old country nigger," knocks off his hat, and adds, "What's you gonna do? Run home to your mama?" Malcolm grabs a whiskey bottle, smashes it to smither-eens against the man's jaw and says, "Don't you ever in your life say anything against my mama." Then he retrieves his hat from

a pretty and adoring woman at the bar, tenderly caresses her cheek, and orders a whiskey. Archie at his table in the next room is so awed by all this that he quickly contrives to buy Malcolm's drink.[41]

What should concern us here is not the question of which version is the more historically accurate – after all, this event is not referred to at all in the autobiography – but rather the excessively melodramatic way in which Lee has rewritten Baldwin's scene. As Rosenbaum comments: 'It's a quintessential Oscar-moment – complete with macho childishness, violent excess, and a comfortable irreverence to history, setting and character.'[42] In fact, both Rosenbaum's and Rafferty's objections relate to a certain tendency in Lee's film towards formal and thematic simplification. While Baldwin's scene, for example, refuses to explain why Archie ends up buying Malcolm a drink – is it because he identifies with him or sees potential in him or wants to exploit him? – Lee's scene, unfortunately, makes his motivation all too clear.

Ultimately, then, the film's didactic intent, its reverential treatment of its subject and its fixing of Malcolm X within a particular, narrowly defined frame, as Black Nationalist icon, are all linked. If the richness of Haley's as-told-to autobiography is realised through the complex inter-relationship of voices in the text – between an older, wiser Malcolm both admonishing a younger, more foolhardy Malcolm for his criminal exploits and staying silent about his later rejection of the narrowness of the Nation's racial ideology – this richness, or rather the ambiguity that results from this richness, is deliberately left out of Lee's film. One imagines that Lee wants to tell his audiences something rather than show them or allow them to think for themselves. As a limited exercise, therefore, Lee's film is effective and one cannot deny that, in the context of Gilroy's remark, it serves an important didactic role as 'starting point in an attempt to recover its own history'.[43] But what of its failings? Lee's concerns as a biographer extend only as far as fixing Malcolm as iconic Black Nationalist hero. Thus, the messiness of his break with the Nation of Islam and the nature of his second conversion are somewhat fudged. Later in the film, following a pilgrimage to Mecca, when Malcolm tells gathered reporters that he wants to develop 'a more flexible approach to solving problems', it is as though Lee's Malcolm is unable to do so because he is so firmly rooted in his former incarnation. Malcolm goes about his business but we see little or nothing of his internal conflicts, nothing of the soul-searching and intellectual 'groping' that accompanies his first conversion. In the film's tumultuous and effectively realised climax, Malcolm is gunned down in Harlem's Audubon ballroom by a posse of Black Muslim assassins but the history lesson, by this point, is effectively over. All that remains is for Nelson Mandela, addressing a classroom of Soweto children, to read a passage from one of Malcolm's most famous speeches, and for different people, different children, to claim his legacy by saying, into the camera, 'I'm Malcolm X.' It is as though Spike Lee, retrospectively, wants to acknowledge Riggs' claim that Malcolm 'constitutes the quintessential unfinished text' only *after* he has fixed and located that text within a particular social, cultural and historical context. One might add that, in the light of Stuart Hall's remarks about the 'end of the innocent notion of the essential black subject'[44] and the related assertion of multiple black identities across increasingly fluid boundaries of race, ethnicity, class, gender and sexuality, the film's unwillingness to acknowledge the heterogeneous nature of blackness and black identities across time and space is something of a missed opportunity.

ALI: THE GREATEST

The last ten years have produced a surfeit of materials, literary and visual, dedicated to Muhammad Ali and his achievements both inside and outside the ring. Prior to Michael Mann's *Ali* (2001), Leon Gast's documentary *When We Were Kings* (1996), focused on the 'Rumble in the Jungle' and related events in Zaire in 1974, was the sole cinematic intervention, but it was accompanied by a deluge of published material. There might have been a seven-year gap between the publication of Thomas Hauser's biography, *Muhammad Ali: His Life and Times* (1991) and David Remnick's *King of the World: Muhammad Ali and the Rise of an American Hero* (1998; UK edition, 2000), but almost immediately thereafter followed Robert Cassidy's *Muhammad Ali: The Greatest of All Time* (1999), Gerald Early's edited volume, *A Muhammad Ali Reader* (1999), Mike Marqusee's *Redemption Song: Muhammad Ali and the Spirit of the Sixties* (2000), and finally Howard Bingham and Max Wallace's *Muhammad Ali's Greatest Fight: Cassius Clay vs. the United States of America* (2000).

With so much having been written about Ali, and given the comprehensive nature of Gast's acclaimed documentary, we might ask why anyone would bother to make a feature film about Muhammad Ali? After all, if not enough was known about Malcolm X and the social and political context that spawned him, then almost too much is known about Ali: about his 1960 Olympic gold medal (which he either simply lost or, more dramatically, threw into a river in his hometown, Louisville, in protest at the continuing racism directed at black Americans[45]); about his first championship fight against Sonny Liston in 1964, a fight that he allegedly stood no chance of winning; about his conversion to the Nation of Islam and name-change from Cassius Clay to Muhammad Ali; about his 'radical' political and religious views; about his refusal to be drafted into the US Army in 1967 to fight in Vietnam ('no Viet Cong ever called me nigger') and subsequent decisions taken to indict him and strip him of his titles and right to fight; about his triumphant, against-all-odds comeback culminating in the 'Rumble in the Jungle' where he defeated George Foreman in Zaire in 1974; about his slow, painful march towards retirement and ignominious defeats suffered at the hands of Larry Holmes and Trevor Berbick in the early 1980s; and latterly about his hard-fought battle against the debilitating effects of Parkinson's disease.

'There exists a great fear today,' Gerald Early writes in his introduction *to A Muhammad Ali Reader*, 'or at least there should, that Muhammad Ali, no stranger to the most intense sort of adulation reserved for certain psychopaths, mystics and movie stars, may become absolutely overesteemed by the society in which he lives.'[46] Early's point is not that Muhammad Ali is somehow unworthy of such esteem or indeed critical attention – far from it, in fact – but rather that for a new generation his ascent to the realm of 'Great American Martyr' or 'our new Martin Luther King' or even 'our new Lincoln' actually puts him 'in danger not only of having his considerable significance misunderstood, but also, ironically, of being diminished as a public figure and a black man of some illustrious complexity'.[47] It was the Atlanta Olympics in 1996 that sealed Ali's social and political rehabilitation and the moment when he lit the Olympic flame somehow completed his transformation into a 'safe' all-American hero and precipitated the books, journal and magazine articles, television specials and films that followed. The fact that a retired heavyweight champion who was at one stage of his career feared and even detested by the majority of white Americans for his 'extreme' religious and political views should now, as a result of illness, forgetfulness, guilt or nostalgia, find himself drowning in a 'bathos of sainthood' says much about our contemporary cultural and political moment:

> [W]hen it comes to . . . Muhammad Ali these days, the public, especially whites, nearly weep. James Baldwin was right: that a certain insistence that the black male figure represent his humanity through the narrow prism of social protest elicits this contradiction, a blurring of the very effects that his social protest was meant to induce. This white response . . . may be a reflection of racism, but it seems more profoundly to be a sign of some organic confusion . . . at that very heart of our perception of ourselves.[48]

Such observations are, by no means, aimed at the recent publications about Ali, of which Remnick's *King of the World* and Marqusee's *Redemption Song* are particularly instructive about the social and political context for Ali's rise to predominance in the 1960s, but rather are made as a starting point for thinking about Michael Mann's *Ali*: an expensive, high-profile film made by an illustrious white director for a major Hollywood studio. That is to say, the question of whether *Ali* merely reiterates what we already know, or ends up celebrating Muhammad Ali's public achievements in order to further the kind of agenda alluded to by Baldwin and then Early, constitutes the critical platform upon which our interrogation of the film will be constructed. But in this respect, as we shall see, the assumption behind the question of why make a feature film about Muhammad Ali is reversed: a film may be needed precisely in order to rescue Ali from universal sainthood and insert him back, as a complex and contradictory figure, into the social and historical context that made him. For Ed Guerrero, such a task is far beyond the reach of the Hollywood mainstream, with its attendant ideology of racial domination and difference that constructs black people as Other and subordinate.[49] As we established earlier, however, there is sometimes less 'rigid a dichotomy between studio and independent films'[50] than Guerrero's claim suggests. More than any other film made in recent years, Mann's *Ali* suggests that it may be possible for a white filmmaker (or a black one, for that matter) to make a critically engaged and formally innovative historical film about a black subject within Hollywood that both 'visions' and 'revises'[51] its historical moment in such a way that throws its all-too-familiar subject into sharp, all-too-unfamiliar relief.

The film opens with a bravura fifteen-minute sequence that inter-cuts Ali's training and pre-fight preparation for his first bout with Sonny Liston in February 1964 with subjective flashbacks of a younger Ali and with momentary glimpses of his relationships with significant figures in his life: with Angelo Dundee (Ron Silver), his trainer, and Drew 'Bundini' Brown (Jamie Foxx), his cornerman and motivator; with his father (Giancarlo Esposito) and Howard Cosell (John Voight), the ABC sports commentator; and with Malcolm X (Mario Van Peebles). As the singer Sam Cooke (David Elliot) stands in front of an exuberant crowd gathered in Miami's Harlem Square Club and belts out an ecstatic medley of soul anthems, culminating in the wonderful 'Bring it on Home to Me', we see a tracksuited Ali (Will Smith) running along a deserted Miami street at dusk. The scene cuts back to Cooke and then to Ali as a police car cruises past him, one of the white officers asking him, 'What are you running from, son?' 'Remember,' Dundee later reminisced, 'this was Miami, pre-civil rights . . . the Deep South, and Muhammad would run across the MacArthur Causeway to the gym and I got calls from the police saying that there's some tall skinny black guy running – and did I know anything about it.'[52]

More cutting takes us between Cooke and Ali, now training inside the gym, hitting the speed bag as the camera hones in on his blank face, and then closer, on just his eyes. Interwoven into the sequence are flashbacks to moments from Ali's younger life: watching his father painting religious murals featuring a white, blue-eyed Jesus inside a black Baptist church, and then, as a twelve-year-old, following his mother through a crowded Louisville bus to the 'coloreds' section at the back and looking, with horror, at the mutilated face of Emmett Till, a fourteen-year-old black boy attacked by a lynch mob because he winked at a white girl in Alabama, on the front of someone else's newspaper. As the speed bag gives way to the skipping rope, the scene cuts to a close-up of Malcolm X addressing an audience gath-ered inside a Miami mosque. Ali, we see, is seated at the back of the mosque, listening intently; the nod that Malcolm X gives Ali when he notices him attests to their closeness. Cooke's 'Bring it on Home to Me' draws near to its climax and the scene cuts again, this time to the pre-fight weigh-in, as Ali and his partner-in-crime Bundini taunt

Liston, calling him a 'big ugly bear', and side-step questions from gathered journalists about Ali's religious beliefs. Finally, we see Ali, Bundini and Dundee in the back of a car, silent, heading to the Miami Convention Center, and then a white-robed Ali walking purposefully along a dark hallway surrounded by his entourage heading for the ring and the fight which would launch his boxing legend.

It is a wonderful opening because it establishes some of the key figures, public and private, and relationships that will shape the trajectory of the film and Ali's life. And it does so in a subtle, carefully nuanced way that withholds any definitive meaning. What, after all, are we meant to make of Ali's blank stare and eyes as he trains? And how are we supposed to read or make sense of the various links and connections that the sequence alludes to? That is, how does the murder of Emmett Till or the casual racism of the police officers relate to his friendship with Malcolm X? How does Bundini's reference to his own 'voodoo powers' relate to the 'performative' aspect of Ali's behaviour in the pre-fight weigh-in with Liston? And how does the introspective 'private' Ali of the training gym make sense of the extrovert 'public' Ali of the boxing ring and media circus, and vice versa?

It is such an impressive opening, too, because it also establishes a number of important tropes that the film will build upon and develop. First and most important is the implicit realisation that the film will not, as Lee's *Malcolm X* sought to do, attempt to explain Ali to us in such a way as to rule out perhaps contradictory ways of understanding him. In the same way that history itself remains tantalisingly available but ultimately unfathomable, so the idea that we can ever truly know someone else, in Mann's film, is presented as both desirable: we do want to know who Ali is; and yet unattainable: we can watch Ali box, watch him interact with others, watch the way he reacts, we can listen to what he says but it doesn't necessarily mean that we will '*know*' him, at least in any definitive way. Certainly there is no attempt to *tell* us who Ali is. Gazing into his blank eyes while he punches the speed bag, the interpretative burden is passed from filmmaker to viewer: the question 'Who is he?' soon becomes 'How can we begin to make sense of his behaviour, of what he does and says?' Make sense, that is, of the contemplative 'private' Ali and of the loquacious, brash 'public' Ali? Of the Ali who is so adept at determining his own identity and yet dependent upon the insight and wisdom of others (Dundee, Malcolm X, and the like)? Of the curiously passive, even apolitical, figure who walks away from the subtly racist enquiries of the police and the media, and yet whose mentor, Malcolm X, instructs a crowd that includes Ali: 'Anyone who puts his hand on you? Do your best to see he doesn't put his hand on anybody else again'? At once the opening sequence stitches Ali into a narrative of black social history, that is to say it asks us to understand him in the context of Civil Rights and Black Nationalism, of the Nation of Islam, of soul music and social protest, and of Sam Cooke and Malcolm X, without ever suggesting that the cumulative effects of such influences will necessarily produce someone whose identity is determined from the outside in, rather than vice versa; determined according to a social and/or political formula. Lee's *Malcolm X* attempts to do likewise, to place Malcolm X into a narrative of black social history, but in a clumsy, heavy-handed way that lacks all of the deftness and subtlety of Mann's nuanced treatment of Ali.

Even as the plaintive cries of Cooke's medley are fading in our ears, the first Ali–Liston fight is upon us and what the film immediately asks us is to reflect on the unexpected nature of Ali's eventual victory and the two fighters' differences, as boxers and public figures. After all, with hindsight Ali's 'greatness' is unquestionable but few, if any, of the fight commentators at the time believed Ali would beat Liston. For starters, Ali's lithe, graceful, committed boxing style, in contrast to Liston's, which was pugnacious and bullish, signifies this difference. Linking the aesthetics of boxing and politics, Sean O'Hagen argues that Ali 'invented a form of radical black politics that, like his boxing style, was new, stylish and proud'.[53] Moreover, if Liston (Michael Bent), whose reaction in the film to Ali's taunts ('I'm gonna fuck you up') reveal his jailhouse upbringing and the fact that he 'accepted the role as bad Negro as his lot after he discovered that he would not be permitted any other',[54] then what of Ali? It might be tempting, with hindsight, to cast him as the correlative 'good Negro' or, rather, to insert him into what Michele Wallace has called 'the binary opposition of "negative" versus "positive" images' or the 'positive/negative image cultural formula' which has 'too often set the limits of Afro-American cultural criticism'.[55] In other words, if Liston is characterised as the 'bad Negro' then such a model requires that someone else assume the opposite mantle. Remnick's point is that such a fighter *did* exist: Floyd Patterson, who doesn't feature in Mann's film, 'cast himself as the Good Negro . . . a deferential champion of civil rights, integration, and Christian decency'.[56] Ali, though, refused to be slotted into this kind of model ('I had to prove you could be a new kind of black man,'[57] he told Remnick) and Mann's film effectively represents this diffidence, this ambivalence, this unwillingness on Ali's part to be assigned to either one category or the other, and, as a corollary, his desire to both determine his own sense of self and allow himself to be determined by others.

Mann's multi-faceted Ali remains available to us and yet somehow elusive as well. In public spaces and setting, we see the figure we expect to see, the playful, adroit, confident, cocksure Ali, a black Walt Whitman celebrating himself and his boxing achievements in hyperbolic rhyming couplets, and throwing down the political gauntlet to the white establishment and status quo. For Paul Arthur, Ali's 'theatricalized self-presentations' foster 'analogies to African-American musical styles as well as to the broader culture of spontaneous, improvised enactment'[58] and, developing this line of argument, Gerald Early argues that Ali's ability to mimic and yet subvert black *and* white archetypes, what Henry Louis Gates might describe as his ability to 'signif(y)'[59] blackness, marks him out as a figure of some complexity:

> [Ali] rarely said anything without a certain kind of mocking quality, and his rage, like his incessant bragging and egoism, was often that of the adolescent. Ali offered the public the contradictory pleasure of having to take him seriously while not having to take him seriously ... In retrospect, Ali struck intense chords of ambiguity as a black public figure. .. Was Ali a star boxer or, through his genius, the utter undermining of boxing? Was he a militant or the complete unmasking of militancy?[60]

Mann's film refuses to answer such a question, opting instead to assign Ali to more than one category; that is to say, assign him as both militant and the unmasking of militancy. So, during an off-air conversation with Howard Cosell discussing the draft issue, Ali privately admits to being bemused by the controversy, telling him 'I'm no Stokely Carmichael, H. Rap Brown', and has to be told by Cosell about his transcendent political impact. At the same time, though, Ali seems only too aware of the issues at stake and later in the film, following a decision by the Illinois Boxing Commission to uphold a ban on him fighting, he tells gathered reporters, 'You want me to go somewhere for you but you won't even stand up for me in America, for my rights and beliefs.' For Paul Arthur, Mann's decision to show-case the former Ali at the expense of the latter – to confect a 'strangely depoliticized Ali at whose ardent and often exemplary involvement in the social activism of his time he barely hints'– is a 'telling evasion' that 'takes a toll on the film's dramatic fabric'[61] but one might ask, as a retort, how else Mann could have done justice to the kind of ambiguity to which Early alludes? Certainly such a task is not made easier by having to work within the confines of the Hollywood system. For the surest way of extinguishing ambiguity is to do what Hollywood films have always tended to do: make it clear, by pursuing deliberate formal and thematic strategies, why people do what they do, act in the way they do. That is to say, Hollywood films tend to *tell* us, in no uncertain terms, what we should be thinking and why. It is rare, and even quite remarkable, therefore, that Mann's representation of Ali manages to capture something of Early's argument and it is worthwhile pausing to think about how else it manages to do so.

In public, then, Will Smith's Ali seems all too aware of the role he wants to play and the person he wants to be. Shortly after the Liston fight, during a trip to Harlem with Malcolm X, he is asked by a white journalist whether he intends to be 'a people's champion like Joe Louis'. His response does not appear to be carefully planned but it intuitively summarises his ambitions. 'I'm going to be a people's champion,' he tells the reporter. 'But I don't have to be the way you want me to be. I'm going to be what I want.' It's a line that he reiterates later in the film, once he has refused to be drafted by the US Army. 'I ain't gonna be what anybody else wants me to be,' he tells Howard Bingham (Jeffrey Wright), his photographer friend. 'I'm not afraid to be what I want. And think how I want.' In this moment, as with his earlier and now much publicised retort to a reporter asking him about the draft ('I ain't got no quarrel with them Viet Cong/No Viet Cong ever called me nigger'), it is almost as though he stumbles, intuitively rather than accidentally, across what will become his defining moment. This reading of the film is instructive because it positions Ali both as acutely aware of his identity and of the white power structures that he is defining himself in opposition to – as Sean O'Hagen puts it, as someone 'who authored his own identity' and who 'invented his own character as he went along'[62] – and yet also as someone whose self-knowledge is always, at best, provisional and contingent.

Whereas Leon Gast's documentary *When We Were Kings* either shows us footage of Ali in Zaire performing in public, baiting

Foreman or talking up his own chances of victory, or features various talking heads (for example, Spike Lee, Norman Mailer, George Plimpton) *telling* us about Ali, Mann's film is able to convey this sense of provisionality by effectively *withholding* from us clear-cut reasons that explain why the 'private' Ali acts or thinks as he does. So when Ali terminates his relationship with Sonja (Jada Pinkett-Smith), his first wife, because she refuses to act in a manner appropriate to her role as a Muslim, his certainty that he has done the right thing evaporates. And when he picks up an item of her clothing and smells it with a degree of what seems to be a sexually-tinged longing, we are left to ponder his previously stated assertion that 'I always know when I know.' In other words, *does* he know? Certainly his claim, to her, that 'how I am says something' is informed by an acute awareness of his own iconic status but whether he understands his feelings for her, and his sexual needs, quite so well is left unclear. Similarly, his rejection of Malcolm X, for disagreeing with Elijah Muhammad, is characterised by a related and contradictory sense of certainty and doubt. For there is real warmth underpinning his initial greeting of Malcolm X when they meet in Ghana, but, having established this warmth, the film shows us Ali saying to Malcolm X two or three times, as if in a trance, 'You shouldn't have argued with the honorable Elijah Muhammad' and breaking off their relationship without another thought. To claim that it is almost as if Elijah Muhammad himself is standing behind Ali telling him what to say and what to think is unfair, because it suggests that Ali has somehow been brainwashed, or that his decision for turning his back on Malcolm X is not based on a deeply-held faith, but what it does indicate is the difficulties faced by us and Mann in trying to understand or know him, or to situate him as a fixed figure within a clear-cut historical narrative. For one thing, given that Malcolm came to view Elijah Muhammad as a manipulator, we are left to reflect upon whose opinion is the 'right' one, particularly in the context of Ali's own shabby treatment by the Nation of Islam later in the film.

Gast, for one, is adamant that Ali's relationship with the Nation of Islam was an exploitative one: 'He was manipulated by the leaders of the Nation of Islam and he turned over vast sums of money to them. Herbert Mohammad, the son of . . . Elijah, was his manager. Ali would never say no to [him] about a fight because he was the son of his spiritual leader.'[63] Mann's film, though, tackles this relationship in a far more nuanced manner, one that shows the influence that the

Nation had over Ali's boxing career and hints at the exploitative nature of this relationship without ever suggesting that Ali was either innocent or naive in his dealings with the Nation. During Ali's wilderness years, following the draft controversy, he drifts apart from Herbert and is eventually suspended from the Nation, but once, through his own actions, he has earned himself a shot at Joe Frazier's world title, Herbert informs him that the suspension has been lifted. Ali's initial response, 'You saying I can be a Muslim again?', is underscored by a mixture of incredulity and suppressed anger, and when Herbert tells him that he can make them 'five million dollars for Frazier', Ali asks: 'Are we talking management, talking money or talking religion?' His follow-up statement, 'I love the Nation . . . but it don't own me' indicates to Herbert, at least, that their relationship is at an end. But, having established his independence, to the consternation of Belinda (Nona Gaye), his second wife, Ali then calls on Herbert to 'make the Frazier deal'. At once we as viewers are compelled to ask: why? Why would Ali, having been banished from the Nation at his lowest point, allow them back into his inner circle? The previous scene has ruled out naivete or innocence, for he seems very much aware of the shoddy way he has been treated and is keen to establish his own autonomy and agency as a boxer and public figure.

Ali's forgiveness of Herbert and the Nation also extends to Bundini, his old cornerman, whose descent into drug addiction and alcoholism culminates in the selling of one of Ali's championship belts for five hundred dollars to a barber in Harlem. If Herbert calls upon Ali to become the model of a devout Muslim, then Bundini embodies an alternative path or route for Ali to follow: that of existential freedom. 'God don't care about you!' he tells Ali. 'Don't care about me! In all of everything, we mean nothing . . . And that's good 'cause that's why we're free. Free is real and realness is a motherfucker.' For Bundini, then, freedom is unconditional and dependent upon an ability to somehow transcend one's social, political and religious moorings, but Mann's film refuses to sanction this version of freedom, or represent Ali's life in teleological terms as progress from religious devotion, and thus exploitation, to existential freedom. During the film's closing scenes, focusing on Ali's fight with Foreman in Zaire, it is hard to escape the contradictory feeling that Ali has both utterly transcended his particular historical moment and become 'a modern existential hero'[64] and yet is trapped as a figure in his own social, political and historical moment: as a

Muslim, a black man, and even as an American. In other words, that his freedom is conditional on his context. And this perhaps is the greatest achievement of both Ali himself and the film: that both he and it are ultimately able to resist the relentless modern tendency towards categorisation and the fixing of meaning; to suppress or eliminate, in the words of Zygmunt Bauman, 'everything that could not or would not be precisely defined'.[65] Because just as Ali, as Remnick puts it, 'would not fit any stereotypes [or] follow any set standard of behavior',[66] so Mann's film courts ambivalence to the point whereby Ali, unlike Lee's Malcolm X (who we know too well), is set free from his celebrants as well as his detractors. As we have seen elsewhere in this book, this kind of achievement is rare for a mainstream Hollywood film but is proof that it is possible to make a thoughtful, subtle, ambivalent historical film within the system that is 'successful' precisely because it requires a response from us as viewers which is critical and intellectual as much as it is emotional.

NOTES

1 Manthia Diawara, 'Black American Cinema: The New Realism', in Diawara, ed., *Black American Cinema* (London and New York: Routledge, 1993), p. 4.

2 Ed Guerrero, *Framing Blackness: The African-American Image in Film* (Philadelphia: Temple University Press, 1993), p. 201.

3 Diawara, *Black American Cinema*, p. 4.

4 Guerrero, *Framing Blackness*, p. 2.

5 Ed Guerrero, 'Be Black and Buy', in Jim Hillier, ed., *American Independent Cinema* (London: BFI, 2001), p. 69.

6 Ibid., p. 73.

7 See Tom Dawson, 'Year of the Panther', *What's On in London*, 8 November 1995, p. 6.

8 Ibid.

9 Mario Van Peebles in David Gritten, 'The Panthers: Heroes or Villains', *The Independent on Sunday*, 4 June 1995, p. 27.

10 Janet Hoberman makes the point in *The Village Voice* that the film's press kit included a detailed statement from Parker in which he claimed that *Mississippi Burning* 'would never have been made if the heroes weren't white' (26 December 1988, p. 83).

11 Tommy L. Lott, 'Hollywood and independent black cinema', in Steve Neale and Murray Smith, eds., *Contemporary Hollywood Cinema* (London and New York: Routledge, 1998), p. 211.

12 For Ozzie Davis and James Baldwin references, see Hilton Als, 'Picture

This', *The Village Voice*, 10 November 1992, p. 39; for Guru reference, see Sean O'Hagen, 'Hero Worship', in *The Sunday Times* magazine, 11 October 1992, p. 73; for Angela Y. Davis reference, see Angela Y. Davis, 'Mediations on the Legacy of Malcolm X', in Joe Wood, ed., *Malcolm X: In Our Image* (New York: St Martin's Press, 1992), p. 37.

13 Marlon Riggs, 'Sexuality, Television, and Death: A Black Gay Dialogue on Malcolm X' (with Ron Simmons), in Wood, *Malcolm X: In Our Image*, p. 141.

14 Terrence Rafferty, 'Still Life', *The New Yorker*, 30 November 1992, p. 160.

15 Stuart Hall, 'New Ethnicities', in Bill Ashcroft et al., eds, *The Post-Colonial Reader* (London and New York: Routledge, 1995), p. 226.

16 See Joe Wood, 'Malcolm X and the New Blackness, in Wood, *Malcolm X: In Our Image*, p. 13.

17 Ibid.

18 Amiri Baraka in an 'open' letter quoted in John Cassidy, 'Malcolm X film pits black against black in Hollywood', *The Sunday Times*, 11 August 1991, p. 17.

19 Ellis Cashmore, 'Every brother ain't a brother', *New Statesman and Society*, 20 November 1992, p. 31.

20 Rafferty, 'Still Life', p. 160.

21 Guerrero, *Framing Blackness*, p. 4.

22 Ibid., p. 199.

23 Ibid., p. 201.

24 Lott, 'Hollywood and independent black cinema', p. 211, 220.

25 Spike Lee quoted in David Sillitoe, 'Putting the X factor on celluloid', *The Guardian*, 16 January 1993, p. 27.

26 Spike Lee quoted in Sean O'Hagen, 'Hero Worship', *The Sunday Times Magazine*, 11 October 1992, p. 73.

27 Paul Gilroy quoted in O'Hagen, 'Hero Worship', p. 72.

28 Guerrero, *American Independent Cinema*, p. 69.

29 Manthia Diawara quoted in Lott, 'Hollywood and independent black cinema', p. 219.

30 Kolker, *A Cinema of Loneliness*, p. 317.

31 Guerrero, *Framing Blackness*, p. 1.

32 Rafferty, 'Still Life', p. 162.

33 Spike Lee quoted in Jonathan Rosenbaum, *Movies as Politics* (Berkeley, CA and London: University of California Press, 1997), p. 148.

34 Alex McGregor, 'Harlem Knights', *Time Out*, 26 February 1992, p. 17.

35 Spike Lee quoted in ibid.

36 Martin Worth quoted in ibid.

37 Spike Lee quoted in Hilton Als, 'Picture This', p. 43.

38 Rafferty, 'Still Life', p. 162.

39 Rosenbaum, *Movies as Politics*, p. 149.

40 Ibid.
41 Ibid.
42 Ibid., pp. 149–50.
43 Ibid., p. 72.
44 Hall, 'New Ethnicities', pp. 224–5.
45 In his book, *King of the World: Muhammad Ali and the Rise of an American Hero* (London: Picador, 2000), David Remnick notes that whereas *The Greatest*, an 'autobiography' (ghostwritten by Richard Durham) claimed that Cassius Clay (as he then was) threw his gold medal into the Ohio river, this was a fabrication and in fact he simply lost it (see pp. 89–90).
46 Gerald Early, 'Introduction: Tales of the Wonderboy', in Early, ed., *A Muhammad Ali Reader* (London: Yellow Jersey Press, 1999), p. vii.
47 Ibid.
48 Ibid.
49 See Guerrero, *Framing Blackness*, p. 2.
50 Lott, 'Hollywood and independent black cinema', p. 211.
51 For distinction between these terms, see Robert Rosenstone in Robert Brent Toplin, ed., *Oliver Stone's USA: Film, History and Controversy* (Lawrence, KS: University Press of Kansas, 2000), pp. 34–5.
52 Remnick, *King of the World*, p. 115.
53 Sean O'Hagen, 'The One and Only King', *The Observer*, review, 16 December 2001, p. 1.
54 Remnick, *King of the World*, p. xiii.
55 Michele Wallace, *Invisibility Blues: From Pop to Theory* (London and New York: Verso, 1990), p. 1.
56 Remnick, *King of the World*, p. xiii.
57 Ibid.
58 Paul Arthur, 'Lord of the Ring', *Film Comment*, December 2001, p. 32.
59 Gates uses the term 'signif(y)' to refer to the subversive processes by which Euro-American languages, voices, forms, and so on, are appropriated and ironically re-worked through the lens of African-American oral or vernacular culture. For a fuller explanation, see Henry Louis Gates, *The Signifying Monkey: A Theory of Afro-American Literary Criticism* (New York: Oxford University Press, 1988).
60 Early, *A Muhammad Ali Reader*, pp. xiii–xiv.
61 Arthur, 'Lord of the Ring', p. 33.
62 O'Hagen, 'The One and Only King', p. 1.
63 Leon Gast in Kevin Toolis, 'The King and I', *The Guardian*, Weekend, 3 May 1997, p. 34.
64 O'Hagen, 'The One and Only King', p. 1.
65 Zygmunt Bauman, *Modernity and Ambivalence* (Cambridge: Polity, 1991), p. 8.
66 Remnick, *King of the World*, p. 207.

Chapter 7

HOLLYWOOD'S POST-COLD WAR HISTORY: THE 'RIGHTEOUSNESS' OF AMERICAN INTERVENTIONISM

In the giddy optimism that accompanied the fall of the Berlin Wall in 1989 and the attendant disintegration of the Cold War, commentators, particularly from the American right, looked to a rose-tinted future in which the United States bestrode the world as its only superpower.[1] Most famously, or notoriously, Francis Fukuyama, then the Deputy Director of the State Department's Policy Planning Staff, argued that the 'triumph of the West' was evidenced 'in the total exhaustion of viable systematic alternatives to Western liberalism' and that the end of the Cold War marked 'the end point of mankind's ideological evolution and the universalization of Western liberal democracy as the ultimate form of human government'.[2] Fukuyama's predictions about the hegemonic global dominance of a form of Western liberal democracy coded as American may have come to pass, but the implicit global stability and order that he might have expected to result from such a situation has not materialised. Rather, the post-Cold War era has done much to justify the fears of other commentators who believed the world would be a far more dangerous and unpredictable place following the end of the ideological struggle between East and West. International stability, far from being assured by the unfettered spread of liberal democracy and market capitalism, has been threatened by the forces of ethnic nationalism, religious fundamentalism, international terrorism and other emergent threats to security. US President George Bush argued that a 'New World Order . . . characterized by the rule of law rather than the resort to force' would emerge from the Cold War,[3] but instead the era has witnessed the proliferation of conflict and instability, and the emergence of what Gore Vidal has described as 'perpetual war for perpetual peace'.[4] As such, 'the end point of mankind's ideological evolution' has actually

187

witnessed the outbreak of violent, internecine conflict in places such as the former Yugoslavia, Somalia, Rwanda and Chechnya, and other major wars and large-scale acts of violence such as the Gulf War, the 11 September 2001 attacks, and the subsequent US-led 'War on Terror', and the invasions of Afghanistan and Iraq.

Inevitably, Hollywood has not been shy about wading into this contemporary historical terrain with a steady stream of films in recent years that focused upon the role of the US in various unilateral and multilateral military interventions (for example, *Courage Under Fire*, *Three Kings*, *Behind Enemy Lines* and *Black Hawk Down*). The question for us is how these films work to produce or unsettle particular established or consensual views about the inherent 'righteousness' of US military actions and, as a result, how they undermine or reinforce traditional understandings of the benign meta-narrative of American history, even as this is being rearticulated in our contemporary cultural and political moment. Hollywood cinema, as Mark Lacy argues, has become 'a space where "commonsense" ideas about global politics and history are (re)produced and where stories about what is acceptable behaviour from states and individuals are naturalised and legitimated'.[5] Our concern is to determine how films about US-led post-Cold War military interventions engage with questions concerning the politics of intervention, the nature of historical 'truth', the American relationship with the rest of the world, the changing face of armed conflict, the ethics of warfare, and the role of technology in shaping the nature of military engagement. As with other films we have addressed in this book, we are also interested in how effectively these films function as pedagogically useful historical texts. That is, not as films which 'tell the truth' about history, but rather interrogate particular episodes and events of the near-past in a provocative, challenging and, above all, open-ended fashion.

In this chapter, we focus on two films in particular: *Three Kings* (1999) and *Black Hawk Down* (2001). Although both address US military interventions in the post-Cold War era, they constitute two very different types of film that illustrate the different approaches to representing American history currently being pursued by the major Hollywood film studios. *Three Kings* was produced by Warner Brothers, part of one of the largest media conglomerates in the United States, and stars instantly recognisable big-name actors (George Clooney, Mark Wahlberg), yet in many ways it resembles an independent film. Screenwriter and director David O. Russell claims he was given essentially free reign in making what he calls an 'independent-minded studio picture'.[6] The film is set in the immediate aftermath of the Gulf War in 1991 and revolves around the fictional story of four American soldiers who drive into Iraq to find a haul of gold bullion seized from Kuwait by Saddam Hussein's army. The film adheres to many of the conventions of the combat genre and in some respects is an updated version of the World War II caper *Kelly's Heroes* (1970), in which Clint Eastwood leads a group of American GIs behind enemy lines to steal some Nazi gold. That said, Russell's film is much more than a tired generic re-tread. *Three Kings* raises questions about the legitimacy and morality of the US mission in the Gulf, depicting the moral anxieties faced by some US soldiers as a result of the fighting and alluding to the confused, contradictory impulses governing the US intervention. It constitutes a thought-provoking, critical engagement with the history of the Gulf War that embraces ambiguity and controversy. *Black Hawk Down*, on the other hand, is more representative of a troublingly common approach to historical movie-making in contemporary Hollywood that largely eschews critical inquiry in favour of spectacle and visceral emotion. Produced by Jerry Bruckheimer (the man behind *Pearl Harbor* and a host of other big budget action movies) and directed by British director Ridley Scott, best known for the science fiction classics *Alien* and *Bladerunner*, and more recently the historical epic *Gladiator*, *Black Hawk Down* focuses on the events of 3 October 1993, when eighteen US Army Rangers were killed and seventy-seven wounded during a failed attempt to arrest Somali 'warlord' Mohammed Farah Aideed. Despite the director's claims that 'I went into it wanting to be as accurate as possible',[7] *Black Hawk Down* gives us little historical context for the events it portrays, nor does it engage with the political ramifications of the death and destruction we observe. Rather, as Lisle and Pepper contend, it is a visual and sonic assault on the senses that leaves little room for contemplation and seems to act largely as an extended advertisement for a 'horizontally integrated entertainment portfolio from Sony' that included computer games, books, videos, DVDs and other merchandising.[8] As such, it joins a growing library of films (including *The Patriot*, *Saving Private Ryan* and *Pearl Harbor* analysed earlier) that celebrate history, and in particular war and violence, as 'consumable spectacle'[9] and therefore become, in Lacy's words, 'another way of attempting to order human society that has become part of corporate culture'.[10]

VISIONING, REVISIONING AND CONTESTING HISTORY

Throughout this book we have praised films that challenge their viewers to *think* about how the historical events they portray can be interpreted. Historical films should not be an open and shut assertion of a viewpoint but raise questions, not all of which they answer. They should give context to their subject matter, engage with historical questions and encourage debate about the meaning of the past. Ultimately, we agree with Robert Rosenstone, that good historical films will not only 'vision' the past but also 'contest' and 'revision' traditional historical wisdoms. One of the central questions that we have addressed in this book is whether or to what extent Hollywood's post-Cold War historical films either service and legitimise or question and challenge an affirmative and quite traditional version of nation and national identity. Do they adhere to or subvert the dominant 'official' view of American history or what we have called the benign meta-narrative of the United States?

Three Kings immediately disturbs the conventional view of the Gulf War. Operation Desert Storm was likened to a video game played out nightly on CNN, with segment after segment of technical, detached footage from the cockpits of US bomber jets showing laser-guided bombs and missiles dropping from great heights to wipe out inanimate targets such as buildings or tanks. Everything looked precise, clinical and essentially without human cost. The media coverage and official portrayal of the Gulf War was so detached from the bloody, destructive reality of modern warfare that Jean Baudrillard famously contended that 'The Gulf War did not take place'.[11] The emphasis on the 'surgical' nature of the coalition's attacks obscured the thousands of Iraqis killed and wounded in the nightly bombardments of towns and cities, and the constant pummelling of the Republican Guard. To a great degree, the Gulf War saw the institutionalisation of what has been somewhat mockingly termed 'a doctrine of immaculate coercion' whereby the US relies heavily on air power to prosecute its foreign-policy objectives in order to avoid suffering high casualty rates during conflicts. As Lacy points out, this 'virtual war' functions to 'distance not only pilots and strategists from the reality of death that they are orchestrating, but also to distance the citizenry back home from the suffering that is being carried out under the banner of virtuous war'.[12] In the opening scene of *Three Kings*, however, we are instantly confronted with the all-too-real human consequences of the

Gulf War. US Army Reserve Sergeant Troy Barlow (Mark Wahlberg) shoots dead an Iraqi soldier. He does so from some distance but runs straight over to the body of the young man, who we see close up, struggling for his last breaths as he chokes blood through a fatal neck wound. Troy's colleague Conrad Vig (Spike Jonze) shares the audience's shock at seeing death at close quarters: 'Dag, I didn't think I'd get to see anybody shot in this war.'

Throughout the film, Russell refuses to let us forget or shy away from the specific, individualised, horrific consequences of war. When Conrad complains that, aside from Troy's killing of the single Iraqi, he 'didn't get to see any action', the seasoned Major Archie Gates (George Clooney) gathers his cohort around the mangled, burned corpses of Iraqi soldiers. The camera cuts up close across the charred remains, forcing the viewer to contemplate, as Gates does, the horror of being on the receiving end of Operation Desert Storm: 'We dropped a lot of bombs out here; also buried a lot of guys alive.' The image recalls those from the so-called 'Highway of Death', where some 1,500 Iraqi vehicles were bombed and strafed as they retreated from Kuwait at the end of the war.[13]Although the media gave a good deal of coverage to the destruction on the road to Basra, the images shown were largely devoid of bodies. Philip Taylor argues that: 'Questions of taste and decency intervened . . . to remove the true horror from the footage.'[14] Dead Iraqis were notably absent from most media coverage during the war, particularly in the US, thus reinforcing the impression that this was a clinical war where targets were carefully chosen to minimise human suffering. The print media also contributed to this perception. *Life* magazine, for example, ran a special weekly series entitled 'In Time of War' yet its pictorial rendering of the war featured only one genuine photograph of a dead Iraqi.[15] The most striking and shocking image of the war featured a close-up of the charred corpse of an Iraqi soldier still sitting upright in a burned out vehicle. The photograph appeared in Britain in *The Observer* but was not published in the US until well after the war.[16] In *Three Kings*, however, Russell has no qualms about showing in graphic detail the lethal effects of the Gulf War on its participants, both Iraqi and American. As George Clooney observes, Russell's 'idea was to resensitise people to violence. He didn't just want to show the effect of the gunshot, he wanted to show it literally.'[17] This intention is most fully realised through the use of an internal shot of a cross-section of a human gut to show the damage a bullet does once it has entered the body. Russell claimed that he had used a real cadaver to achieve the ultimate degree of realism. Although he later admitted the organs were created by his special effects crew, the scenes using the internal shot are nonetheless groundbreaking and take the impact and verisimilitude of combat filmmaking to a new level. They also puncture the received wisdom that the Gulf War's destruction was somehow clinical and bloodless, and disrupt the practice of much war cinema of distancing audiences from the consequences of the violence.

Black Hawk Down also has no qualms about showing the devastating impact that modern weaponry and warfare can have on the human body. In keeping with other recent war films that feature epic battle scenes (for example, *Saving Private Ryan*, *The Thin Red Line*), we are not spared images of bullets and explosions ripping flesh apart and severing limbs. In fact, the whole film acts as a memorial to the eighteen Americans who were killed during the 'firefight' on the streets of Mogadishu and whose names are reverentially shown on screen as the film ends. The credits also mention that as many as a thousand Somalis perished but this fact and the questions of morality and proportionality it raises are notably absent in the film itself. As Lynn Barber observes, *Black Hawk Down* is 'startlingly free of any moral context or concern'.[18] From the perspective of Mogadishu's civilian residents, the 'firefight' was actually a massacre perpetrated by the Americans. Not only is this viewpoint given no airing in the film, but the deaths of the Somalis are also treated in an entirely different manner from those of the Americans. When Somalis are shot, on the whole, they simply fall to the ground in a style not unlike the sanitised comic-book violence of TV shows like *The A-Team*. Unlike the Americans, they do not writhe in agony or cry out for their mothers while they grasp for obliterated limbs. They are dispatched as though they were little more than ants being crushed underfoot. During the battle, we see a few child soldiers, one armed Somali boy is spared by US soldiers, and we see two armed Somali women, one of whom is killed. There is little indication, however, that around thirty per cent of the Somali casualties during the operation were women and children, and many of the men were unarmed civilians.[19] Although one or two warnings are issued to the Americans to 'Be careful what you shoot at because people do live there' and 'hostiles advancing . . . be advised, women and children among them', on the whole we do not get a clear picture of the impact the fighting is having on the civilian population. As Yusuf Hassan of the BBC in Somalia argues, the residents of Mogadishu are 'not characterised' because the film is 'not telling their story'. Yet, as he relates, the nature of the resistance to the American incursion was far more complicated than the film allows: 'I know that the people who were fighting were not only supporters of Aideed. Many of them were just people in the neighbourhood who got caught up in this fire and were trying to defend their homes, as they thought they were under attack.'[20]

By contrast, the costs to the civilian population in Iraq of weeks of US-led bombing are made plain in *Three Kings* and the Iraqis themselves are given a voice. When Troy is captured and tortured by Iraqi soldiers, his interrogator speaks eloquently and passionately about the personal consequences of the coalition's air campaign: 'You bombed my family, do you know that? You blow up my home, my whole street. My wife is crushed by big fucking block of concrete. She lose her legs. . . My son. My son was killed in his bed. He is one years old. He is sleeping with his doll when the bomb come.' To drive home the point, we are shown the concrete ceiling falling on the boy, destroying his cot. But Russell does not simply show us the consequences for Iraqi civilians. He attempts through Troy to establish empathy with the human suffering in Iraq for both supporters and opponents of Saddam Hussein. Troy tries to make a connection with his torturer by telling him he is also a father. But the Iraqi asks: 'Can you think how it would feel inside your heart if I bombed your daughter?' We are then confronted by an image of Troy's young wife cradling her baby in her arms as her kitchen wall explodes in flames behind her and envelopes them both. The image is deliberately manipulative but challenges the audience to consider how they would react if, rather than merely seeing and reading about the cynically named 'collateral damage' in some detached, distant land, the consequence of US military interventions abroad was the daily threat of death and destruction being rained down on their own suburban havens, killing and maiming their own family members. The thought of it, as Troy concludes, is 'worse than death'. In this scene, therefore, Russell refuses to allow audience complacency over the consequences of American military action, encourages the film's viewers to question the meaning of the Gulf War and the rationale for the US-led intervention, and unsettles any clear-cut division between 'them' and 'us'.

The confusion and chaos of war are also central elements in *Black*

Hawk Down. But where *Three Kings* constructs its scenes of violence in ways that raise questions about the consequences of war, the nature of modern fighting, and the political justifications for and ramifications of all the death and destruction being represented on the screen, *Black Hawk Down* embraces the visceral spectacle of the fighting in ways that close off any critical engagement with the larger consequences of what is happening. Scott's is the latest in a growing number of 'blockbuster' films we have identified in this book (*The Patriot*, *Saving Private Ryan*, *Pearl Harbor*) that privilege sensation and spectacle over critical historical inquiry. As Lisle and Pepper argue, *Black Hawk Down* combines rapid editing and long shots, emphasises sound effects over dialogue, features an ensemble cast of character actors rather than a single renowned star, and bookends the film with brief, on-screen captions that establish the 'true facts' of the conflict in Somalia in order to, in Robert Kolker's words, 'reduce the spectator to an accepting position' – a position that asks, if not requires, one to sacrifice critical thinking and succumb to the easy attractions of spectacular action sequences and sensational stimuli.[21]

There is widespread agreement among critics of *Black Hawk Down* that, 'whatever its politics, the film is aesthetically brilliant'.[22] Despite his scathing denouncement of the film's content, for example, George Monbiot admits it is 'gripping, intense and beautifully shot'.[23] Lynn Barber says of Ridley Scott that 'Everyone agrees that the look of his films is consistently superb' and fellow director Alan Parker has called him 'the greatest visual artist living today'.[24] The result is that it is difficult for viewers to detach themselves from the 'two-and-a-quarter hours of directionless, cacophonous, kick-ass operatics' that is *Black Hawk Down*.[25] Much of the film is simply a barrage of carefully crafted imagery. As Lisle and Pepper point out, 'the long battle scenes in the middle of the film contain no dialogue at all, and are simply spectacular cinematic amalgamations of gun fire, running soldiers, evocative music, swarming Somalis and crashing helicopters'.[26] Scott argues that he was simply trying to give the audience some sense of what it must have been like to fight on the streets of Mogadishu: 'That's my job, it's what I do . . . putting the audience actually in the scene, in the delivery and on the receiving end. Making them feel it.'[27] In this sense, perhaps, Scott could be credited with following one of Rosenstone's requirements for a historical film by giving us a 'vision' of the past, but, as we have argued elsewhere in this book when analysing the films of Steven Spielberg, for example, to make audiences feel is not the same as allowing them to think. Scott's film trades on the visceral excitement and horror of battle without engaging with what it might mean, or what its consequences are, and without allowing his audience sufficient distance or space with which to contemplate such questions. Spectacle alone may enable action films in particular to perform well at the international box office but such a preference tends to obstruct the ability of a film to convey anything useful about the particularity of historical events.

Three Kings allows far more room for audience contemplation and raises serious questions about why the Gulf War was fought and what it actually achieved. Most of its characters are bewildered by the circumstances around them. In the opening two minutes of the film, the audience is not only unsettled by the sight of the dying Iraqi soldier but is also confronted with ambiguity and confusion over how they should interpret what they are watching. When the Iraqi dies, Conrad is intrigued and another of the American soldiers moves excitedly to take a photograph of the corpse. But Troy turns away with a pained expression, seemingly wiping tears from his eyes. Since he was brandishing both a gun and a white flag, was the Iraqi surrendering or posing a threat? Troy is himself unsure what he is authorised to do when he first spots the Iraqi soldier. The war has just ended, we have been told by a caption, but Troy is clearly unsure about the current rules of engagement. 'Are we shooting people or what?' he asks a colleague, who replies with the same question. Troy then responds: 'I don't know the answer, that's what I'm trying to work out.' Already it is apparent we will not be getting a clear, straightforward view of the Gulf War or indeed be told what to think about it. The opening-credits sequence that follows hints at where the film might be heading, but then immediately obfuscates the initial interpretation. US troops are shown in jubilation, celebrating the 'liberation of Kuwait'. They give a rousing chant of 'God Bless the USA' but the patriotic anthem then transmogrifies into the thumping anti-authority rap of Public Enemy. Where other American combat films telegraph how an audience should feel with their rousing, emotional, orchestrated soundtracks – Barber's 'Adagio for Strings' in *Platoon*, John Williams' score for *Saving Private Ryan*, Hans Zimmer's score for *Pearl Harbor* – the sonic eclecticism of *Three Kings* reflects the ambiguity of much of the film's content. Elsewhere in the film we get an incongruous mismatch of sounds: Bach followed by the Beach Boys; Chicago followed by an Iraqi group.

A wide variety of music is also used in *Black Hawk Down*. In a homage to *Apocalypse Now* and a host of other Vietnam films, US helicopters fly into action to Jimi Hendrix's 'Voodoo Chile'. Elsewhere we are 'treated to a multi-ethnic mix'[28] including Elvis Presley, Senegalese singer Baaba Maal, American grunge rockers Alice In Chains, Algerian artist Rachid Taha, English punk rocker Joe Strummer, and the score of Bruckheimer favourite Hans Zimmer. But unlike *Three Kings*, where the eclecticism of the music disrupts and challenges our reading of the film, in *Black Hawk Down* the soundtrack assigns clear meaning to characters and situations. As George Monbiot has noted, the appearances of the Somalis 'are accompanied by sinister Arab techno, while the US forces are trailed by violins, oboes and vocals inspired by Enya'.[29]

Just as the soundtrack never settles in *Three Kings*, neither does our view of the war. Confusion and chaos seems to reign and all that is clear is that the many different players in this conflict all have different motivations and objectives. The film makes little attempt, however, to engage with the complexities of the situation in Iraq. The film is set in the south, so there is barely a mention of the Kurds, but neither do we gain any real sense of the other divisions within Iraq, not least those between Shias and Sunnis. We simply know that there are pro-Saddam Iraqis and anti-Saddam Iraqis – loyalists and 'rebels', the latter being 'good' and the former on the whole 'bad'. That being said, the portrayals of the Iraqis do move beyond cartoonish caricatures. There is some complexity and ambiguity, for instance, in the portrayal of those who remain loyal to Saddam. It is clear during Troy's rescue that it is fear of Saddam's retribution rather than faith in his leadership that keeps many Iraqi soldiers loyal. Troy's torturer also argues that 'I only join Saddam Hussein army to make good living for my family. Good house. Now, I can't get out.'

These limited attempts in *Three Kings* to explore the complex loyalties and identities of the Iraqis are far more accomplished, however, than the almost complete lack of engagement with the motivations of the Somalis in *Black Hawk Down*. Although Mark Bowden's book, which provided the source material for the film, gives context to the actions of the Somalis and details the complicated clan divisions and rivalries that made the conflict so difficult to resolve, the film virtually ignores them.[30] The Somalis are portrayed as a marauding mass of ill-disciplined, bloodthirsty madmen, reviving stereotypical images of 'Africans' as savages to be either controlled or exterminated. We know nothing about why they might regard the

Americans with such fury and hatred. They are simply 'faceless and expendable'.[31] Even the few Somalis we see who are obviously civilians are given no opportunity to voice their opinions about the UN intervention and the actions of the Americans, or indeed what they might make of the conflict between their own people. As Elvis Mitchell concluded in the *New York Times*: 'the lack of characterization converts the Somalis into a pack of snarling dark-skinned beasts, gleefully pulling the Americans from their downed aircraft and stripping them. Intended or not, it reeks of glumly staged racism.'[32] The situation is made worse, according to Yusuf Hassan, because 'despite the fact that there are tens of thousands of Somali refugees in the United States, Britain and elsewhere, who could in principle have been used as extras in the film, the black actors used are of other nationalities who are physically totally different'.[33] Scott admits he had trouble finding appropriate extras: 'I had a lot come up from Congo. I couldn't get as many Somalians [sic] as I wanted.'[34] The racial politics of the film is not, however, only problematic in its depiction of the Somalis. There is only one black soldier among the Americans, who are otherwise all white. This depiction is perhaps unavoidable since the Army Rangers and Delta Force troops the film focuses upon were in reality dominated by white soldiers. This racial imbalance among the US Army's elite forces was of concern to various Congressional and Pentagon reports on racial discrimination in the armed services that were published during the mid-1990s.[35] *Black Hawk Down* makes no attempts, however, to address the obvious question of whether deploying a predominantly white force, most likely with racists among their ranks, was the most appropriate way to confront a volatile situation in the Horn of Africa.

Three Kings rejects the simple racism of *Black Hawk Down* and challenges the trend in several other post-Cold War films of portraying Arabs as the uncomplicated, post-communist representation of evil in the world (see, for example, *True Lies* (1994) starring Arnold Schwarzenegger). The possibility that the Gulf War had racist undertones reflective of unresolved racial tensions in the US itself is raised in two brief scenes in particular. Near the film's beginning, Chief Elgin (Ice Cube) chastises Conrad for his racist language: 'I don't wanna hear dune-coon or sand-nigger from him or anybody else.' In a brilliant observation on 1990s political correctness and the accommodationist tendency of post-Cold War rhetoric we have addressed elsewhere, Russell has Troy respond: 'Look, the point is, Conrad, that

towel-head and camel-jockey are perfectly good substitutes.'
'Exactly,' agrees Chief. American racism is again brought into sharp
relief later in the film when Gates, Troy and Chief burst into a bunker
where Iraqi soldiers are watching the soon-to-become-infamous
video of LA police officers beating Rodney King. Chief looks on curiously, not fully comprehending what he is seeing but perhaps all too
familiar with such scenes. Neither this nor the earlier incident is
taken any further by Russell. They are simply left there for the audience to contemplate and draw their own conclusions. During Troy's
torture scene, however, American racism is unambiguously condemned and the parallel bluntly drawn between what continues to
happen in the US and what is happening in Iraq. To Troy's obvious
surprise, his torturer's opening salvo in the interrogation is to accuse
American society of forcing the pop singer Michael Jackson to try to
make himself white. The Iraqi concludes forcefully that 'Your sick
fucking country make the black man hate himself just like you hate
the Arab and the children that you bomb over here.'

Although he inflicts intense pain and discomfort upon Troy, the
torturer is not portrayed as a sadistic, evil 'other', like numerous
enemy torturers in earlier films such as *Rambo: First Blood Part II* and
The Deer Hunter, and indeed in *Black Hawk Down*. He is, in fact, hand-
some and clean-cut, speaks calmly despite his obvious anger, and
thereby succeeds in giving a human face to the enemy. His thoughtful arguments make the audience consider the motivations of Iraqis
who serve in the armed forces and how they might equate with
Americans doing their own president's bidding. We are even given
some indication of how the United States may have created its own
nemesis in Iraq, since the torturer admits that he was trained by
American Special Forces during the war with Iran, learning not only
his English but also how to use weapons and how to inflict torture.
Troy, at least, seems convinced by his torturer's essential humanity,
choosing to spare his life after Gates rescues Troy and shoots the torturer in the leg.

The torture scene is one of many in *Three Kings* where characters
enter into debates about what the causes and objectives of the Gulf
War might actually be. Troy is convinced by the official rhetoric that
the US has fought the war to 'save the Kuwaiti people', reverse Iraq's
illegal invasion of another sovereign state and 'stabilise the region'.
These were three of President Bush's stated objectives in the war. He
believed that Saddam Hussein had 'become the epitome of evil . . . in

his treatment of the Kuwaiti people', that the invasion must be reversed because 'every use of force unchecked is an invitation to further aggression', and that Iraqi expansion would destabilise the area by making Jordan, Yemen and other Arab states 'probably tilt toward' Iraq.[36] In *Three Kings*, Troy's torturer makes it abundantly clear what he believes is the main reason for the American intervention: oil, which he proceeds to pour down Troy's throat. Many critics of the administration and opponents of the war agreed that oil interests were the primary reason for intervention. Anti-war demonstrators in Washington, New York and elsewhere, for example, rallied to the call of 'No Blood For Oil' and chanted 'Hell, no, we won't go – we won't fight for Texaco'.[37] Bush's advisers agreed that oil production and pricing would be affected by Iraq's action. As a result, the President admitted publicly, the American and global economies were under threat. Bush emphasised, however, not the strategic and economic rationale for intervention but the moral imperative of defeating Saddam Hussein's expansionist aims. Bush increasingly personalised the conflict by demonising the Iraqi leader and portraying the confrontation over Kuwait as a test of American post-Cold War resolve that would finally eradicate the self-doubt that had dogged US foreign policy since the defeat in Vietnam.[38]

Black Hawk Down allows very little discussion of the larger context and consequences of the intervention in Somalia. The opening images of the film are accompanied by a series of captions that establish the 'facts' of the situation: a famine of 'biblical proportions' has been 'caused' by 'years of war among rival clans', resulting in the deaths of 300,000 civilians from starvation; 'Mohamed Farrah Aidid [sic]', the 'most powerful of the warlords' who 'rules the capital Mogadishu' has exacerbated the situation by seizing aid supplies and using hunger as a 'weapon'; the United States had 'restored order' and delivered food by deploying 20,000 Marines; after the Marines were withdrawn, Aideed had 'declared war' on the remaining UN peacekeepers, 'slaughtering' twenty-four Pakistani soldiers and targeting Americans; Washington had then deployed elite forces to 'remove Aidid [sic]' and 'restore order'. This is certainly more context-setting than films such as *Saving Private Ryan* give us, but it is not unproblematic. As Lisle and Pepper argue, the captions frame the conflict in terms that lay all the blame for the crisis on the Somali 'warlords', and Aideed in particular, while 'securing the position of the US and the UN as heroic saviours'. As a result, 'the "rightness" of the Somalia intervention is, therefore, unquestioned from the beginning'.[39] Beyond these initial captions and a few brief explanatory comments during the film's first few minutes, however, the characters do not engage in any lengthy discussion of the reasons for their intervention or the possible consequences of their actions. They are simply soldiers doing a job. Only one of them, Ranger Staff Sergeant Matt Eversmann (Josh Hartnett), seems aware that there may be some political debate over the justifications and objectives of his mission but he is soon put in his place by a colleague who, in one of the most telling lines of the film, makes clear that 'once that first bullet goes past your head, politics and all that shit just goes right out the window'. This is precisely what happens in *Black Hawk Down* – as soon as the first bullets start to fly during the operation to seize Aideed's men, any political or historical engagement disappears completely and the film becomes an overwhelming barrage of explosions, gun battles and tense stand-offs as the Americans try to extricate themselves from the streets of Mogadishu at whatever cost to their attackers or those caught in the crossfire. The film may well give a relatively faithful account of how the chaotic battle unfolded, and it is certainly effective at gripping the audience, but the recreation of the events of Mogadishu is rendered meaningless without a wider engagement with its consequences, such as the impact it had on the willingness and ability of the US and the UN to intervene in future conflicts. The events of 3 October 1993 had far-reaching effects not only on Somalia's future but also devastatingly so on Rwanda the following year, the conflict in Bosnia and later Kosovo, the relationship between the United States and the UN, and the apparently emerging norm of 'humanitarian intervention'. None of this larger context is even hinted at in *Black Hawk Down*, thus severely limiting its effectiveness as a cinematic contribution to historical discourse.

The best historical films, like *Three Kings*, not only engage with or effectively 'vision' the past, but also attempt to 'contest' and 'revision' the history we think we know. On 1 March 1991, following victory in the Gulf, President Bush declared: 'By God, we've kicked the Vietnam syndrome once and for all.'[40] *Three Kings* repeats the claim and then challenges it with an unstinting critique of how the war ended. In the film's opening scenes, reporter Adriana Cruz (Nora Dunn) observes that officials are saying the US 'exorcised the ghost of Vietnam with a clear moral imperative' but it is soon clear that Russell believes morality to have been scorned for other interests in the Gulf. It is here that the screenwriter/director takes a stand and advocates a particular interpretation of the Gulf War and its consequences that directly challenges and criticises the Bush administration's perspective. Major Gates certainly does not believe the official line on the war: 'I don't even know what we did here. Just tell me what we did here?' His commanding officer replies: 'What do you want to do? Occupy Iraq and do Vietnam all over again? Is that what you want?' Throughout the film, Russell is deeply critical of the Bush administration's decision to stop the war soon after the liberation of Kuwait rather than prosecuting the war to Baghdad and overthrowing Saddam Hussein, or at the very least to give full support to the Shia and Kurdish uprisings in the south and north of Iraq. Gates explains that 'Bush told the people to rise up against Saddam. They thought they'd have our support; they don't. Now they're getting slaughtered.' During the air-war phase of Operation Desert Storm, President Bush did publicly call upon the 'Iraqi military and the Iraqi people to take matters into their own hands – to force Saddam Hussein, the dictator, to step aside, and to comply with the United Nations resolutions and then rejoin the family of peace-loving nations'.[41] When the uprisings began, however, the US adopted a policy of non-intervention by appealing to the same principle of state sovereignty it had declared as a justification for using force to liberate Kuwait. The administration argued there was no mandate from the UN to pursue the war further or interfere in Iraqi internal affairs. They also refused to assist the uprisings, however, because Bush and his advisers feared the dismantling of the Iraqi state would lead to regional instability and furthermore that they were concerned about becoming entangled in a civil war that could lead to a Vietnam-style quagmire.[42]

Bush's National Security Adviser Brent Scowcroft later argued that it is 'stretching the point to imagine that a routine speech in Washington could have gotten to the Iraqi malcontents and have been the motivation for the subsequent actions of the [Shias] and Kurds'.[43] In *Three Kings*, however, Russell leaves no doubt that Bush's call to arms did reach Saddam Hussein's opponents in Iraq and that they expected American help. An Iraqi resistance leader chastises the Americans for failing to support his cause: 'we try to get rid of Saddam, Bush leaves us twisting in the wind. Where is America now? . . . What good is it if you leave us here to be slaughtered? The big army of democracy beats the ugly dictator and saves the rich

Kuwaitis but you go to jail if you help us escape from the same dictator.' Earlier, when Gates, Troy, Chief and Conrad first enter an Iraqi village, they are met with cries of 'The Americans are here! It is safe to come out. We can fight Saddam!' Civilians then emerge from their homes and begin to throw stones at the Republican Guard soldiers stationed in their village, while calling out: 'Down with Saddam's army! Free Iraq!' However, although they state that 'We are here for your protection and safety, stay calm', the Americans are reluctant to get involved. Throughout the film, the Americans struggle with their sense of morality and their orders not to intervene in Iraqi affairs. Even after a young Iraqi woman is summarily executed with a bullet to the head by one of Saddam Hussein's loyalists while her small daughter watches, Troy denies that they should help the civilian uprising: 'This is not what we're here for. Let's go.' Gates, however, is overwhelmed by the compulsion to intervene and uses force to free the civilian prisoners in the village and then helps them to reach safety at the Iranian border. Ultimately, he puts his moral compulsions ahead of personal gain by sacrificing the gold and risking court martial to help the Iraqis escape even though it is 'in violation of US policy'. The clear message from Russell is that President Bush should have done more to help the Iraqi uprising and that US foreign policy needs to live up more consistently to the moral justifications in its rhetoric. That said, given that the film ends with a quite traditional set of images – heroic US soldiers temporarily foregoing their own selfish interests and disobeying official orders so they can help 'innocents' to flee persecution – one could also argue, as Mark Lacy does, that the soldiers and indeed the film end up problematically restoring 'a "just" moral order'[44] with the Americans firmly at its apex, just as President Bush had argued in his conception of a New World Order. Despite such claims, however, *Three Kings* remains an example of how a film can be both entertaining and thought-provoking, following a relatively conventional storyline whilst nonetheless contesting and revisioning accepted historical interpretations in a sophisticated manner.

CONCLUSIONS: 11 SEPTEMBER 2001 AND THE FUTURE OF HOLLYWOOD AS AMERICAN HISTORIAN

Throughout this book, we have sought to read and interpret Hollywood films that feature episodes and events from American history through a number of related critical lenses, asking of these films three key questions: first, what kind of history is being told in these films; second, what value do they have as pedagogical tools or rather how might we able to simultaneously hold on to the notion that they constitute a useful intervention in debates about American history and also identify their particular ideological commitments; and third, how or to what extent do these films either contest or re-affirm what we have called the benign meta-narrative of American history? As such, we have argued that a handful of films (that is, *Ali*, *JFK*, *Ride with the Devil*, *The Thin Red Line*, *Three Kings*), to a greater or lesser extent, contest traditional or straightforward understandings of what happened in the past, unsettle the assumption that Hollywood films should unequivocally service an affirmative national ideology, and afford viewers the critical space to think about what they are watching and encourage debate about the meaning of historical inquiry. The majority of Hollywood films, however, have tended to fulfil a more limited function: compressing and fixing historical 'truths'; articulating a wholly or largely uncritical narrative of national advancement; and encouraging audiences to feel rather than to think – to encourage audiences to passively consume spectacular images of an American past emptied of significance, controversy or even meaning. At the heart of such debates has been the question of whose history is being told and for whom? That is to say, whether an undif-ferentiated American history is being packaged for an exclusively American audience or whether the apparently universal appeal of certain American stories means that these Hollywood films are now being made as much for audiences in Europe and Asia as in the United States. Our findings, gleaned from readings of a disparate collection of films, have been by no means uniform, though certain trends have become noticeable. Chief among these has been the discrepancy between form and content. Whereas the content of many historical films made by Hollywood may appear to underscore the belief that these are American films, featuring American historical events, made for American audiences, their form tells a slightly different story: that is, their reliance on spectacular action sequences, their provision of trite shocks and constant reassurance, and their insistence that audi-ences succumb to the easy stimuli and sensation provided by com-puter-generated images of overdetermined historical events robbed of their particular significance, mean that they are just as intelligible and perhaps also appealing to audiences in Hong Kong as in Houston. It is no surprise, then, that the editors of *Cineaste* recently argued that the celebration of war and violence in mainstream films as 'consumable spectacle' is 'one of the most pernicious Hollywood trends of recent years'.[45]

As we look to the future and speculate how Hollywood's role or function as American historian might evolve in the next few years, the spectre of 11 September 2001 casts a shadow over the entire social, political and cultural landscape in Hollywood, the United States and across the globe. Although it was filmed before the attacks on the World Trade Center and the Pentagon, the case of *Black Hawk Down* provides us with a number of useful clues or pointers as to future trends. First, it is instructive of how the relationship between Hollywood filmmakers and the US government will become closer. Ridley Scott's film was made with a remarkable level of cooperation from the Pentagon, which supplied not only helicopters and transport planes but also military personnel to act as extras and advisers. This support was granted largely because the ideological interests of the two parties coalesced.[46] *Black Hawk Down* succeeded in taking what was essentially 'one of the most embarrassing and disastrous episodes of American foreign intervention'[47] and turned it into an uplifting piece of patriotic affirmation. The film did so by ignoring deeper questions of causation, morality and political significance, and instead emphasised the individual courage and valour of American soldiers who managed to extricate themselves from a seemingly impossible situation. In the immediate aftermath of the attacks in New York and Washington DC, the outpouring of patriotic sentiment and the near evaporation of political dissent created an apparent unanimity of purpose that brought Hollywood filmmakers and US politicians into even closer cooperation. Two months after 11 September 2001, President George W. Bush's senior political advisor Karl Rove held a meeting with several dozen senior Hollywood executives from companies including CBS, Viacom, Sony, DreamWorks and MGM to discuss 'how the film industry might contribute to the [war on terror] and disseminate the Bush message'.[48] Jack Valenti, president of the Motion Picture Association of America, claimed afterwards that the distribution of first-run films to US troops stationed abroad and cooperation making public service films, rather than the actual content of feature films, were the main items on the agenda.[49] Nonetheless, if filmmakers do require the administration's assistance in any form, it is hard to see how the Bush White House would grant cooperation to any future Hollywood films whose content did not meet with its explicit approval.

Our second point, given the success of *Black Hawk Down* at least at the domestic US box office, and other films like *Pearl Harbor*, *Saving Private Ryan* and *The Patriot* at the global box office, is that the growing tendency of Hollywood filmmakers to embrace the visceral spectacle of violent conflict at the expense of any sustained critical engagement with the wider consequences of American history and the contexts framing it will continue apace. As the cross-fertilisation between movies and computer games intensifies, and the ambitions of filmmakers and producers are increasingly aimed predominantly at the task of re-creating the 'experience' of history through technical aspects (for example, rapid cutting, hand-held camera, grainy film-stock, constant barrage of visceral images), which are themselves transferable to computer games, what is inevitably lost is any kind of coherent engagement with the events being represented. Lisle and Pepper argue that filmmakers like Scott can lay claim to cinematic verisimilitude while simultaneously absolving themselves of any political responsibility. Scott's claim that he is both 'putting the audience in the scene' and, at the same time, telling the story from a 'neutral' or 'objective' stance makes it easier for audiences to be seduced by such images because their political content is always secondary to their aesthetic appeal.[50] Since these kinds of films have played so well internationally, we might expect more spectacular history films to be produced in which the goals of verisimilitude, narrative coherence and political relevance are sacrificed for stories in which historical realism is measured solely in terms of how closely the 'experience' equates to those simulations of conflict (that is, wars on CNN, video games, previous Hollywood movies) that now stand-in for the 'real' in the eyes of global consumers.

Our third point is that the reception of *Black Hawk Down* in the US and internationally draws attention to two significant trends which require our further consideration. As Lisle and Pepper note, Scott's film tapped into a rich patriotic vein opened up by 11 September 2001. It was a major box office success in the US, where it earned $108.6 million and became a cause célèbre for the American right and the so-called 'neo-conservatives'. Vice President Dick Cheney and Secretary of Defense Donald Rumsfeld attended a gala screening in Washington and copies of the film were also flown out to boost morale among US troops in Afghanistan.[51] The international reception of the film was rather different, however, with *Black Hawk Down* a relative failure abroad. Despite its emphasis on spectacular action that, as we have argued, has tended to be popular among audiences globally, the film took only $50.5 at the international box office and achieved only a very limited first-run in the usually lucrative markets of France, Germany and Japan – notably countries that would later oppose or only belatedly support the US-led war in Iraq.[52]

We can therefore draw two tentative and seemingly contradictory conclusions. On the one hand, a very definite emphasis on spectacular action sequences has enabled recent blockbuster films like *Saving Private Ryan* and *Pearl Harbor* to perform very well not only at the domestic US but also the international box office, in spite of their aggressively pro-American stance and perspective. On the other hand, in the repoliticised post-September 11th world, with various incarnations of anti-Americanism on the rise, it seems that film audiences, particularly in those countries ambivalent or opposed to the US-led 'War on Terror', have responded in a lukewarm manner to blatant images of American heroism provided by films like *Black Hawk Down*. As such, the direct effects of the September 11th attacks and the ongoing 'War on Terror' either on Hollywood's general output, or on its role as American historian, are still difficult to discern. Certainly we need to resist lazy attempts to characterise September 11th as some kind of 'return to the year zero' or as the beginning of an entirely new epoch. In some respects, the post-September 11th cultural and political landscape is simply an exaggerated version of what preceded it. Still, in the context of Hollywood, what does seem to be different, post-September 11th, is that the conspicuously large number of films that featured episodes and events from American history throughout the 1990s has somewhat abated. In the current situation, even a film like *Black Hawk Down*, which flirts with controversy (that is, its subject is an event that was perceived at the time to be a failure on the part of the US military) but which ultimately celebrates the 'rightness' of American actions, may be unlikely to get funded. It is certainly hard to imagine another *Three Kings*, this time about the current war in Iraq, being made in the short or medium-term future. Instead, historical filmmakers have turned to the politically safer subject of the Alamo and, as they did in the 1950s during the years of the McCarthyite repressions, to ancient Greek and biblical sources; hence, 2004 sees the release of John Lee Hancock's version of *The Alamo*; Wolfgang Petersen's $140 million nostalgic paen to 'old-fashioned' wars, *Troy*; Oliver Stone's version of the life of Alexander the Great, entitled *Alexander*; and Mel Gibson's already phenomenally popular film *The Passion of The Christ*. *The Alamo* was initially planned, in the words of Disney's Michael Eisner, to 'capture the post-September 11 surge in patriotism'.[53] The level of success achieved by *The Alamo* at the US and international box office will, in part, determine how or even whether Hollywood engages with American history in the short run, though poor 'first-weekend' takings at the US box office and accusations that the subject matter (that is, American soldiers dying for their country) was somehow inappropriate, given the corresponding and worsening situation in Iraq, suggest that forays into such territory will, in the near future, be limited. In the medium and long term, the challenge of how to interpret the American past through the increasingly complicated lens of our contemporary political and cultural moment is one that Hollywood will, no doubt, meet again. Whether it does so in a sophisticated, pedagogically useful way that engages with and problematises the discourse of historical inquiry or simply succumbs in an ever more infantalising way to the easy allure of the blockbuster and the spectacular remains to be seen, though the current prospects for the former appear slim.

NOTES

1 See, for example, Charles Krauthammer, 'The Unipolar Moment', in Graham Allison and Gregory F. Treverton, *Rethinking America's Security: Beyond Cold War to New World Order* (New York: W. W. Norton, 1992), pp. 295–306.
2 Francis Fukuyama, 'The End of History', *The National Interest*, No. 16, Summer 1989, pp. 3, 4.
3 George Bush, 'Address to the 46th Session of the United Nations General Assembly in New York City, September 23, 1991', *Public Papers of the Presidents of the United States: George Bush, 1991*, http://bushlibrary. tamu.edu/research/papers/1991/91092301.html (23/5/04).
4 Gore Vidal, *Perpetual War for Perpetual Peace* (New York: Nation Books, 2002).
5 Mark J. Lacy, 'War, Cinema and Moral Anxiety', *Alternatives*, 28, 2003, p. 614.
6 Quoted in Andrew Pulver, 'Exploding the Myth of Desert Storm', *The Guardian*, G2, 1 March 2000, p. 12.
7 Quoted in Giles Foden, 'You Can't Diddle With The Truth', *The Guardian*,

11   January 2002, http://film.guardian.co.uk/interview/interview pages/0,6737,630681,00.html (08/05/03).

8   Debbie Lisle and Andrew Pepper, 'The New Face of Global Hollywood: *Black Hawk Down* and the Politics of Meta-Sovereignty', *Cultural Politics*, July 2005.

9   'Editorial', *Cineaste*, Vol. XXVII No. 3, Summer 2002, p. 1.

10   Lacy, 'War, Cinema and Moral Anxiety', p. 616.

11   Jean Baudrillard, *The Gulf War Did Not Take Place* (Bloomington, IN: Indiana University Press, 1995).

12   Lacy, 'War, Cinema and Moral Anxiety', p. 612.

13   See Lawrence Freedman and Efraim Karsh, *The Gulf Conflict 1990–1991: Diplomacy and War in the New World Order* (London and Boston: Faber and Faber, 1993), pp. 402–6, 408; Trevor McCrisken, *American Exceptionalism and the Legacy of Vietnam* (Basingstoke: Palgrave Macmillan, 2003), pp. 148–9.

14   Philip M. Taylor, *War and the Media: Propaganda and Persuasion in the Gulf War* (Manchester: Manchester University Press, 1992), p. 258.

15   John MacArthur notes that 'the most gruesome pictures in the four special issues of *Life* were of corpses from the Iran–Iraq war'. John R. MacArthur, *Second Front: Censorship and Propaganda in the Gulf War* (Berkeley, CA: University of California Press, 1993), pp. 154–5.

16   Taylor, *War and the Media*, p. 258; MacArthur, *Second Front*, p. 155.

17   Quoted in Pulver, 'Exploding the Myth of Desert Storm', p. 13.

18   Lynn   Barber,   'Scott's   Corner',   *The   Observer*,   6   January   2002, http://film.guardian.co.uk/interview/interviewpages/0,6737,628186,00. html (08/05/03).

19   See Karin von Hippel, *Democracy By Force: US Military Intervention in the Post-Cold War World* (Cambridge: Cambridge University Press, 2000), p. 60.

20   Quoted in Jonathan Fryer, '*Black Hawk Down*: Coincides with US Patriotic Mood', http://news.bbc.co.uk/1/hi/world/africa/1773466. stm (08/05/03).

21   Lisle and Pepper, 'The New Face of Global Hollywood'. In this article, Lisle and Pepper argue that Scott's pursuit of aesthetic perfection and the film's flirtation with a bewilderingly diverse range of political positions and messages makes it 'practically impossible to locate any definite ideological commitment' and that, as a result, 'we need a new critical idiom in order to determine how ideology is working' not just in *Black Hawk Down* but also in blockbuster cinema generally.

22   Ibid.

23   George Monbiot, 'Both Saviour and Victim: *Black Hawk Down* Creates a New and Dangerous Myth of American Nationhood', *The Guardian*, 29 January 2002.

24 Quoted in Barber, 'Scott's Corner'.

25 Peter Bradshaw, *'Black Hawk Down'*, *The Guardian*, 18 January 2002.

26 Lisle and Pepper, 'The New Face of Global Hollywood'.

27 Quoted in Foden, 'You Can't Diddle With The Truth'.

28 Lisle and Pepper, 'The New Face of Global Hollywood'.

29 Monbiot, 'Both Saviour and Victim'.

30 See Mark Bowden, *Black Hawk Down: A Story of Modern War* (New York: Penguin USA, 2000).

31 Philip Strick, *'Black Hawk Down'*, *Sight and Sound*, February 2002, p. 41.

32 Elvis Mitchell, 'Film Review: Mission of Mercy Goes Bad in Africa', *The New York Times*, 28 December 2001, http://query.nytimes.com/gst/full page.html?res=9903E3D61031F93BA15751C1A9679C8B63 (08/04/04).

33 Quoted in Fryer, *'Black Hawk Down'*.

34 Quoted in Foden, 'You Can't Diddle With The Truth'.

35 See, for example, *An Assessment of Racial Discrimination in the Military: A Global Perspective* (Washington, DC: US Government Printing Office, 1994).

36 George Bush and Brent Scowcroft, *A World Transformed* (New York: Alfred A. Knopf, 1998); George Bush, 'Address to the Nation Announcing the Deployment of United States Armed Forces to Saudi Arabia, August 8, 1990', *Public Papers of the Presidents of the United States: George Bush, 1990* (Washington, DC: United States Government Printing Office, 1991); George Bush, 'Remarks at a Fundraising Luncheon for Rep. Bill Grant, September 6, 1990', *Public Papers, 1990*; Colin L. Powell with Joseph E. Persico, *My American Journey* (New York: Random House, 1995), p. 463; Robert W. Tucker and David C. Hendrickson, *The Imperial Temptation: The New World Order and America's Purpose* (New York: Council on Foreign Relations Press, 1992), p. 81.

37 John Robert Greene, *The Presidency of George Bush* (Lawrence, KS: University of Kansas Press, 2000), p. 124.

38 See McCrisken, *American Exceptionalism and the Legacy of Vietnam*, pp. 142–7.

39 Lisle and Pepper, 'The New Face of Global Hollywood'.

40 Bush, 'Remarks to the American Legislative Exchange Council, March 1, 1991', *Public Papers, 1991*.

41 Bush, 'Remarks to the American Association for the Advancement of Science, February 15, 1991', *Public Papers, 1991*.

42 See McCrisken, *American Exceptionalism and the Legacy of Vietnam*, pp. 150–2.

43 Bush and Scowcroft, *A World Transformed*, p. 472.

44 Lacy, 'War, Cinema and Moral Anxiety', p. 631.

45 'Editorial,' *Cineaste*, Vol. XXVII No. 3, Summer 2002, p. 1.

46 Lisle and Pepper, 'The New Face of Global Hollywood'; Elizabeth Snead,

'The Special Operation of *Black Hawk Down*', *The Washington Post*, 13 January 2002, p. G01.

47 Barber, 'Scott's Corner'.

48 'Editorial', *Cineaste*, p. 1.

49 Quoted in Gary Gentile, 'The Role of a Lifetime: Hollywood Executive Asked to Help With War on Terror', ABC News On-line, 11 November 2001, http://abcnews.go.com/sections/business/DailyNews/strike_hollywood011101.html (8/4/04).

50 Lisle and Pepper, 'The New Face of Global Hollywood'.

51 Ibid.

52 Lisle and Pepper, 'The New Face of Global Hollywood'; J. Hoberman, 'The Art of War', *The Village Voice*, http://www.villagevoice.com/issues/0225/hoberman2.php (08/05/03); Joe Burlas, '*Black Hawk Down* Reflects Army Values', US Army News Service, 16 January 2002.

53 Quoted in Sharon Waxman, 'It was like directing a football game', *The Guardian*, G2, 26 March 2004, p. 8.

SELECT BIBLIOGRAPHY

Adams, Michael C. C., *The Best War Ever: America and World War II* (Baltimore, MD: Johns Hopkins University, 1994)

Allison, Graham and Treverton, Gregory F., *Rethinking America's Security: Beyond Cold War to New World Order* (New York: W. W. Norton, 1992)

Ambrose, Stephen E., *The Victors: Eisenhower and His Boys – The Men of World War II* (New York: Simon & Schuster, 1998)

Auster, Albert and Leonard Quart, *How the War was Remembered: Hollywood and Vietnam* (New York: Praeger, 1988)

Basinger, Jeanine, *The World War II Combat Film: Anatomy of a Genre* (Middletown, CT: Wesleyan University Press, 2003)

Baudrillard, Jean, *The Gulf War Did Not Take Place* (Bloomington, IN: Indiana University Press, 1995)

Bauman, Zygmunt, *Modernity and Ambivalence* (Cambridge: Polity, 1991)

Beidler, Philip D., *The Good War's Greatest Hits: World War II and American Remembering* (Athens, GA and London: University of Georgia Press, 1998)

Biskind, Peter, *Easy Riders, Raging Bulls: How the Sex-Drugs-and-Rock'n'Roll Generation Saved Hollywood* (New York: Simon & Schuster, 1998)

Bowden, Mark, *Black Hawk Down: A Story of Modern War* (New York: Penguin USA, 2000)

Brands, H. W., *What America Owes the World: The Struggle for the Soul of Foreign Policy* (Cambridge: Cambridge University Press, 1998)

Burgoyne, Robert, *Film Nation: Hollywood Looks at US History* (Minneapolis: University of Minneapolis Press, 1997)

Bush, George and Brent Scowcroft, *A World Transformed* (New York: Alfred A. Knopf, 1998)

Buzzanco, Robert, *Vietnam and the Transformation of American Life* (Oxford: Blackwell, 1999)

Cameron, Kenneth, *America on Film: Hollywood and American History* (New York: Continuum, 1997)

Chambers, John Whiteclay, II and David Culbert, eds, *World War II, Film and History* (New York and Oxford: Oxford University Press, 1996)

Countryman, Edward, *Americans: A Collision of Histories* (London and New York: I. B. Tauris, 1996)

Custen, George, *Bio/Pics: How Hollywood Constructed Public History* (New Jersey: Rutgers University Press, 1992)

Davies, Jude and Carol R. Smith, *Gender, Ethnicity and Sexuality in Contemporary American Film* (Edinburgh: Edinburgh University Press, 2001)

DeGroot, Gerard J., *A Noble Cause?: America and the Vietnam War* (Harlow: Longman, 2000)

Diawara, Manthia, ed., *Black American Cinema* (London and New York: Routledge, 1993)

Dick, Bernard F., *The Star-Spangled Screen: The American World War II Film* (Lexington, KY: University of Kentucky Press, 1996)

Doherty, Thomas, *Projections of War: Hollywood, American Culture, and World War II* (New York: Columbia University Press, 1993)

Dower, John W., *War Without Mercy: Race and Power in the Pacific War* (New York: Pantheon, 1986)

Early, Gerald, ed., *A Muhammad Ali Reader* (London: Yellow Jersey Press, 1999)

Folly, Martin, *The United States and World War II: The Awakening Giant* (Edinburgh: Edinburgh University Press, 2002)

Foote, Shelby, *The Civil War: A Narrative* (London: Pimlico, 1992)

Fousek, John, *To Lead the Free World: American Nationalism and the Cultural Roots of the Cold War* (Chapel Hill, NC: University of North Carolina Press, 2000)

Freedman, Lawrence and Efraim Karsh, *The Gulf Conflict 1990–1991: Diplomacy and War in the New World Order* (London and Boston: Faber and Faber, 1993)

Giroux, Henry A., *Breaking In To Movies: Film and the Culture of Politics* (Malden, MA and Oxford: Blackwell, 2002)

Goldberg, David Theo, *Racial Subjects: Writing on Race in America* (London and New York: Routledge, 1997)

Greene, John Robert, *The Presidency of George Bush* (Lawrence, KS: University of Kansas Press, 2000)

Gregg, Robert W., *International Relations on Film* (Boulder, CO: Lynne Rienner, 1998)

Guerrero, Ed, *Framing Blackness: The African-American Image in Film* (Philadelphia: Temple University Press, 1993)

Hardt, Michael and Antonio Negri, *Empire* (Cambridge, MA and London: Harvard University Press: 2000)

Hellmann, John, *American Myth and the Legacy of Vietnam* (New York: Columbia University Press, 1986)

Hillier, Jim, ed., *American Independent Cinema* (London: BFI, 2001)

Hoyt, Edwin P., *The GI's War: American Soldiers in Europe During World War II* (New York: Cooper Square Press, 2000)

Hutton, Will, *The World We're In* (London: Abacus, 2003)

Jay, Gregory J., *American Literature and the Culture Wars* (Ithaca: Cornell University Press, 1997)

Jeffords, Susan, *The Remasculinization of America: Gender and the Vietnam War* (Bloomington, IN: Indiana University Press, 1989)

Kolker, Robert, *A Cinema of Loneliness: Penn, Stone, Kubrick, Scorsese, Spielberg, Altman*, 3rd ed., (Oxford and New York: Oxford University Press, 2000)

Kovic, Ron, *Born on the Fourth of July* (New York: Corgi, 1990)

Lewis, Jon, ed., *The New American Cinema* (Durham and London: Duke University Press, 1998)

Linderman, Gerald F., *The World Within War: America's Combat Experience in World War II* (New York: The Free Press, 1997)

MacArthur, John R., *Second Front: Censorship and Propaganda in the Gulf War* (Berkeley, CA: University of California Press, 1993)

Mackey-Kallis, Susan, *Oliver Stone's America: 'Dreaming the Myth Outward'* (Boulder, CO: Westview Press, 1996)

Marqusee, Mike, *Redemption Song: Muhammad Ali and the Spirit of the Sixties* (London: Verso, 2000)

McCrisken, Trevor B., *American Exceptionalism and the Legacy of Vietnam: US Foreign Policy Since 1974* (Basingstoke: Palgrave Macmillan, 2003)

Miller, Mark Crispen, ed., *Seeing Through Movies* (New York: Pantheon, 1990)

Neale, Steve and Murray Smith, eds, *Contemporary Hollywood Cinema* (London and New York: Routledge, 1998)

Newman, John M., *JFK and Vietnam: Deception, Intrigue and the Struggle for Power* (New York: Warner Books, 1992)

Nichols, Bill, *Representing Reality: Issues and Concepts in Documentary Films* (Bloomington, IN: Indiana University Press, 1992)

O'Connor, John E. and Martin A. Jackson, eds, *American History/American Film* (New York: Frederick Ungar, 1979)

Omi, Michael and Howard Winant, *Racial Formation in the United States: From the 1960s to the 1990s*, 2nd ed., (New York and London: Routledge, 1994)

Penman, Michael, ed., *Perspectives on the American Past Vol. 1: To 1877* (Chicago: Heath, 1996)

Powell, Colin L. with Joseph E. Persico, *My American Journey* (New York: Random House, 1995)

Quart, Leonard and Albert Auster, *American Film and Society Since 1945*, 2nd ed., (Westport, CT: Praeger, 1991)

Raphael, Ray, *A People's History of the American Revolution* (New York: Harper Perennial, 2002)

Remnick, David, *King of the World: Muhammad Ali and the Rise of an American Hero* (London: Picador, 2000)

Ray, Robert, *A Certain Tendency of Hollywood Cinema 1930–1980* (Princeton: Princeton University Press, 1985)

Rollins, Peter, ed., *Hollywood as Historian: American Film in a Cultural Context* (Lexington, KT: University of Kentucky Press, 1983)

Rosenbaum, Jonathan, *Movies as Politics* (Berkeley, CA and London: University of California Press, 1997)

Rosenstone, Robert A., ed., *Revisioning History: Film and the Construction of a New Past* (Princeton: Princeton University Press, 1995)

Rosenstone, Robert A., *Visions of the Past: The Challenge of Film to Our Idea of History* (Cambridge, MA: Harvard University Press, 1995)

Ross, Karen, *Black Images in Popular Film and Television* (Cambridge: Polity, 1996)

Ryan, David, *US Foreign Policy in World History* (London and New York: Routledge, 2000)

Ryan, Michael and Douglas Kellner, *Camera Politica: The Politics and Ideology of Contemporary Hollywood Film* (Bloomington, IN: Indiana University Press, 1990)

Scott, Ian, *American Politics in Hollywood Film* (Edinburgh: Edinburgh University Press, 2000).

Sebag-Montefiore, Hugh, *Enigma: The Battle for the Code* (London: Weidenfeld & Nicolson, 2000)

Sklar, Robert, *Movie-Made America: A Social History of American Movies* (New York: Random House, 1975)

Slotkin, Richard, *Gunfighter Nation: The Frontier Myth in Twentieth Century America* (New York: Athenum, 1992)

Slotkin, Richard, *The Fatal Environment: The Myth of the Frontier in the Age of Industrialization* (Norman, OK: University of Oklahoma Press, 1998)

Sobchak, Vivian, ed., *The Persistence of History: Cinema, Television and the Modern Event* (London and New York: Routledge, 1996)

Spector, Ronald H., *Eagle Against the Sun: The American War with Japan* (New York: Viking, 1984)

Stam, Robert, and Toby Miller, eds, *Film and Theory: An Anthology* (Oxford: Blackwell, 2000)

Stam, Robert, *Film Theory* (Oxford: Blackwell, 2000)

Taylor, Philip M., *War and the Media: Propaganda and Persuasion in the Gulf War* (Manchester: Manchester University Press, 1992)

Tomblin, Barbara Brooks, *G.I. Nightingales: The Army Nurse Corps in World War II* (Lexington, KY: University Press of Kentucky, 1996)

Toplin, Robert Brent, ed., *Hollywood as Mirror: Changing Views of 'Outsiders' and 'Enemies' in American Movies* (Westport, CT: Greenwood Press, 1993)

Toplin, Robert Brent, ed., *Oliver Stone's USA: Film, History and Controversy* (Lawrence, KS: University Press of Kansas, 2000)

Tucker, Robert W. and David C. Hendrickson, *The Imperial Temptation: The New World Order and America's Purpose* (New York: Council on Foreign Relations Press, 1992)

Van Der Vat, Dan, *The Pacific Campaign* (Edinburgh: Birlinn, 1992)

Vidal, Gore, *Perpetual War for Perpetual Peace*, (New York: Nation Books, 2002)

von Hippel, Karin, *Democracy By Force: US Military Intervention in the Post-Cold War World* (Cambridge: Cambridge University Press, 2000)

Wood, Joe, ed., *Malcolm X: In Our Image* (New York: St Martin's Press, 1992)

Wyatt, Justin, *High Concept: Movies and Marketing in Hollywood* (Austin, TX: University of Texas Press, 1994)

Zizek, Slavoj, *The Ticklish Subject* (London and New York: Verso, 1999)

INDEX

217